Effective Project Management

Second Edition

Robert K. Wysocki
Robert Beck, Jr.
David B. Crane

Wiley Computer Publishing

John Wiley & Sons, Inc.
NEW YORK · CHICHESTER · WEINHEIM · BRISBANE · SINGAPORE · TORONTO

Publisher: Robert Ipsen
Editor: Theresa Hudson
Associate Developmental Editor: Kathryn A. Malm
Managing Editor: Angela Smith
Associate New Media Editor: Brian Snapp
Text Design & Composition: Publishers' Design and Production Services, Inc.

Designations used by companies to distinguish their products are often claimed as trademarks. In all instances where John Wiley & Sons, Inc., is aware of a claim, the product names appear in initial capital or ALL CAPITAL LETTERS. Readers, however, should contact the appropriate companies for more complete information regarding trademarks and registration.

This book is printed on acid-free paper. ∞

This publication is designed to provide accurate and authoritative information in regard to the subject matter covered. It is sold with the understanding that the publisher is not engaged in professional services. If professional advice or other expert assistance is required, the services of a competent professional person should be sought.

Microsoft® Project 2000 © Microsoft Corporation.

All rights reserved. Microsoft® Project 2000 and Microsoft® are registered trademarks of Microsoft Corporation in the United States and other countries.

Library of Congress Cataloging-in-Publication Data:

ISBN 0-471-36028-7

Printed in the United States of America.

10 9 8 7 6 5 4

Contents

Preface to the Second Edition   **xi**

About the Authors   **xv**

Part One   Introduction   **1**

Chapter 1   What This Book Is All About   **3**

Changes in the Business Environment   5
    Organizational Structures   5
    Software Applications   5
    Cycle Time   5
    Right-Sizing   6

The Growth of Project Management as a Profession   6

The Need for a New Training Paradigm for Project Managers   7

Why We Wrote This Book   7

How This Book Is Structured   8
    Part One, Introduction to Project Management   8
    Part Two, Staging   8
    Part Three, Planning   9
    Part Four, Implementation   10
    Part Five, References   11

How to Use This Book   11

Who Should Read This Book   12

The Case Exercises on the CD-ROM   12

Chapter 2   How to Become a World-Class Project Manager   **13**

Start Now   15

Demand for Project Managers   15

Customer-Driven Organizations 16
Evolution from Function to Process 16
Task Forces 18
Project-Driven Organizations 20

Traditional Organizational Environments 22
Functional Structures 23
Matrix Structures 24

Project Management in Contemporary Environments 28

Project Support Office 30

Job Functions and Tasks for Project Management 32

Competencies and Skills of the Project Manager 34
Classifying Projects 34
Classifying Project Managers 36
Assessing Competencies and Skills 37
Application of Bloom's Taxonomy 47

A Career Planning Template 50
Where Are You? 50
Where Do You Want to Go? 50
How Will You Get There? 51

Becoming a World-Class Project Manager 52

Chapter 3 **Case Study: O'Neill & Preigh** **53**

The Projects 55

Overview of the Business Situation 55

Description of Project Initiatives 56
Project 1: Office Supplies Containment 57
Project 2: Gold Medallion Organ 57

Professional Staff Resources 58

Part Two **Staging** **61**

Chapter 4 **What Is a Project?** **63**

Definition of a Project 65
Sequence of Activities 65
Unique Activities 65
Complex Activities 66
Connected Activities 66
One Goal 66
Specified Time 67
Within Budget 67
According to Specification 67

What Is a Program? 68

Project Parameters   68
    Scope   69
    Quality   69
    Cost   70
    Time   70
    Resources   71

The Scope Triangle: Time, Cost, and Resource Availability   71
    Scope Creep   72
    Hope Creep   73
    Effort Creep   73
    Feature Creep   73

Project Classifications   74

Chapter 5 **What Is Project Management?**   **77**

Principles of Project Management   79
    Defining   79
    Planning   80
    Executing   81
    Controlling   82
    Closing   82

Project Management Life Cycle   83
    Phases of Project Management   84
    Levels of Project Management   90

Quality Management   91
    Continuous Quality Management Model   93
    Process Quality Management Model   93

An Overview of Risk Management   95
    Risk Analysis Example   96

Relationship between Project Management and Other
Methodologies   99

The Pain Curve   102

Part Three **Planning**   **105**

Chapter 6 **Scope the Project**   **107**

Define the Project   109

Develop Conditions of Satisfaction   109

Create the Project Overview Statement   113
    Parts of the POS   114
    Attachments   122

Using the Joint Project Planning Session to Develop
the POS   124

Approval Process   125
    Participants in the Approval Process   127
The Project Definition Statement   129

Chapter 7   Identify Project Activities   133

The Work Breakdown Structure   135

Uses for the WBS   137

Generating the WBS   138
    Top-Down Approach   139
    Bottom-Up Approach   141
    WBS for Small Projects   142
    Intermediate WBS for Large Projects   142

Six Criteria to Test for Completeness in the WBS   143
    Measurable Status   144
    Bounded   145
    Deliverable   145
    Cost/Time Estimate   146
    Acceptable Duration Limits   146
    Activity Independence   146

Approaches to Building the WBS   147
    Noun-Type Approaches   148
    Verb-Type Approaches   149
    Other Approaches   150

Representing the WBS   151

**Chapter 8   Estimate Activity Duration, Resource Requirements,
             and Cost   157**

Duration   159
    Resource Loading versus Activity Duration   160
    Variation in Activity Duration   162
    Six Methods for Estimating Activity Duration   163
    Estimation Precision   167

Resources   167
    People as Resources   168

Estimating Duration as a Function of Resource Availability   170
    Assign as a Total Work and a Constant Percent/Day   170
    Assign as a Duration and Total Work Effort   171
    Assign as a Duration and Percent/Day   171
    Assign as a Profile   171

Estimating Cost   172

Using a JPP Session to Estimate Activity Duration
and Resource Requirements   173
    Determining Resource Requirements   174

Chapter 9	**Construct and Analyze the Project Network Diagram**	**177**
	The Project Network Diagram	179
	Benefits to Network-Based Scheduling	180
	Building the Network Diagram Using the PDM	181
	Dependencies	184
	Constraints	186
	The Use of the Lag Variable	191
	Analyzing the Initial Project Network Diagram	197
	Schedule Compression	197
	Management Reserve	200
	Using the JPP Session	203

Chapter 10	**Finalize the Schedule Based on Resource Availability**	**207**
	Resources	209
	Leveling Resources	209
	Acceptably Leveled Schedule	212
	Resource Leveling Strategies	212
	Slack	213
	Shifting the Project Finish Date	213
	Smoothing	214
	Alternative Methods of Scheduling Activities	214
	Work Packages	216
	Purpose of a Work Package	217
	Format of a Work Package	218

Chapter 11	**Organize and Conduct the Joint Project Planning Session**	**223**
	Joint Project Planning Sessions	225
	Planning the JPP Session	226
	Attendees	227
	Facilities	230
	Equipment	230
	The Complete Planning Agenda	230
	Deliverables	231
	Project Proposal	232
	Contents of the Project Proposal	233

Part Four	**Implementation**	**235**

Chapter 12	**Recruit, Organize, and Manage the Project Team**	**237**
	Project Manager vis-a-vis the Functional Manager	239
	Conflicting Objectives	239
	Projects as Motivation and Development Tools	240

Recruit the Project Team 244
The Project Manager 245
The Core Team Members 247
The Contracted Team Member 251
Types of Proposals 253
Types of Contracts 254

Organize the Project Team 255
Authority 255
Responsibility 256

Establish Team Operating Rules 256
Decision Making 257
Conflict Resolution 258
Consensus Building 259
Brainstorming 259
Team Meetings 260

Summary 261

Chapter 13 Monitor and Control Progress 263

Control versus Risk 265
Purpose of Controls 265
High Control—Low Risk 266
Low Control—High Risk 266
Balancing the Control System 267

Control versus Quality 268

Progress Reporting System 268
Types of Project Status Reports 268
How and What Information to Update 272
Frequency of Gathering and Reporting
Project Progress 274
Variances 274

Graphical Reporting Tools 276
Gantt Charts 276
Milestone Trend Charts 278
Cost Schedule Control 281
Using the WBS to Report Project Status 286

Level of Detail 288
Activity Manager 288
Project Manager 288
Senior Management 289

Project Status Review Meetings 289

Change Control 291

Problem Escalation	294
The Escalation Strategy Hierachy	297
Problem Management Meetings	298

Chapter 14   Close Out the Project   301

Steps in Closing a Project	303
Get Client Acceptance	303
Ceremonial Acceptance	303
Formal Acceptance	304
Install Project Deliverables	304
Document the Project	304
Documentation Contents	305
Post-Implementation Audit	306
The Final Report	308
Celebrating Success	309

Part Five   References   311

Appendix A   Managing Multiple Projects   313

Shared Resources	315
Organizational Considerations	316
Staffing Considerations	318
Project-Related Considerations	319
Slack Management	322
Project Delay	322
Strategic and Tactical Issues	323

Appendix B   What's on the CD-ROM   325

Bibliography   327

Index   337

Preface to the Second Edition

The original edition of *Effective Project Management* was published in 1995. The only thing significant about that date is that the book is now several years old. In those years, we have learned a lot from those of you who we have been fortunate to help. We will be forever indebted to you, our readers; you have helped make this book a great success.

For us, project management has become a habit that was not easily acquired. You need to know that. To become an effective project manager requires a behavioral change—and those aren't easy. Our best advice is to find a few "getting started" pearls in the pages of this book. Use them. Get comfortable with them. Make them part of your life. Make them indispensable so that you feel short-changed if you neglect to use them. Once you have reached that point, you are ready for more. Add another tool. Add another technique. In time you will find that your project management arsenal is complete and you have the confidence to go forward into the unpredictable and exhilarating world of the project manager fully ready to do your best.

We have tried to be as helpful as possible by making our book a real addition to your library. Much of what you find in the pages that follow is the compendium of many years' experience. In fact, we total over 70 years experience among us. We've been through a lot. We've made a lot of mistakes. Follow our advice and you will not repeat history.

There are several factors that led to this new edition:

- Microsoft Project98 is on the market, with Project2000 expected shortly, and the simulation CD-ROM needed to be updated to be compatible with this version.

- Several continuing education programs and professional societies have adopted our book in their curriculum.

- We have had a lot of feedback from our business associates and readers on how we might improve the presentation.

- We read the book for the first time since 1995 and found a number of improvements we would like to make.

- Terri Hudson, our editor, says it's time for a revised edition.

There are four major changes in this edition. The first major change is the overhaul and reorganization of the entire book. It now contains 14 chapters that present the material in an easier to digest sequence.

Second, the case studies have been expanded to two projects from our favorite fictitious company, O'Neill & Preigh, a leading manufacturer of church furnishings and equipment. As you go from chapter to chapter, we use one of the cases to illustrate the concepts and the other as the basis for an exercise for you. The exercises and their solutions can be found on the CD-ROM. We trust you won't peek until you have tried your hand with the exercises.

Third, we have completely rewritten Chapter 2. The revised chapter, "How to Become a World-Class Project Manager," offers a complete guide to becoming a world class project manager. In our consulting practices we have noticed a remarkable shift towards investments in the workforce. Nowhere is that more obvious than in the tremendous growth of project management in organizations. Much of this has been fueled by the organizational changes that have taken place. Those changes have given birth to a new (or in some cases, renewed) interest in integrating sound project management practices in organizations. The missing ingredients are the design and implementation of an enterprise-wide project management methodology and the training to support it. What we offer in Chapter 2 is a model of a project manager career path and the skills and competencies needed to move along that career path. To our knowledge, this is the first detailed presentation of a project manager career path to appear in print. Those of you who would like to become exemplary project managers will find this material enlightening and invaluable.

And finally, we added several topics that bring the book more in line with the Project Management Institute's PMBOK.

In writing this book we found, as so many other writers have, that we could have gone on for several more months with additional tools and techniques honed through years of experiences. Our editor would not have been pleased had we done that. We have, however, put as much good practical advice and practices in these pages as possible. Our hope is that you will come to appreciate the value from the fruits of our labor. We truly want this to be your single guide to learning project management. We think we have something unique in our approach.

Thank you for adding our book to your project management library. Enjoy reading it as much as we have enjoyed writing it. If you get a chance, let us hear from you. Visit us at eiiinc.com or email us at rkw@eiiinc.com.

About the Authors

Robert K. Wysocki, PhD, has been an information systems manager, systems and management consultant, author, training developer and provider, and professor of information systems. He has written seven books on project management and information systems management. He is a frequent speaker at conferences and professional society meetings.

Mr. Wysocki is co-founder and president of Enterprise Information Insights, Inc., a management consulting practice incorporated in 1990. EII specializes in the design, development, and integration of business-driven project management practices in the information technology organization. In this capacity, EII has completed engagements in project management methodology design and integration, project management training program design and delivery, project support office establishment, process quality management programs and career planning and professional development of project managers.

Mr. Wysocki earned a B.A. in Mathematics from the University of Dallas and an M.S. and Ph.D. in Mathematical Statistics both from Southern Methodist University. He is a member of the Project Management Institute, the American Society of Training & Development, the International Association for Human Resource Management, the International Society for Performance Improvement, the National Career Development Association, and the Society for Human Resource Management.

David B. Crane is a respected authority in project management consulting and training. Over the past 25 years he has delivered consulting services and training to over 5,000 employees of major firms throughout the United States.

Mr. Crane is the founder and principal of D.B. Crane and Associates, Inc., a company focused on providing project management training, consulting, and the development of add-on tools for project management software. During the last fifteen years he has worked with over 150 corporations in the fields of computer software, hardware, automotive engineering, energy, municipal engineering, and manufacturing. His work with these corporations has involved both education and the implementation of methods and tools to control and reduce development cycle time. In this capacity Mr. Crane has facilitated the design and implementation of schedule recovery plans to assure on time delivery of major new products.

Mr. Crane is a member of the Project Management Institute; he majored in Psychology at Gordon College in Wenham, Massachusetts, and studied engineering at Northeastern University. He has served as a member of the Boston University, Corporate Education Center adjunct faculty for the past seven years, where he provides training and consulting services for the Center for Management Development.

Robert Beck, Jr. has been a computer service engineer, instructor, systems engineer, product manager, training developer, technical writer, lecturer, marketing representative, and computer business consultant. He has over 35 years experience in the data processing industry beginning as a Customer Engineer and Instruction Manager. Subsequent to this, Mr. Beck has held field and staff positions as Systems Engineer, Program Manager, Market Support Representative, and Systems Consultant. For the past several years he has concentrated on Information Resource Management, Client/Server technologies, Networking, Project Management, and Multimedia.

As owner of the Enterprise Technology Company, Mr. Beck specializes in systems integration and networking. For the past five years ETC has assisted small businesses and other organizations in the implementation of their first data processing systems, upgrades to their existing systems, as well as the introduction of computer networks, intranets, and Internets.

As an IBM Consulting Systems Engineer, Mr. Beck has led many engagements with Fortune 100 companies in the Financial, Manufacturing, and Retail industries pertaining to all facets of information technology. In the retail industry he has concentrated on systems integration where he has led the implementation of EDI, Point Of Sale kiosks, WAN and in-store networks, and multimedia application development. Mr. Beck has been recognized for his skills managing vendor/Client project teams through design, implementation, and operations of complex IT infrastructures.

Introduction

We think you will find our treatment of project management a refreshing change from the usual fare you have been subjected to. In keeping with the format of the first edition, there will be plenty of opportunity to practice the tools and techniques that we have used successfully for many years and are now sharing with you. Short, practical exercises and comprehensive simulated problems reinforce your practice of newly acquired knowledge. You'll also find a rich source of practice-oriented materials, many of which are not to be found in other books on the subject.

With this edition we introduce our project manager career path model in Chapter 2, "How to Become a World-Class Project Manager." There is a structure to projects that leads to four classes of project manager. Each class is characterized by skill profiles and competency levels. These lead to a natural definition of skill-based career paths.

In Chapter 3, "Case Study: O'Neill & Preigh," you are introduced to a hypothetical manufacturer of church furnishings and equipment. In their attempt to remain competitive, O'Neill & Preigh is introducing two projects, which you will follow from day one to day last through a number of case exercises in many of the chapters. Most chapters present problems from these two projects. One of the projects is used to illustrate concepts and practices while the other is left as exercises for you. You will have to analyze the situation and look for alternative solutions to any problems you may uncover. We hope you will find these exercises stimulating and enjoyable.

Good luck!

What This Book Is All About

Chapter Learning Objectives

After reading this chapter you will be able to:

✔ Explain how the changing business climate has affected project management
✔ Understand the growing importance of project management in contemporary organizations
✔ Appreciate the need for project management training and the specific training needs of project managers

Practice is everything.

—DIOGENES LAERTIUS
GREEK HISTORIAN AND WRITER

Changes in the Business Environment

Change is constant! We hope that does not come as a surprise to you. Change is always with us and seems to be happening at an increasing rate. Every day we face new challenges and the need to improve yesterday's practices. As John Naisbett says in *The Third Wave*, "Change or die." For experienced project managers as well as "wanna be" project managers, the road to breakthrough performance is paved with uncertainty and with the need to be courageous, creative, and flexible. If we simply rely on a routine application of someone else's methodology, we are sure to fall short of the mark.

Organizational Structures

The familiar command and control structures introduced at the turn of the century are rapidly disappearing. In their place are task forces, self-directed work teams, and various forms of projectized organizations. In all cases, empowerment of the worker lies at the foundation of these new structures. With structural changes and worker empowerment comes the need for all of us to have solid project management skills.

Software Applications

Many of you may remember the days when a computer application had to meet the needs of just a single department. If there was a corporate database, it was accessed to retrieve the required date, which was passed to an applications program that produced the requested report. If there was no data or if we did not know of its existence, we created our own database or file and proceeded accordingly. In retrospect, our professional life as systems developers was relatively simple. Not so any more. To be competitive we now develop applications that cross departmental lines, applications that span organizations, applications that are not clearly defined, applications that will change because the business climate is changing. All of this means that we must anticipate changes that will affect our projects and be skilled at managing those changes.

Cycle Time

The window of opportunity is narrowing and constantly moving. Organizations that can take advantage of opportunities are organizations that have reduced cycle times. Taking too long to roll out a new or revamped product can result in a missed business opportunity. Project managers must know how and when to introduce multiple release strategies and compress project schedules to help meet these requirements. We spend considerable time on these strategies in later chapters.

Right-Sizing

With the reduction in management layers, a common practice in many organizations, the professional staff needs to find ways to work smarter, not harder. Project management includes a number of tools and techniques that help the professional manage increased work loads.

Middle Management

Peter Drucker, in a landmark paper ("The Coming of the New Organization," *Harvard Business Review*, January/February 1988), depicts middle managers as either those who receive information from above, reinterpret it, and pass it down or those who receive information from below, reinterpret it, and pass it up the line. Not only is quality suspect but the computer is perfectly capable of delivering that information to the desk of any manager who has a need to know. Given these factors, plus the politics and power struggles at play, why employ middle managers? As technology advances and acceptance of these ideas grows, we have seen the thinning of the layers of middle management. Do not expect them to come back; they are gone forever. The effect on project managers is predictable and significant. Hierarchical structures are being replaced by organizations that have a greater dependence on project teams, resulting in more opportunities for project managers.

The Growth of Project Management as a Profession

We are beginning to see companies implementing career-path programs for project managers. Projects are classified according to such characteristics as risk, business value, length, and complexity. Project management skill sets are mapped into these classifications, and project managers are chosen based on a skill set match. Project management curricula are matched to these classifications so that a project manager can develop skills by managing projects of a certain classification and participating in the training associated with that project class.

The Project Management Institute has developed a *Project Management Body of Knowledge* (PMBOK), a curriculum outline to accompany it, and an examination for the professional certification of project managers. The topics in this book relate closely to the PMBOK so that you can learn project management as defined by its premier professional society. We have written this book to be an ideal source of information to help you prepare for the Project Management Professional certification exam.

The Need for a New Training Paradigm for Project Managers

We would like to think that all organizations recognize how important project management is to the success of their business activity. Unfortunately, they do not. Thankfully, however, many of their professional staff do. They have seen radical changes in their jobs in the last few years. As organizations right-sized, many of the responsibilities of those who were let go passed on to those who remained. We are not sure who the winners and losers are in these cases. Jobs changed radically. New responsibilities were added, often without the benefit of training in how to carry out those new responsibilities. In many cases, professionals had to rely on their own resources to find a way. Where do they turn when they want to learn how to be a good project manager?

As project managers, you are in charge of your own careers and professional development. You own your career; don't ever forget that. Your company owns your job; don't ever forget that either. If you are serious about taking charge of your career, you will find considerable help in this book.

Why We Wrote This Book

We believe a number of professionals are looking for some help. We hope that we can fill their needs with this book. When scheduled training is not available or practical, our book can help. It is written to be studied. It is written to guide you as you learn project management. It is written to be a self-paced resource, one that will immerse you in managing projects for a simulated company and a number of its active projects.

How This Book Is Structured

The book consists of five parts organized into 14 chapters and two appendices. We have followed the materials presented in PMBOK, but not necessarily in the same order. Once you have completed this book, you will have covered all nine areas of the PMBOK.

Part One, Introduction to Project Management

Part One introduces project management.

Chapter 2, "How to Become a World-Class Project Manager." This chapter emphasizes the need to develop project management skills to meet the changing needs of the contemporary organization. The Project Office is a newcomer to the enterprise and is briefly discussed.

Chapter 3, "Case Study: O'Neill & Preigh." Chapter 3 introduces the case study company. O'Neill & Preigh is a manufacturer of church equipment and furnishings. Recent downturns in its market position have resulted in the launch of two projects. One focuses on cost reduction, the other on a new product. Exercises related to these projects are provided throughout Chapters 6 through 13 to give you an opportunity to practice the tools and techniques you have learned.

Part Two, Staging

Part Two sets the stage for the rest of the book. Here we define the example project and introduce our five-phase model for project management. Even though the principles of management apply to project management, a number of collateral principles are specific to project management; we want to introduce them right away. You need to think about the management dimensions just as you will think about the block and tackle of project management.

Chapter 4, "What Is a Project?" This chapter defines the term *project*. In many organizations the project label is attached to almost any type of activity. You'll learn the precise definition for project, which we use as the basis for exploring the nature of projects. A model of the project as a system in balance is introduced. A balanced system is defined by the interaction of scope, quality, time, cost, and resources. These are the basic building blocks of a project and are referred to throughout the book. We also define a rule for classifying projects and use that classification to discuss how the methodology can be adapted to project type.

Chapter 5, "What Is Project Management?" Now that what constitutes a project has been explained, this chapter defines project management. Project management has a life cycle patterned after the principles of people management. The model we use has five steps or phases: scope the project, develop the detailed plan, launch the plan, monitor and control progress, and close out the project. This model sets the framework for the remainder of the book. We draw a parallel between the project management life cycle and the software development, new product development, and continuous quality improvement program life cycles. We also introduce the notion of quality management and risk management as integral parts of a complete project management methodology.

Part Three, Planning

Part Three is the heart of the book. It contains six chapters that lead you through the details of developing a project plan. You follow the chronology of events, beginning with developing a clear understanding of the request and the deliverable, followed by the detailed development of the work to be done, the time to complete each item of work, the resources required to do the work, and the timeline for completing the work. The treatment is applications oriented and includes several problems from the two projects commissioned by the senior managers at O'Neill & Preigh.

Chapter 6, "Scope the Project." The planning of a project requires answers to several questions, such as what work is to be done, how long will it take, what resources will be needed, what will it cost, and in what sequence can the work be done. The answers are certainly not independent of one another. Our minds, however, cannot absorb all of these dimensions simultaneously, so we will consider them one at a time. We begin in this chapter by determining the boundaries of the project and defining, through goal and objective statements, what is to be done to meet the deliverables negotiated by the requestor and the provider.

Chapter 7, "Identify Project Activities." Once the scope has been approved, we define the items of work (labeled *activities* in this book) needed to meet the requestor's requirements. Note that the term *tasks* is used by some authors and in some project management software packages. We use *activity* in this book, and we use *task* for another purpose. Activities and tasks are discussed in this chapter.

Chapter 8, "Estimate Activity Duration, Resource Requirements, and Cost." This chapter discusses estimating the clock time needed to complete each activity (labeled *activity duration* in this book), the resources required, and the cost.

Chapter 9, "Construct and Analyze the Project Network Diagram." This chapter constructs a graphical representation of the project work (labeled the *project network* in this book). An analysis of the project network provides an estimate of the project completion date.

Chapter 10, "Finalize the Schedule Based on Resource Availability." We complete the final schedule details for the project in this chapter.

Chapter 11, "Organize and Conduct the Joint Project Planning Session." All of the planning tools and methods come together in Chapter 11. Here we discuss how to plan and conduct the Joint Project Planning session. This chapter closes with a brief discussion of the project proposal, which is the deliverable from the Joint Project Planning session. This proposal is submitted to senior management for final approval and authorization to proceed with the project work.

Part Four, Implementation

Part Four covers the implementation of the project plan. Once the concepts and principles of status reporting, change management, and problem resolution are discussed, you are immersed in a number of exercises from O'Neill & Preigh. These exercises are designed to test your mettle. Various projects and project situations are presented.

Chapter 12, "Recruit, Organize, and Manage the Project Team." The implementation phase begins with management's approval of the project proposal. In this chapter, we discuss the final details of assembling the project team and establishing the rules and procedures governing how the team will work together.

Chapter 13, "Monitor and Control Progress." Despite the best efforts to plan and document the project work, things seldom go according to plan. This chapter introduces a number of monitoring and control tools for analyzing and reporting project progress. These tools include procedures for managing change and resolving problems.

Chapter 14, "Close Out the Project." Finally, when the project work has been completed and accepted by the requestor, a series of closing activities begins. These activities are discussed in this chapter.

Part Five, References

Part Five contains Appendix A, Appendix B, and the bibliography.

Appendix A, "Managing Multiple Projects." This appendix offers a brief discussion of multiple projects with a major focus on resource management.

Appendix B, "About the CD-ROM." This explains how to use the CD-ROM to access case exercises.

The bibliography contains extensive references for those who would like to further their learning and research into project management.

How to Use This Book

This book adapts very well to whatever your current knowledge of or experience with project management might be. If you are unfamiliar with project management, you can learn the basics by simply reading and reflecting. If you wish to advance to the next level, we offer a wealth of practice opportunities through the case exercises. If you are more experienced, we offer several advanced topics. In all cases, the best way to read the book is front to back. If you are an experienced project manager, feel free to skip around and read the sections as a refresher course.

The seasoned professional project manager will find value in the book as well. We have gathered a number of tools and techniques that appeared in the first edition of this book. The Joint Project Planning session, the use of post-it notes and whiteboards for building the project network, the completeness criteria for generating the Work Breakdown Structure, the use of work packages for professional staff development, and milestone trend charts are a few of our more noteworthy and original contributions.

Who Should Read This Book

Even though our industry experience in information technology clearly shows, we have tried to write this book to be industry independent. Whether you are the seasoned project manager professional or the "wanna be" project manager, you will find useful information in this book. We have incorporated a healthy mix of introductory and advanced topics. Much of what we have written comes from our own experiences as project management consultants and trainers.

The Case Exercises on the CD-ROM

We often observe seminars and workshops that build birdhouses to test your mastery of the tools and techniques of project management. We will not insult you with yet another birdhouse-type project. Instead, we guide you through a realistic project and expose you to the warts and traps that you can expect to encounter.

Chapters 6 through 10 and Chapter 13 include case exercises for you to use with the companion CD-ROM. Each exercise is geared to help you practice the skills you've learned in that chapter. Here's what you'll be asked to do:

- Develop the POS and the PDS (Chapter 6)
- Develop a WBS (Chapter 7)
- Estimate activity durations and resource assignments (Chapter 8)
- Construct a project activity network (Chapter 9)
- Level the resource schedule (Chapter 10)
- Record progress for monitoring and control (Chapter 13)

In each chapter, you'll see an overview of the case exercise and a set of instructions for accessing the exercise on the CD-ROM.

CHAPTER 2

How to Become a World-Class Project Manager

Chapter Learning Objectives

After reading this chapter, you will be able to:

✔ Appreciate the dynamics in the business world that have caused project management to be a growing profession
✔ Understand how the practice of project management is affected by organizational structure
✔ List the functions and tasks performed by project managers
✔ Know the difference between competencies and skills
✔ Know the competencies and skills required of an effective project manager
✔ Assess your own competencies and skills
✔ Put a plan together for your own professional development as a project manager
✔ Identify the specific skills that you personally wish to develop

*The direction in which education starts
a man will determine his future.*

—PLATO
DIALOGS

Start Now

It won't happen by accident. If you want to grow up to be a world-class project manager, you need a plan. In this chapter we help you develop that plan and formulate a strategy for implementing it.

The first lesson is simple but not always obvious to many professionals: Your company owns your job, and you own your career. Never default to your company to take care of your career. At the same time, always look for opportunities in your company to further your career in line with your career plan.

Bob Wysocki spent a lot of time as a dinner speaker on the "rubber chicken dinner circuit." The standard talk was entitled "Jobs Are Out—Careers Are In." Attendees always had questions about how to take charge of their careers. At the end of one of these presentations, three women came forward with rather glum expressions on their faces. A much larger bank from a neighboring state had just acquired the bank at which they worked. All three women had 10 to 15 years' experience as business systems analysts but because of overlaps with the acquiring bank's systems development department, they were not needed and were let go. The sad part of the story is that each thought the bank would take care of them; as a result they had not been concerned for their long-term prospects while they were at the bank. Now that they were in the job market, they were surprised to realize that their technical skills were obsolete, as were many of their bank's systems. Sadly, the bank did something *to* them, not for them—it held them back from their careers. They were trapped because they allowed the bank to take charge of their careers.

Let's agree that you will not let this happen to you. It won't, if you follow the advice given in this chapter.

Demand for Project Managers

The demand for project managers has never been greater than it is today. There are at least four reasons for this:

- Organizations have become customer-driven.
- Organizations have evolved from function to process structures.
- Organizations are using task forces more frequently.
- Organizations have become more project-focused.

Let's take a look at each of these reasons in more detail.

Customer-Driven Organizations

Organizations are *customer-driven*. Their processes and practices are designed to relate directly to the customer. Their success is measured using metrics that are directly related to the customer. These organizations often assign responsibility for the care and feeding of a customer's request by turning the request into a project, or projectizing that request, and assigning a specific person (a project manager) to that customer's request.

"If you don't support the customer directly, you support someone who does support the customer directly." In today's organization, the value you add to an organization is measured by how strongly your job responsibilities reflect this statement. If you are not adding value to your organization, your manager might ask, "Why are we continuing to employ you?" Remember that you don't get paid for simply showing up! Customers have come to expect immediate satisfaction. If you don't provide it, they will find someone who will.

What does this mean to the project manager? Simply put, it is essential that you look for ways to add value to your organization by participating in projects that focus on enhancing customer relations and improving the way your company and its business processes relate to the customer. At the same time, you should participate in projects that give you an opportunity to acquire a new skill or enhance an existing one. Even if you don't have a choice in the projects you work on, keep in mind that projects are a way to develop yourself professionally. Opportunities to do that should be sought out and taken advantage of wherever and whenever possible.

Evolution from Function to Process

As companies become more process-focused, the need for multidisciplined project managers increases. This trend may not contribute to a net increase in the number of project managers needed, but it does increase the demand for multidisciplined project managers.

Most customer-driven organizations have made the transition from the once popular *functional silos* (marketing, sales, finance, and so forth) to a more focused *process structure* (order entry to order fullfillment, product research and development, and so forth). This transition makes it possible for the company to define itself in terms of those processes that relate directly to the customer. The reengineering movement enabled much of this transition to take place. Cost containment, reduced time to market, improved productivity, and other programs were the drivers that characterized this transition.

What does this mean to the project manager? There are an unlimited number of opportunities for career development for project managers who work in organizations that have made this transition or are in the process of making this transition. In organizations in the transition phase, there are numerous projects that define and implement business processes to replace functional approaches.

A good example is integrating the steps that the organization undertakes to receive and completely process a customer order. In the functional silo organization, this can involve the following steps:

- Order entry by the sales department
- Credit approval by the accounting department
- Production scheduling by the manufacturing department
- Acceptance into the warehouse by the inventory control department
- Picking and packaging by the shipping department
- Invoicing and collections by the accounts receivable department

These steps are under the control of several different managers in several different departments. Poor communications, delays, and errors are common. In the process-driven organization, all of these steps are integrated under one manager (or process owner, if you will). Problems associated with communications, delays, and errors are greatly reduced as a result.

In organizations that have made the transition, there are opportunities for process quality improvement projects to further hone the new business model. For example, it is very likely that the newly implemented process will not function up to the level expected by management. Improvements may be needed, and a number of short-term projects to make such improvements will be commissioned. These projects provide many opportunities for project managers and their team members to gain a better understanding of their organization's business functions and processes. Later in this chapter we discuss how projects create opportunities for specific skills development and career growth.

Task Forces

Along with all of the changes in organizations, hybrid forms of organizational structures are emerging, such as Fish-net, T-Form, network organizations, and the boundary-less organization. (For more information on these structures, refer to Johansen and Swigart, *Upsizing the Individual in the Downsized Organization*; Lucas, *The T-Form Organization*; Helgesen, *The Web of Inclusion*; Stacey, *Complexity and Creativity in Organizations*; and Davidow and Malone, *The Virtual Corporation*.) Many of these new structures are the direct result of downsizing efforts and empowerment of the worker. These new forms are grouped under the heading *task force*.

We generally think of task forces as taking on a responsibility or charge. They are temporary; once the charge has been met, the task force is dissolved. These situations are similar to a project structure except that the team members are generally assigned to the task force on a part-time basis.

Organizations charter task forces to address a myriad of one-time situations. For example:

- A problem arises unexpectedly, and a task force is commissioned to study the problem and recommend a solution.

- A new employee benefit program has become available, and a task force is formed to evaluate it and its impact on existing benefit programs.

- A suggestion is made to put an employee-find-an-employee program in place, and a task force is commissioned to look into the suggestion.

All of these situations generate associated projects and the need for project managers.

The more interesting variation is the *permanent task force*, as depicted in Figure 2.1. The permanent task force has a specific responsibility, acts independently of the department, and draws on the functional areas for advice and training. The functional areas perform a support role only.

There are four advantages to the permanent task force:

It is the same as pure project form. In this situation the project has high visibility in the organization. Resources are not shared across projects but rather are assigned to the project team and are under the control

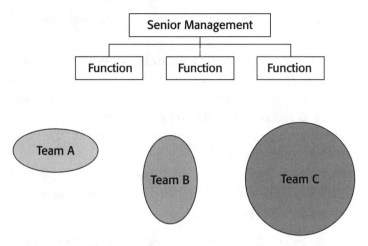

Figure 2.1   The task force structure.

of the project manager. The task force is more adaptable to changing conditions, can make schedule changes more easily, and generally has better cost control as well.

It empowers workers and develops responsibility and authority. The task force is self-contained, which means that the skills needed to accomplish the work of the project must exist among one or more of the team members. Team members with these unique skills will often have more autonomy to complete their tasks in accordance with the project plan.

It generally fosters higher morale. Each team member's importance is recognized because of the particular skill he or she brings to the team, and with that comes increased autonomy and higher morale.

It generates higher levels of productivity and quality. Because their team depends on them for their unique contributions, team members have a heightened sense of commitment, resulting in higher productivity and quality of workmanship.

There are also disadvantages to this structure:

Implementation time is long. Building a team takes time. The team members must learn each other's work habits, interpersonal skills, and conflict styles before they can begin to function as a team rather than just a group of people.

There are few opportunities to develop special skills. Team members contribute their special skills to the project and often have limited opportunities to develop new skills outside of the skills needed by the team.

There is a high risk of failure. Individuals generally have a difficult time transitioning from their focus on self to their focus on team. The training and development needed to make this transition often are not available. There is too much work to be done, the schedule is aggressive, and project managers typically do not appreciate the value of the training and development needed.

There is no clear career path. Just as skill development is limited, so are opportunities for career growth and development. The individual is trapped within the task force structure.

The most common example of the permanent task force structure is the *self-managed* or *self-directed* team. The team has all of the skills it needs to carry out its assigned mission. If any skills are missing, the team is responsible for training its members or acquiring additional team members who possess the needed skills. Teams often will have profit/loss responsibility and hiring and firing authority. In a sense, they are a business within a business. This structure is supportive of effective project management. In fact, effective project management is a prerequisite for good performance of these task forces. Because the team is a permanent structure, it shares the same advantages of the project structure.

Project-Driven Organizations

The project-driven organization aligns its professional staff with projects. In these organizations, a person is assigned to only one project at a time. When that project is complete, he or she is reassigned to another project. Project teams tend to be self-sufficient, that is, they possess all of the skills needed to achieve their goal. Any skills not present among the team are developed through training. This practice maximizes the opportunities for professionals to become project managers and to develop their project management skills. In project-driven organizations, a managerial-level function (a project support office or project portfolio steering committee, for example) assesses project complexity and assigns project managers to projects that match their skill profile.

For those who want the best of all project management worlds, working in the project-driven organization should be your goal. Empowerment of the worker makes it possible for the organization to structure itself more along the lines of a project-driven organization.

The project-driven structure has some advantages:

Everybody understands the work of the whole project. Team members are assigned 100 percent to the project and do not have the diversions that other structures create.

It is highly receptive to new ideas. The success of the team members totally depends on the success of the project. In the true project team all ideas are welcomed and all ideas are discussed.

It offers better individual visibility. The project team is self-contained, with every member accountable for deliverables. There is no place to hide.

It has greater adaptability. The project manager essentially has line authority over the team members. Schedules can be adjusted as needed without having to worry about creating scheduling conflicts due to other assignments.

It is more amenable to planning/scheduling. Because the team is self-contained, planning and scheduling are done without the difficulties encountered in other types of organizational structures.

It has better cost control. The project manager controls all of the resources and therefore has better visibility and control of those costs than in other organizational structures.

There are also some disadvantages to this structure:

It has poor stability. Projects can be cancelled at any time due to changing market conditions, business priorities, and a host of other reasons. In those cases deployment of the team members to other projects may be problematic. The same situation exists when the project is completed.

It demands continuous management attention. Because of the changing portfolio of projects in the organization, more management attention is required than in the case of more stable structures.

There are few opportunities to develop special skills. The individual is assigned to a project, and skill development is limited to the skills needed by the project team. There is no opportunity to expand skills beyond those used in the project.

There is no clear career path. Limited skill development opportunities constrain career development.

The project structure, shown in Figure 2.2, is most supportive of effective project management. In this organizational structure, the project

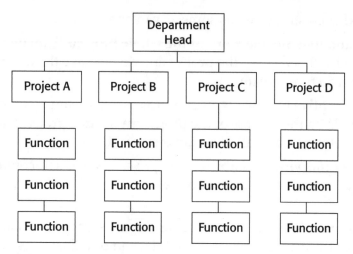

Figure 2.2   The project structure.

team works full-time on the project until its completion. The project manager has line responsibility for the team members. For the project manager, this means having the responsibility for team skill development and deployment. Having the authority to assign and reassign team members to project activities as the needs of the project schedule dictate and not having to negotiate resource reassignment with another manager are both big advantages.

On the other hand, the major disadvantage of the project structure is its inefficient use of resources. If time to market is the dominant constraint, then resource efficiency suffers. On the other hand, if the efficient use of resources is the binding constraint, then time to market suffers. You can't have it both ways!

Traditional Organizational Environments

The previous discussion focused on contemporary organizational structures, but the reality is that many companies are holding fast to the old ways. Because many of you may find yourself in these situations, we would like to offer quick overviews of how project managers fare in such organizations. The environment in which the project team must function can be a great help or hindrance to the successful practice of project management. If you must work within one of these organizational environments, you should at least understand the advantages and disadvantages relative to your professional development as a project manager. To the extent that you can influence your participation, this section will help you build your strategy.

Functional Structures

The *functional structure* is shown in Figure 2.3. Each major functional area is represented as a unit in the organization with a line manager and reporting staff. The unit's scope of responsibility is limited to the functional area in which they work. Work is transmitted to the unit; they do their work and pass it along to the next functional unit. Team work exists within the unit but not across units.

The functional structure is the least conducive for effective project management. In the functional structure, projects frequently have no identity of their own. When the first functional manager finishes working on an activity in the project, the deliverable is "thrown over the transom" to the next functional manager, and so the process continues. Because the project has no champion and no project manager, so to speak, the risk of failure is high. Other disadvantages to the functional structure include these:

Management time needed for between-function problems. Coordination and communication across functional boundaries increase the management time required to move projects forward.

Development opportunities are limited. Individuals are constrained to the project management development opportunities that lie within the functional area. Because projects have little identity in the functional structure, these opportunities are limited.

Communication across functions is more difficult. Poor communications is one of the major reasons why projects fail. The functional structure contributes to that problem rather than alleviating it.

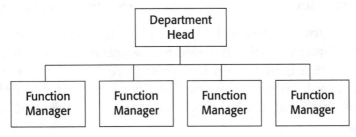

Figure 2.3   The functional structure.

Perhaps the greatest advantage of the functional structure falls on the side of skill development. Because the project work undertaken within a functional unit is typically repetitive and must be completed within the functional unit, the manager has to develop the requisite skills among his or her staff. Other advantages include the following:

Everybody understands his or her task. There is less task variety in the functional structure as compared to the others. Jobs tend to be more repetitive.

It is more stable than other forms. All of the other structures are subject to change as projects start, end, or are cancelled.

It provides for checks and balances. As the work of the project is passed from one function to the next, a check is made to ensure that the deliverable does, in fact, meet requirements.

Standardization within functions is possible. Because of the volatility of the other forms, standardization is not as easily accomplished as in the functional structure.

Matrix Structures

The *matrix structure* is probably the most common organizational environment found in today's organizations, although there is strong evidence that this is changing and businesses are moving toward a hybrid form of project structure. In the matrix organization, there are two entities to consider:

- The functional home of the individual
- The project home of the individual

The functional home deals with development and deployment of individuals to projects. This is where the line manager of the individual is found. The project home is where the individual actually engages in work. The individual team members are accountable to the project manager.

The movement toward down-sizing or right-sizing (or, in some cases, capsizing) has brought with it the need to use resources more efficiently. At the same time it is important that projects retain their identity and visibility in order to increase their probability of successful completion. The structure that accomplishes this best is the matrix structure, shown in Figure 2.4.

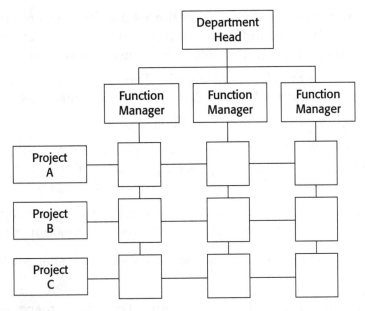

Figure 2.4   The matrix structure.

The matrix structure has all of the advantages of the functional and project structures:

It offers better assessment of skill and development needs. The functional manager is responsible for development and deployment of his or her staff to projects. Based on feedback the functional manager receives from project managers and on the demands placed on them for staff, the functional manager is able to effectively plan for the necessary staff training.

It better utilizes specialized skills. Staff with specialized skills can be deployed across a number of projects. In other structures, that specialization may not be sufficiently required to justify creating a position with those skills.

It is flexible and can adapt to changing environments. As projects start, end, or are cancelled staff can be easily reassigned.

It has few communication problems (dual reporting). The project manager can focus on managing the work; the functional manager can focus on managing the staff. The individual understands the role of the two managers and is able to work more effectively.

Everybody understands the work of the whole. Just as in the projectized organization, the individual is assigned to a project and understands not only the project but his or her role and responsibility in it.

Project objectives are clear and visible. Team members are fully informed on the project objectives, deliverables, schedules, and so forth.

Morale is high. Just as it is in the projectized structure.

It develops future project managers. The functional manager can create an on-the-job development program for each of the staff so that he or she develops needed skills through project assignments.

Project shutdown is not too traumatic. Functional managers simply reassign staff or use the downtime for further skill development.

In addition to sharing advantages, the matrix structure shares a few of their disadvantages:

Success depends on manager interactions. The project manager and functional manager are frequently placed in positions where they must negotiate for who gets assigned to what project. The success of the project depends on their ability to handle those situations effectively.

Project management is difficult. The project manager does not have line authority over his or her team members. The line authority belongs with the functional managers. This means that the leadership skills of the project manager will be called into action.

Potential for politics is greater. Who gets assigned to what project presents opportunities for political maneuverings. A project manager might be willing to give way to the functional manager on one project with the expectation that the favor will be returned on another.

Each project team member has two bosses. This can place the team member in a difficult position. Whose wishes do the team member respond to?

There are conflicting goals (project versus function). Is the project the dominant factor, or is it the function? This distinction must be clearly articulated by senior management. Such issues as assigning priorities and resolving resource contention problems will occur frequently and may have to be resolved above the level of project manager or functional manager.

There is the potential for balance-of-power conflicts. This is a natural result of the politics and goal conflicts that can arise.

Management costs are higher. The dual management structure as well as the heavier burden on senior management contributes to higher management costs.

It is more complex than other forms. No other structure that we have presented has this duality to contend with.

Although there are great advantages to using the matrix structure, it is not that simple to implement. Along with the matrix structure comes a good dose of political baggage. The functional manager is responsible for staff development and deployment. The project manager is responsible for completing projects on time, within budget, and according to specification. These two sets of responsibilities are often at odds with one another. The project manager will always want to negotiate for the "A Team"—the team most skilled and best equipped to handle the requirements of the project—while the functional manager will want to use project work for on-the-job training. The situation is further complicated when the functional manager is also a project manager. To whose projects is the "A Team" assigned?

There are three variations of the matrix structure. The matrix structure shown in Figure 2.4 is called a *functional matrix structure*. In this variation, functional units are strong relative to projects.

The functional matrix structure can be rotated so that projects are strong relative to functional units. In this structure, called *project matrix structures,* functional units provide a support role to projects. Functional managers would prefer the functional matrix because it establishes a more important role for them. Project managers would prefer the project matrix because it gives greater visibility for projects than does the functional structure.

The third variation is called the *balanced matrix*. In this form the project managers report through a project office that reports to the general manager responsible for functional units. Balance is achieved in that both the project managers and the functional managers ultimately report to the same line manager.

For the project manager working in the balanced matrix structure, there are some interesting dynamics to understand. The project manager's line responsibility is to the function/resource manager, whose objective is development and deployment. Let the function/resource manager work for you by sharing your professional goals with him or her. If you know where you are going and the manager knows where you are going, he or she can probably help you get there.

Project Management in Contemporary Environments

Today, there is a trend in organizations to use *cross-functional teams*. Members of cross-functional teams include people from different business functions. This adds several areas of concern for the project manager.

Project managers and team members who manage projects within larger organizations must communicate, sell ideas, negotiate, solve problems, and resolve conflicts across functional and sometimes geographic boundaries. Because the project manager and team are almost always "between" authority and control structures in the larger organization, their people skills must be adept. Having more than one boss is a given in projects in these organizations.

While cross-functional teams are common in those enterprises that focus on business process rather than business function and those that are more customer-centered than in prior years, they do bring some new issues to the table for the project manager:

Ownership. Companies that have evolved to a process focus will often have identified a *process owner*. The process owner is a manager who has the responsibility and authority over a specific process from end to end. Project teams function very successfully in these environments because they have end-to-end responsibility and line responsibility for the staff that are assigned to the process. Companies that are new to the process structure may not have made such delegations. It can be difficult for the project managers in these companies to manage the project because there is no clear line of authority. The task force or self-managed team approach can mitigate some of these problems. In addition, processes span several business functions. This presents a challenge to the team to have a broader understanding of the organization's business functions and to take advantage of the opportunity being presented to learn more about those functions and how they relate to the business processes.

Commitment. As is the case with contracted team members, individuals who have a minor role in the project may not share a commitment to the project. This can become a significant problem unless the project manager takes steps to build that commitment. Those team members who do not have a vested interest in the project may consider themselves as hired help for the project. The project manager should ensure that these professionals understand their role in the success of the project. For example, the team members should know the importance of their work on the project—that their activity is on the critical path or how the output of their efforts contributes to the project objectives, for example. They need to know both the good and bad consequences of their efforts. If possible, the project manager should involve the team members in the planning process and give them an opportunity to contribute their expertise to what is to be done, how it is to be done, and what resource requirements they have for successfully completing their project work.

Authority. Perhaps the major issue in cross-functional teams is line of authority. It should not be determined by default. The stakeholders, especially the contracted team members and resource managers, must have formal statements from the project champion or customer, identifying who is responsible for the project. A formal kick-off presentation, led by the project champion or customer, includes an announcement (verbal and in writing) as to the lines of authority for the project. If the lines of authority are identified at the beginning of the project, there is little chance of confusion or problems downstream in the project.

Process-oriented. With the need to focus the organization's efforts more on customer satisfaction, organizations have turned themselves on their side to reconfigure from functional to process structures. The process structure consists of process owners and process teams. These teams could be *product-based*, that is, they have total responsibility from R&D to customer support and for everything in between. In these situations the project team is a permanent entity and can develop a solid base for project work. The team has the opportunity to establish its own work habits, skill set, meeting format, reporting structure, problem resolution method, and other tools, techniques, and procedures to make project management truly effective. Other organizational structures do not avail the team of these opportunities. Project management in a process-oriented organization has every reason to be successful.

Self-managed teams. Closely related to the process-oriented format are self-managed teams. They have an ongoing responsibility for a function or subfunction, but otherwise they share the same strengths as the process structure. They are self-contained in that all of the skills they need are present in the team. They are devoid of the usual command and control features and generally function just as independently as the process structures.

Interenterprise. Electronic commerce, the information highway, and electronic data interchange have led to new forms of conducting business, such as trading partnerships between suppliers and customers and other neighboring pairs in the food chain. Because of these changes, new application systems that span organizational boundaries are needed. For example, the vendor now has access to its customer's inventory system and can trigger a reorder whenever inventory levels have reached previously established reorder points. Invoicing and payment of invoices are moving toward electronic transactions under the control of both parties' computer systems. In these situations project management is treading new waters. Some of the issues to consider are as follows:

- Which organization provides the project manager, or will there be two project managers?

- Who owns the system?

- How are the differences between technology infrastructures to be reconciled?

- What about public network security? Should we use a private network?

Project Support Office

The *project support office (PSO)* is a staffed function within those organizations that have recognized that the successful completion of projects is a critical success factor. In general, the PSO is a support unit to project managers and their teams that ensures the success of all projects in the portfolio.

The PSO serves six purposes:

Establish, monitor, and enforce standards. This includes such areas as project initiation, project planning, project selection, project prioritization, work breakdown structure templates, risk assessment, project documentation, reporting, software selection and training, post-implementation audits, and dissemination of best practices.

Manage communications. Because communications is at the heart of many project failures, a major reason for the existence of the PSO is to ensure clear and complete communications across all stakeholder groups. This is partially achieved through a series of reports to all levels of management. These reports summarize the status of all projects in the portfolio at a level of detail appropriate to the recipient.

Provide administrative support to the project managers. This extends to preparing proposals, gathering and reporting weekly status information, maintaining the project notebook, and assisting with the post-implementation audit.

Provide training and development. The organization will need a continual supply of new and experienced project managers. Because of their involvement with projects, the PSO has a good sense of areas where skill development is needed and can assist human resources managers, training managers, and line managers with that task. Depending on the type of organizational structure, that role can be a leadership role or a support role. Training curriculum development and training delivery may be assigned to the PSO depending on whether the organization has a centralized training department and whether it has the expertise needed to develop and deliver the needed programs.

Fill a mentoring role. Here the PSO provides safe harbor to project managers for advice, suggestions, and career guidance. Regardless of the organizational structure in which the PSO exists, the project manager does not have any other safe place to seek advice and counsel. The PSO is ideally suited to that role.

Facilitate deployment. Because it is the depository for skills inventories and its staff is knowledgeable of the project portfolio, the PSO is positioned to assist senior managers with the assignment of project managers and the formation of project teams.

There are at least four reasons why an organization would choose to implement a PSO. As the organization grows in the number and complexity of the projects in its portfolio, it must adopt formal procedures for managing the volume. To do this, the organization establishes the procedures that are followed for initiating, proposing, and approving projects.

With the increased volume comes a need for more qualified project managers. Those who would like to become project managers will need to be identified and trained. Those who already are project managers will need additional training to deal effectively with the increased complexity. The PSO is often the depository of the organization's skill inventory of current and developing project managers; because it is aware of the types and complexity of current and forthcoming projects, it is best prepared to identify the training needs of project managers and their teams.

The lack of standards and policies will lead to increased inefficiencies and a compromise on productivity. The increasing failure rate of projects is testimony to that need. Through the establishment and enforcement of standards and practices the PSO can have a positive impact on efficiency and productivity.

Finally, the increased complexity and number of projects places a greater demand on resources. It is no secret that the scarcity of information technology professionals has become a barrier to project success. By paying attention to the demand for skilled project teams and the inventory of skilled team members the PSO can maintain the proper balance through training.

Job Functions and Tasks for Project Management

Project managers are called on to perform a variety of functions and tasks. Many might seem to be removed from the direct management of the project. Here's a list of the most common responsibilities of the project manager:

I. Project planning (strategic and tactical)
    a. Develops preliminary study with project team, identifying business problem, requirements, project scope and benefits
    b. Identifies key project results and milestones
    c. Develops project plan and work breakdown structure and communicates to team and client
    d. Determines needed resources; including client involvement
    e. Estimates timelines and phases
    f. Influences selection of project team members
    g. Assigns project responsibilities based on assessment of individual skills and development needs
    h. Defines clear individual roles and performance expectations
    i. Establishes acceptance criteria
    j. Determines appropriate technological approach

II. Managing the project
   a. Continually reviews project status
   b. Reviews work against key results criteria
   c. Uses systematic method for logging project status, checking against schedule
   d. Uses change management/request procedure
   e. Uses project meetings to measure progress against plan, communicate changes and issues
   f. Assesses skill-needed documentation of meetings, work, conversations, and decisions
   g. Measures quality through testing against requirements
   h. Conducts project reviews and walk-throughs (with appropriate client involvement)

III. Lead project team
   a. Involves team in planning
   b. Uses both formal and informal methods to track project status
   c. Recognizes individual and team accomplishments or results
   d. Manages performance issues in a timely manner
   e. Delegates tasks effectively based on understanding individual strengths and weaknesses
   f. Maintains open door for staff ideas and concerns
   g. Sets performance and development objectives for staff
   h. Schedules and holds regular team meetings

IV. Building client partnerships
   a. Involves working jointly with client in defining project goals and key results
   b. Works with client to ensure alignment of project to overall business goals
   c. Listens and responds actively, documents client needs, changes, and demands
   d. Implements procedures for controlling and handling change
   e. Develops client understanding of the system and trains in systems use
   f. Presents and reports periodically to client
   g. Establishes lines of responsibility and accountability to client

V. Targeting to the business
   a. Manages in accordance with visions and values
   b. Links overall architecture principles
   c. Interfaces effectively with business systems and processes

d. Plans for impacts on related systems/departments to achieve maximum efficiency
e. Understands business needs, time, and cost pressures
f. Keeps current with business and technology developments in competitors
g. Aligns project with corporate and business priorities and direction

Competencies and Skills of the Project Manager

Projects are unique. Some are simple for a variety of reasons (they are short-term, have low business value, and use well-developed and understood technologies). Others are more complex (they use bleeding-edge technologies, involve high risk, require scarce or expensive resources, and are long term). The type of project manager who can successfully manage these differing types of projects will also be different. The model that we discuss in this section assumes that appropriately matching project type with project manager type will greatly increase the probability of the project's success.

We have built a skill model based on links between project managers and projects. Projects are classified into one of four categories, where each project category is defined by a complexity metric. Similarly, project managers are classified into one of four classes, where each project manager class is defined by a skill profile. Through our model we can profile the skills required of the project managers for projects of a given complexity. Finally, by evaluating an individual on the skill set we can determine their qualifications for managing a project of a given complexity. Let's see exactly how this approach works by looking at the details of each of the component parts.

Classifying Projects

First we consider classifications of project managers based on classifications of projects. Figure 2.5 classifies projects according to business and technology dimensions. The Complexity Assessment Grid was developed by the Center for Project Management and is reproduced here with permission.

Given a project, the complexity assessment process begins by measuring as many as 40 variables that define the characteristics of the project and, through a proprietary algorithm, maps them into two dimensions: business environment and technical environment. A typical project can thus be plotted as a data point on the complexity assessment matrix. The data point will fall into one of four categories:

Type I projects. These bear all of the characteristics of Type II and III projects in that they use complex technologies and have high business value. They are the most demanding of the four types and are often mission-critical.

Type II projects. This type may use new or complex technologies and while business value may be low or moderate, these projects can be distinguished from Type I projects.

Type III projects. These are characterized by their high business value even though they may have low or moderate technical complexity. These projects are therefore distinguished from the other two by their high business content.

Type IV projects. These projects have low business value and use well-established technology. In fact, these are projects that may have been repeated several times and are now routine.

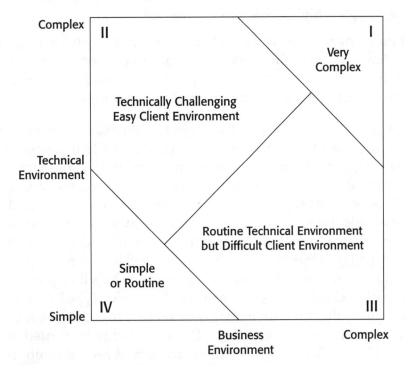

Figure 2.5 Project complexity assessment.
Compliments of the Center for Project Management.

Classifying Project Managers

Project managers can also be classified. The more seasoned project managers are qualified to manage the most complex and mission-critical projects. On the other hand, new project managers might be limited to less complex and noncritical projects.

There are four classifications for project managers, which directly relate to the project classifications:

Team leader. Team leaders have responsibility for part of the project. They are generally assigned responsibility for an activity and can have a small number of staff assigned to the activity whose work they will manage.

Project manager. This individual will have management responsibility for projects that are classified as simpler, less complex, lower risk, or not mission-critical. They are the more junior of the two classes of project manager.

Senior project manager. These are the more experienced of the two project manager classes. They are qualified to manage projects that are more complex, higher risk, or mission-critical.

Program manager. This classification is reserved for those individuals who have achieved the highest level of professionalism and experience in project management. They will often manage project managers on very complex or multiproject undertakings.

Each of these levels relates to the project complexity assessment grid. Type IV projects can be managed by anyone of the four classes of project manager but will most frequently be managed by those who have demonstrated team leader qualifications. By choosing the appropriate Type IV project the project manager and project team can learn and practice new skills. Type II and III projects can be managed by anyone who has demonstrated project manager or higher qualifications but will most likely be managed by someone who has reached project manager status. Depending on the mix of technical and business skills they possess, they will be assigned to either Type II or Type III projects. Type IV projects are the domain of the program manager or senior project manager classes. The most critical of the large Type IV projects may be treated as programs and be staffed by a program manager and several senior project managers or project managers.

The career path for project managers follows these four types. Experience and additional training eventually lead to promotions along the career path. Later in this chapter we profile each type of project manager based on the competencies and skills needed to be effective at that class.

Assessing Competencies and Skills

If anyone has a foolproof method for identifying a professional who will make a competent project manager, please contact one of us. We can show you how to make a lot of money. In fact, it is very difficult to identify someone with the requisite competencies.

Two levels of characteristics determine success or failure as a project manager: *skills* and *competencies* (see Figure 2.6). At the visible level are skills whose level of mastery can be measured and that a person can acquire through training. Estimating time and estimating cost are two examples. That is the easy part. More difficult are competencies, those traits that lie below the surface, out of the range of the visible. We can see them in practice, but we cannot measure them in the sense of determining whether a particular person has them and, if so, to what degree. Noticing and interpreting nonverbal behavior is one example. Competencies are also the traits that are more difficult to develop through training. Some of them can be hereditary.

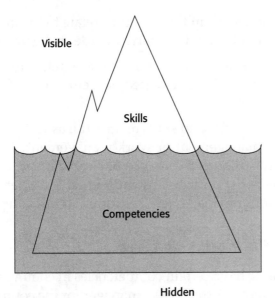

Figure 2.6   Project manager competencies and skills.

To establish an individual's competency level we recommend that some form of assessment be done by the individual's coworkers. Often 360 assessment approaches will be used. In the typical 360 assessment situation, the assessors might be the individual's manager, peer professionals, subordinates, and customers. A common practice is to have the individual complete a self-assessment and compare it to the coworkers' assessments. While this approach is simplistic, it is practical and has surfaced rather insightful conclusions regarding individual performance.

We have also developed a skill assessment tool that can be an effective self-assessment tool as well as a 360 assessment tool. In addition to using the business, personal, interpersonal, and management categories of the competency assessment, the skill assessment includes project management skills as a fifth category. Effective project managers require competencies and skills that are specific to the discipline in which the project they manage lies, and they require a set of nondiscipline-specific competencies and skills that are classified into one of four categories. The well-rounded project manager has skills and competencies in all of these categories:

Business. These competencies and skills relate to the business and business processes in general and do not involve specific business function knowledge.

Personal. Competencies and skills in this category relate to the individual. These skills do not involve another party in order to be practiced.

Interpersonal. Competencies and skills in this category relate to the individual. These skills involve at least two people, neither one of which is the manager of the other.

Management. These competencies and skills relate to all aspects of management, either people management or work management. Also included are skills related to the performance of strategic and tactical management functions not specific to any individual. Competencies and skills specific to project management are found in this category.

Competency Profile of the Project Manager

All levels of project manager have certain competencies in common. The competency assessment examines the project manager for the competencies that are required to be an effective project manager; it can help you match your current competencies against those that are required of world-class project managers. What results from this examination is a gap between the competencies you have and those that you will need to add to your profile as you increase your project management responsibilities. This assessment forms the core of your personal learning contract.

Figures 2.7 through 2.10 provide a capsule description of the business, personal, interpersonal, and management competencies required of an effective project manager. It is a good exercise to review this list and

---

Business Competencies

Business Awareness

Ensures that the project is linked to the organization's business plan and satisfies a business objective by solving a business problem.	5	4	3	2	1
Evaluates the impact of industry and technology developments.	5	4	3	2	1
Balances ideal technical approaches and project scope against business deadlines and priorities to find the best compromise.	5	4	3	2	1
Quickly adapts to changing business conditions.	5	4	3	2	1

TOTAL BUSINESS AWARENESS SCORE [   ]

Business Partnership

Follows up with business partners, throughout the cycle of the project, to ensure full understanding of the business partners' needs and concerns.	5	4	3	2	1
Seeks meaningful business area participation during the design process.	5	4	3	2	1
Conducts business-oriented walk-throughs	5	4	3	2	1
Structures the activities of the project team, so that systems staff work closely with a business partner.	5	4	3	2	1

TOTAL BUSINESS PARTNERSHIP SCORE [   ]

Commitment to Quality

Pushes for more efficient ways to do things.	5	4	3	2	1
Sets and enforces high standards of quality for self and others.	5	4	3	2	1
Develops a quality plan coordinated with the project plan.	5	4	3	2	1
Monitors performance against quality plan and objectives.	5	4	3	2	1

TOTAL COMMITMENT TO QUALITY SCORE [   ]

Figures 2.7 Business competencies.

Personal Competencies

Initiative

Develops innovative and creative approaches to problems when faced with obstacles or limitations.	5	4	3	2	1
Takes calculated risks.	5	4	3	2	1
Takes persistent action to overcome obstacles and achieve solutions.	5	4	3	2	1
Puts in whatever effort is needed to get the job done.	5	4	3	2	1

TOTAL INITIATIVE SCORE [   ]

Information Gathering

Actively solicits input from all groups that may be affected by the project.	5	4	3	2	1
Seeks information or data from various sources to clarify a problem.	5	4	3	2	1
Identities and consults individuals and groups that can expedite project activities or provide assistance.	5	4	3	2	1
Gets enough information to support design and implementation decisions.	5	4	3	2	1

TOTAL INFORMATION GATHERING SCORE [   ]

Analytic Thinking

Develops an overall project plan including resources, budget, and time.	5	4	3	2	1
Translates business goals into project goals and project goals into detailed work breakdown structures.	5	4	3	2	1
Uses project management software to develop plans and track status.	5	4	3	2	1
Generates and presents logical, clearly reasoned alternatives.	5	4	3	2	1

TOTAL ANALYTIC THINKING SCORE [   ]

Conceptual Thinking

Considers the project within the context of a broader view of how the business and technology will be changing over the next several years.	5	4	3	2	1
Uses understanding of business and technical objectives to prioritize effectively (for example: project tasks, test cases, issues to be resolved).	5	4	3	2	1
Anticipates and plans for the impact of the project on other systems.	5	4	3	2	1
Develops a clear vision or conceptual model of the deliverables.	5	4	3	2	1

TOTAL CONCEPTUAL THINKING SCORE [   ]

(continues)

Figure 2.8 Personal competencies.

Personal Competencies

Self Confidence

Presents a confident and positive attitude to set the tone for the team.	5	4	3	2	1
Confronts problems with others quickly and directly.	5	4	3	2	1
Controls own feelings and behavior in stressful situations.	5	4	3	2	1
Works effectively under pressure.	5	4	3	2	1

TOTAL SELF CONFIDENCE SCORE ☐

Concern for Credibility

Maintains credibility by consistently delivering what has been promised.	5	4	3	2	1
Stays on top of the details of the project effort, to be able to answer questions authoritatively and maintain credibility.	5	4	3	2	1
Answers questions honestly, even if it is awkward to do so.	5	4	3	2	1
Promptly informs management and the customer about any difficulties.	5	4	3	2	1

TOTAL CONCERN FOR CREDIBILITY SCORE ☐

Flexibility

Adjusts readily to changes in the work environment.	5	4	3	2	1
Adjusts own managerial style, depending on the people and situation.	5	4	3	2	1
Uses or shares resources to best accomplish organizational goals.	5	4	3	2	1
Delegates tasks and activities to others.	5	4	3	2	1

TOTAL FLEXIBILITY SCORE ☐

Figure 2.8 *(continued)*

personally assess how your competencies measure up. The list was originally developed by the Corporate Education Center of Boston University in cooperation with several of its major corporate accounts. It has since been revised through experience with several other clients and has been adapted here with permission. The scoring algorithm in Figures 2.7 through 2.10 was developed by Enterprise Information Insights, Inc. and is used here with permission.

Interpersonal Competencies

Interpersonal Awareness

Tries to know team members, to understand what motivates them.	5	4	3	2	1
Understands the issues and concerns of other individuals and groups.	5	4	3	2	1
Notices and interprets non-verbal behavior.	5	4	3	2	1
Is objective when mediating conflicting positions of team members.	5	4	3	2	1

TOTAL INTERPERSONAL AWARENESS SCORE ☐

Organizational Awareness

Identifies and seeks the support of key stakeholders affected by the project.	5	4	3	2	1
Proactively engages groups and individuals with technical and/or financial overseeing responsibilities.	5	4	3	2	1
Takes the time to understand and consider the political dynamics among groups involved in the project.	5	4	3	2	1
Uses relationships with people from other units within the organization to resolve issues or provide assistance.	5	4	3	2	1

TOTAL ORGANIZATIONAL AWARENESS SCORE ☐

Anticipation of Impact

Adapts style or approach to achieve a particular impact.	5	4	3	2	1
Manages expectations by ensuring that what is promised can be delivered.	5	4	3	2	1
Arranges for a senior manager to attend the initial project meeting and explain the project's mission and objectives.	5	4	3	2	1
Considers the short and long term implications of project decisions.	5	4	3	2	1

TOTAL ANTICIPATION OF IMPACT SCORE ☐

Resourceful use of Influence

Develops strategies that address other people's most important concerns.	5	4	3	2	1
Enlists the support of his/her management to influence other managers.	5	4	3	2	1
Enlists cooperation by appealing to people's unique expertise.	5	4	3	2	1
Involves project team members in the detail planning of the project, so that they will have ownership of the plan.	5	4	3	2	1

TOTAL RESOURCEFUL USE OF INFLUENCE SCORE ☐

Figure 2.9 Interpersonal competencies.

Management Competencies

Motivating Others

Ensures that team members understand the project's goals and purpose.	5	4	3	2	1
Provides rewards and recognition to people as milestones are reached.	5	4	3	2	1
Initiates informal events to promote team work.	5	4	3	2	1
Takes appropriate action to assist and counsel marginal performers.	5	4	3	2	1

TOTAL MOTIVATING OTHERS SCORE [＿＿＿]

Communications

Organizes and meets regularly with a management team composed of representatives from all areas affected by the project.	5	4	3	2	1
Plans and holds regular, frequent meetings with the project team to discuss status, resolve issues, and share information.	5	4	3	2	1
Ensures that presentations are well organized.	5	4	3	2	1
Tailors his/her language to the level of the audience.	5	4	3	2	1

TOTAL COMMUNICATIONS SCORE [＿＿＿]

Developing Others

Gives team members assignments or training to provide opportunities for growth and development.	5	4	3	2	1
Provides direct, specific, constructive feedback and guidance to others regarding their performance.	5	4	3	2	1
Empowers team members to create challenge and stretch their abilities.	5	4	3	2	1
Provides closer supervision for inexperienced people.	5	4	3	2	1

TOTAL DEVELOPING OTHERS SCORE [＿＿＿]

Planning

Develops and maintains a detailed master plan that shows resource needs, budget, time schedules, and work to be done.	5	4	3	2	1
Assesses project design and implementation approach often to ensure that the project properly addresses the business problem to be solved.	5	4	3	2	1
Ensures a common understanding and agreement on the project scope and objectives and on any subsequent changes.	5	4	3	2	1
Maintains control of accepted changes to the project plan and ensures that any changes are communicated to all team members.	5	4	3	2	1

TOTAL PLANNING SCORE [＿＿＿]

(continues)

Figure 2.10　Management competencies.

Management Competencies

Monitoring and Controlling

Regularly obtains status information from each project team member on their assigned tasks, monitors resource usage, schedules variances, and keeps the project on schedule.	5	4	3	2	1
Identifies the economic and schedule consequences of requested and/or mandated scope changes and communicates these to management.	5	4	3	2	1
Accepts responsibility for resolving project issues, especially scope changes, focusing on solutions, recommendations, and actions.	5	4	3	2	1
Conducts a post-project review to identify what went well, what should have been done differently, and what lessons were learned.	5	4	3	2	1

TOTAL MONITORING & CONTROLLING SCORE [＿＿＿]

Figure 2.10   (*continued*)

The Project Manager Competency Assessment consists of 72 questions. The answers are processed through a mock factor analysis and scores are derived for 19 competencies. For the purposes of this book we have simplified the scoring algorithm and present it in a manual format so that you can complete a self-scoring analysis and evaluation. The rating scale is as follows:

5 = Strongly agree

4 = Agree

3 = Neutral

2 = Disagree

1 = Strongly disagree

Evaluate yourself on each of the competencies and circle the number that best corresponds with how you would respond. Then, add the score value for each of the competency areas. Compare your scores to the interpretations found in Table 2.1.

The resulting scores for each of the competencies can roughly indicate where you should concentrate your development activities. You might

Table 2.1   Resulting Scores

SCORE RANGE	PROJECT MANAGER COMPETENCY LEVEL
4–7	Does not meet minimum competency level
8–10	Meets team leader minimum competency level
11–15	Meets project manager minimum competency level
16–18	Meets senior project manager minimum competency level
19–20	Meets program manager minimum competency level

want to ask your coworkers to assess your competencies, and compare their responses to yours. You'll discover that others do not perceive you as you perceive yourself. Don't disregard their results; their perceptions are reality regardless of how closely they agree with reality as you see it. Remember that the total profile is what counts. As a project manager you are only as strong as your weakest competency.

Skill Profile of the Project Manager

Unlike competencies, *skills* are traits that are visible and can be assessed. The skill levels of the project manager are assessed with Bloom's Taxonomy of Educational Objectives–Cognitive Domain. Bloom's Taxonomy is a six-level taxonomy that measures cognitive abilities:

- Knowledge
- Comprehension
- Application
- Analysis
- Synthesis
- Evaluation

It is based on observable and verifiable events as they relate to each of the skills. The following sections define each of the six levels.

Level 1.0 Knowledge (I Can Define It)

Knowledge, as defined in this level of Bloom's Taxonomy, involves *remembering or recalling* ideas, materials, or phenomena. For measurement purposes, the recall situations involve little more than bringing to mind the appropriate material. Although altering the material may be required, this is a relatively minor part of the task. The student is asked to relate and judge materials. He or she is expected to answer questions or problems that are posed in a form that is different in the test situation than in the learning situation.

You can think of the mind as a file system and knowledge as the information stored in that file. The purpose of the knowledge test situation is for the student to identify in the problem or task the appropriate signals, cues, and clues that will most effectively retrieve whatever knowledge is filed or stored. Knowledge does not mean that the student can actually perform or use the knowledge in a practical manner; the student only needs to be able to retrieve it.

Level 2.0 Comprehension (I Can Explain How It Works)

Comprehension refers to those objectives, behaviors, or responses that represent an understanding of the literal message contained in a communication. In order to understand a communication, the student can change the communication in his or her mind or in his or her overt responses to a form that is more meaningful. There also can be responses, which represent simple extensions beyond what is given in the communication itself. In other words, the student responds in his or her own words with an explanation of the communication that displays an understanding of the message that was sent.

Level 3.0 Application (I Have Limited Experience Using It in Simple Situations)

While the first two skill levels are knowledge-based, the *application* level and the next three are experience-based. This skill level involves using abstractions and concrete situations. The abstractions can be in the form of general ideas, rules of procedures, or generalized methods. The abstractions also can be technical principles, ideas, and theories, which must be remembered and applied.

If the student uses an abstraction correctly, given an appropriate situation in which no mode of solution is specified, he or she has demonstrated application. The ability to apply generalizations and conclusions to real-life problems and the ability to apply science principles, postulates, theorems, or other abstractions to new situations demonstrate understanding at the application level.

Level 4.0 Analysis (I Have Extensive Experience Using It in Complex Situations)

Analysis is the breakdown of a communication into its constituent elements or parts so that the relative hierarchy of ideas is made clear and/or the relations between the ideas expressed are made explicit. The analyses are intended to clarify the communication, to indicate how the communication is organized and the way in which it manages to convey its effects, as well as its basis and arrangement. Analysis deals with both the content and form of material.

Level 5.0 Synthesis (I Can Adapt It to Other Uses)

Synthesis tests the student's ability to put together elements and parts to form a whole. This involves working with pieces, parts, elements, and so on, and arranging and combining them in such a way as to constitute a pattern or structure not clearly there before.

Level 6.0 Evaluation (I Am Recognized as an Expert by My Peers)

The *evaluation level* tests the student's judgment about the value of material and methods for given purposes. Quantitative and qualitative judgments about the extent to which material and methods satisfy criteria and the use of a standard appraisal are demonstrations of understanding at the evaluation level. The criteria may be those determined by the student or those that are given to him or her.

Application of Bloom's Taxonomy

Bloom's Taxonomy has been applied by Enterprise Information Insights to the skill profile required to manage projects of a given complexity. For each of the four project classes described earlier, a skill profile of the successful manager of each project class was determined. One way of understanding this is to envision a matrix of skills (the rows of the matrix) by project manager class (the columns of the matrix). At the intersection of a row (skill) with a column (project manager class) a value from 1 to 6 indicates the skill level that is required for a project manager of that class. Figures 2.11 through Figure 2.15 give the skill levels for project management, management, business, interpersonal, and personal as a function of project manager class. Note how skill levels change for each class of project manager. Project managers can identify skills development needs as they consider progression through the ranks of project management.

Project Management Skills	IV	III	II	I
Charter Development	3	4	4	4
Complexity Assessment	—	3	3	4
Cost Estimating	3	4	4	5
Cost Management	3	4	4	5
Critical Path Management	3	4	4	4
Detailed Estimating	3	4	4	5
Project Planning (WBS, network, PERT, etc)	3	4	4	4
Project Closeout	3	4	4	5
Project Management Software Expertise	4	4	4	4
Project Notebook Construction & Maintenance	3	4	4	4
Project Organization	—	3	3	5
Project Progress Assessment	2	3	3	4
Resource Acquisition	2	4	4	5
Resource Leveling	2	4	4	5
Resource Requirements	2	4	4	5
Schedule Development	3	3	3	4
Scope Management	3	4	4	5
Size Estimating	3	4	4	5

Figure 2.11   Project management skills of project managers.

Management Skills	IV	III	II	I
Delegation	3	4	4	5
Leadership	3	4	4	5
Managing Change	—	4	4	4
Managing Multiple Priorities	3	4	4	5
Meeting Management	3	4	4	5
Performance Management	—	3	3	4
Quality Management	3	3	3	4
Staff and Career Development	—	—	—	4
Staffing, Hiring, Selection	—	4	4	4

Figure 2.12   Management skills of project managers.

Business Skills	IV	III	II	I
Budgeting	—	3	3	4
Business Assessment	—	4	4	4
Business Case Justification	—	—	—	4
Business Functions	3	3	3	4
Business Process Design	—	3	3	3
Company Products Services	—	3	3	3
Core Application Systems	3	3	3	3
Customer Service	—	—	—	3
Implementation	4	5	5	5
Planning: Strategic and Tactical	—	3	3	3
Product/Vendor Evaluation	—	—	—	4
Standards, Procedures, Policies	3	4	4	4
Systems and Technology Integration	—	4	4	4
Testing	4	4	4	4

Figure 2.13   Business skills of project managers.

Interpersonal Skills	IV	III	II	I
Delegation	3	4	4	4
Conflict Management	3	4	4	4
Flexibility	3	4	4	4
Influencing	—	3	3	4
Interpersonal Relations	3	4	4	4
Negotiating	—	3	3	4
Relationship Management	—	4	4	5
Team Management/Building	3	4	4	4

Figure 2.14   Interpersonal skills of project managers.

Personal Skills	IV	III	II	I
Creativity	3	4	4	5
Decision Making/Critical Thinking	—	4	4	5
Presentations	—	4	4	4
Problem Solving Trouble Shooting	4	4	4	5
Verbal Communications	3	4	4	4
Written Communications	3	3	3	4

Figure 2.15   Personal skills of project managers.

A Career Planning Template

When Alice in Wonderland answered that she didn't know where she was going, the Mad Hatter replied "Then it doesn't make any difference which way you go." While you may take any path you choose and you may have a successful career, the odds are definitely not in your favor. Companies want employees who can add value. They aren't going to keep you around if you can't demonstrate that you do add value. You won't get paid for simply showing up! In our experience few professionals give even a passing thought to their future. If you don't believe me, try a little experiment. Ask 10 people the following questions:

1. Do you like your job?

2. Do you have a career goal? If so, describe it.

3. Are you satisfied with your accomplishments so far?

It is unlikely that even one of the 10 people will say yes to all three questions. That's sad. We claim to be professionals yet we don't seem to be able to spend the time to plan our futures as professionals. The most frequent response to the question "What do you want to be when you grow up?" is "I want to have a job." This will not work in today's business environment. We need to have a specific goal and a strategy for getting there.

Where Are You?

Before you can start on your journey to becoming a world-class project manager, you have to know your starting position. Where are you? In other words, what do you know about project management? What are your competencies and skills? The best beginning strategy is to take the self-assessments in the previous sections. Ask a few coworkers to offer their opinions, too. Be honest. You have no one to fool but yourself.

Where Do You Want to Go?

Fifteen years ago I asked my then 6-year-old son what he wanted to be when he grew up. "A lawyer," he answered without hesitation. He is now 21 and a senior studying mechanical engineering with thoughts of working for a large toy manufacturer. The very fact that he had a goal was the important thing. Goals will most likely change. We are all smarter tomorrow than we are today. But at least if you have a goal you have a direction to set out in.

Your goal may be short term or long term. It really doesn't make any difference. Get one. One response we frequently hear is "I don't know what I want to be when I grow up." We think that you really do have a very important short-term goal; that is, to find a goal. Read, observe, participate, talk to professionals, get a mentor, get a career counselor.

How Will You Get There?

I'm glad you finally made it to this section. Now that you have a short-term or long-term goal, we can get down to some serious planning. First, let's agree that to attain your goal you will adopt a step-by-step strategy. We know the first step (Where are you?). We know the last step even though it may only be to reach the top of the next hill. (Where are you going?). What we don't have are the steps that lead from the start to the finish (How will you get there?).

Step 1: Gap Analysis

The first step to achieving your goal is to compare what you know with what you need to know to get to your goal. The differences are the *gaps*. We will work on these gaps based on some measure of importance and as opportunities for learning and training arise.

Step 2: Prioritize the Gaps to Get to the Next Project Manager Class

Your career path as a project manager will take you through the four classes of project manager one at a time and in the order of increasing complexity. That career path is team leader to project manager to senior project manager to program manager. Within that career path are options. You may be more interested in technical rather than business types of projects. In that case you would look to move from Type IV to Type II to Type I projects. The more business-oriented project manager would similarly consider a path from Type IV to Type III to Type I projects, but those with a business slant. Your goal may be to stop somewhere along the way and not attain the ultimate rank of program manager. Knowing that next step will help you prioritize your gaps.

Step 3: Look for Learning Opportunities to Close the Gaps

At this point you have a prioritized list of gaps that you need to close in order to move to the next class of project manager. Keeping the top three or four in mind, look for learning and on-the-job opportunities that address the needed skills. The opportunities are endless if you pay attention and act proactively. Formal training is the most obvious. What does your company offer? What is available through outside training providers? Informal training is a little less obvious but equally as effective. Get in the habit of reading as a first pass at learning a new skill.

Projects are a hidden treasure for those who are considering on-the-job training. Get to know something about the projects that are coming up and who are the likely project managers. If you need to develop a skill that one of these projects will require or that one of the project managers is particularly good at, get involved with the projects and/or the project manager. You can't yet claim to have the skill, but you can do something on the project that will expose you to situations where the skill is practiced. Observation is a good form of learning. If you are fortunate, you may be able to work in a closely related part of the project and see the skill being practiced first hand. If you don't know much about planning and conducting a project planning session, get on the planning team or at least get in the planning sessions. Be a gopher, get coffee, take care of handouts. Do something that exposes you to a great project planner in action. You would have to be dead to not learn something!

Step 4: Go Back to Step One

On occasion you should revisit your gap analysis. Your skills will have changed; your goals can change, too. You may have reached that next step in the career path. It's time to take a skills inventory again, recalculate the gaps, and reset the priorities. You will repeat this step many times, and you may never finish until your professional career reaches its natural end.

Becoming a World-Class Project Manager

You now have a good understanding of what it takes to become a world-class project manager and how you stack up to that goal. In the remaining chapters we will help you with Levels 1.0 and 2.0 of Bloom's Taxonomy and give you a little practice at Level 3.0 as well.

Case Study: O'Neill & Preigh

Practice is the best master.

—LATIN PROVERB

Information's pretty thin stuff, unless mixed with experience.

—CLARENCE DAY
AMERICAN ESSAYIST AND HUMORIST

The Projects

As the Latin proverb says, "Practice is the best master." We believe that, and rather than have you just read about project management, we want you to *do* project management. This chapter introduces you to two projects that will run in parallel through the entire text. The first project, entitled "Office Supplies Containment," is our example project. We use it to illustrate tools and techniques discussed in the chapters. The other project, entitled "Gold Medallion Organ," is an exercise for you to try. Many of the chapters contain exercises that you will try. The details for each exercise are contained in the accompanying CD-ROM. Answers are also provided, but we trust that you will not peek until you have given the exercises a try. Have fun!

Overview of the Business Situation

O'Neill & Preigh is an 800-year-old manufacturer of church equipment. Originally established in a small village on the outskirts of Rome, it now operates out of corporate offices in Lancaster, Pennsylvania. It is recognized as the market leader in both stock and custom-built furnishings for churches of all denominations. Its quality and craftsmanship are undisputed as the best in the industry. It sells its products in international markets through its own sales staff as well as through distributor channels in major cities around the world.

All is not good, however. For the past six quarters O'Neill & Preigh's business has dropped off dramatically. The senior management team agrees that their problems are both internal and external.

Internally, the company has always operated rather loosely. Business has been excellent for so many years that growth has come without the need for processes and procedures. The few processes and procedures that are in place were put there by their managers out of necessity, rather than as the result of a strategic planning effort. Operating budgets are held at the officer level, so department managers have not been involved in operational-level details. They simply go about the business of doing those things they have been doing for years without giving much thought to the business reasons for doing so. The department managers have not questioned the need for change. The company's long history has established it as an organization that focuses on the highly skilled craft of building custom furnishings, for which the company is both very proud and world-renowned. You could say that O'Neill & Preigh is more an organization of artisans than an organization of business managers. One of the consequences of this method of operating is poor cost control; until recently, the company never had to worry about its efficiency and effectiveness. The computer has made little inroad into business operations. The accounting office has computerized payables, receivables, payroll, and inventory, but little else.

Externally, the changing market is a cause for concern. O'Neill & Preigh's president, Del E. Lama, reported at the quarterly "State of the Business" meeting of the senior officers that part of the company's problem is the aggressive pricing strategies of a Southeastern Asian conglomerate that recently introduced its product to the American market. While the Asians do not compete on quality, it seems that the American market now is more price-sensitive than in the past. Del exhorted his management team to take a good hard look at the business. He went on to talk about a likely reengineering effort and a reexamination of the information systems that support the business. Here he is concerned that the few computer applications they have were developed in the company's decentralized, laissez-faire style. Maybe it was time to look at information as a competitive weapon and see what might be done to increase its future impact. Del has also heard much about information technology and automated manufacturing, and he wonders whether the company, in its zeal for craftsmanship, hasn't overlooked opportunities to remain competitive without sacrificing quality. To spearhead this computerization effort he hired his grandson, Sal Vation, to join the firm as director of information resources. Sal had just graduated from a prominent New England business school with an MBA in information systems.

Needless to say, the management team was taken aback. They certainly used computers, but only as a backroom tool. Computers ran their accounting functions, and that was just fine. Del was talking about a whole new way of doing business. Many would find that uncomfortable.

Description of Project Initiatives

As a result of Del's bleak report, several managers stepped forward with ideas for projects that might help pull the company back to its former greatness and still maintain its image of world-class quality. They were, after all, committed to the company and proud to be associated with O&P. Two projects will soon be proposed to the management team. They are briefly described next.

Project 1: Office Supplies Containment

The management team has a long history of not bothering department managers with operating issues. Times were good, and there was little reason to be heavy-handed. The budget for office supplies was always administered by Nick Uldyme, the vice president for finance. Departments charged their office supplies expenses against a corporate budget; they did not have departmental office supply budgets. Nick was happy to report the numbers, but he was not too interested in procedures and controls for controlling expenses. The result: the corporate budget for office supplies was generally overspent by 4 percent. Until now no one expressed much concern.

Because of Del's bleak report, Nick decided that the time had come to tighten the corporate belt. Office supply expenses had always been suspect, but until now he simply ignored that area of the budget. Things were different now. He decided to initiate a project that would establish an office supplies budgeting process with controls and checkpoints to bring some rationale to office supply expenditures. Because he didn't have a specific avenue of attack to pursue, Nick decided to explore various ideas for cost containment and see what he could do.

Project 2: Gold Medallion Organ

Hal E. Lewya is the vice president of manufacturing for O&P. He has been with the company for many years, having been aggressively recruited away from a leading manufacturer of church musical instruments. Hal has always been the champion for new and innovative instrumentation. In fact, after only a few weeks on the job, he presented an idea for a new line of church organs. He believed strongly in using current technology, and he had devised an idea for replacing the usual pulls and stops with a touch screen. The performer could easily configure the organ with a few quick finger moves, rather than by the physical process usually required. The old guard did not receive his idea very well. They saw it as a compromise of the traditions for which O&P had been known. Somehow computers and craftsmanship didn't mix very well in their minds. Del's proclamation changed the game, however, and Hal was preparing to resurrect his idea. Surely they would buy it this time.

Before going forward with his proposal, Hal decided to polish it up a bit. After all, a lot of technology breakthroughs have occurred since he first put his ideas on paper almost two years ago. He began by listing the features and functions he saw in his new organ:

- All stops and pulls would be replaced with a color touch-screen menu.
- The touch screen would be physically integrated into the design of the organ. It would have to be as inconspicuous as possible.
- The screen would use a graphic interface. There would be no text to read.
- Once the performer had set the configuration, the screen would display a description of the configuration that had been input. This was a final check that the correct data had been entered.
- The organ should be online to the O&P offices for remote diagnostics and tuning.

Hal knew that his proposal would not be received enthusiastically. O&P was a company of craftsmen, not of technologists. He expected that an outside contractor would have to be hired to develop the touch-screen application. The contractor would have to work with the craftsmen to create the integrated look that he envisioned. That was going to be a big challenge.

One thing in his favor, however, was that Del E. Lama was open to new ideas. That the company was in trouble could be just the way to sell his idea. His initial proposal would have to be carefully worded.

Professional Staff Resources

Here are the profiles of the key O&P professional staff who will be working on either or both of the two projects. You will meet others as you work on the case exercises.

President, Del E. Lama. Del has been with O&P longer than he, or anyone else, can remember. Del is steeped in the old ways; he designed and built many of the products that are still in the O&P product line and that have been among their most successful. He is not a strong leader but has done well in his job as president. The management team looks up to him because of his even-handedness in dealing with personnel issues. He has nurtured a corporate culture that speaks of family values and concern for the individual. His openness is his greatest strength. He knows that business as usual is not going to work. It is time for change, and he is encouraging his senior managers to come forward with new ideas.

VP finance, Nick Uldyme. Nick has been around for some time and has worked his way up from accounting clerk to his present position as vice president of finance. He tends to spend his time on activities that are more operations related, and he hasn't established himself as a member of the senior management team. He reports what happens with little interest in strategic issues, efficiency, or effectiveness.

VP manufacturing, Hal E. Lewya. Hal has been with O&P for 30 years. He is a true craftsman who has been quite successful with O&P. Even though he has a high regard for the craft he is open to new ideas to improve the business as long as quality is not sacrificed.

VP marketing, Clara Voyant. Clara truly has the talent to design effective marketing programs. She has the uncanny ability to see pearls of wisdom in data where others see only numbers. She welcomes the challenges that the current business situation presents.

VP administration, Olive Branch. Olive doesn't make waves and avoids confrontation whenever possible. She would rather spend the time finding common grounds on which agreements can be reached than use the power of her position to dictate.

IS manager, Sal Vation. Sal is the grandson of the president, Del Lama. He just received his MBA with a specialization in information systems from a prominent New England business school. His uncle hired him to bring O&P into the computer age although he is not sure exactly what that will mean to the company. Sal is surely taking some risk given the culture.

Programmer, Sy Yonara. Sy is unique among IS professionals. He is unequalled in his ability to solve very complex systems design problems. He is also unequalled in his ability to deliver complex solutions that no one can understand. He seems to delight in other people's confusion. Sy is very much a loner. He doesn't like to work with people, and they respond in kind: people don't like to work with Sy. If it weren't for his exceptional analytic and programming skills he would be long gone.

Programmer, Terri Tory. Terri is definitely not a team player. She is a very skilled programmer, but she works effectively only if she is responsible for an activity from start to finish. She makes it clear that she doesn't want to complete work begun by others.

Programmer, Manuel Labor. Manuel is a hard-working junior programmer. Give him a well-defined programming task, and you can count on him to deliver. His skill set is limited, but he learns quickly and has demonstrated a definite potential for growth.

Systems analyst, Anna Lyst. Anna is the only systems analyst at O&P. Many have commented on her ability to see the heart of a given problem, offer a number of solutions, and work with users through to implementation. She is an effective negotiator. Her only shortcoming is her intolerance of incompetent or poorly committed professionals. She makes no bones about letting them know of her disdain, not so much through words as through actions.

Senior accountant, Paul Bearer. Paul has just been promoted to project manager for the Office Supplies Containment project. It is his first experience as project manager. He has just returned from a three-day seminar in project management and is looking forward to his first opportunity to "show his stuff."

Receivables clerk, Bill U. Slowly. Bill has been an accounts receivable clerk ever since there were accounts receivable. He is trustworthy and accurate, but don't look to him for any breakthrough strategies.

These are the major players in the two case studies. You will meet others as the cases unfold. You now have the background you need to begin your study of project management. So let's get started!

PART TWO

Staging

This part sets the foundation for project management.

Chapter 4, "What Is a Project?" defines the term project. In many organizations the project label is attached to almost any type of activity. There is a precise definition for project that you should use as the basis for exploring the nature of projects. This chapter also introduces a model of the project as a system in balance. It is defined by the interaction of scope, quality, time, cost, and resources. These are the basic building blocks of a project and are referred to throughout the book. The rule for classifying projects is also described in this chapter. You will use that classification to discuss how the methodology can be adapted to project type.

With a clear understanding of what constitutes a project, project management is defined in Chapter 5, "What Is Project Management?" Project management has a life cycle patterned after the principles of people management. The model we use has five steps or phases:

1. Scope the project
2. Develop the detailed plan
3. Launch the plan
4. Monitor and control progress
5. Close out the project

This model sets the framework for the remainder of the book. We'll also show you the parallelism between the project management life cycle and the software development, the new product development, and the continuous quality improvement program life cycles. Quality management and risk management as integral parts of a complete project management methodology are also discussed.

What Is a Project?

Chapter Learning Objectives

After reading this chapter you will be able to:

✔ **Define a project**

✔ **List a project's characteristics**

✔ **Distinguish a project from a program, activity, and task**

✔ **Understand the three parameters that constrain a project**

✔ **Know the importance of defining and using a project classification rule**

✔ **Understand the issues around scope creep, hope creep, effort creep, and feature creep**

Things are not always what they seem.

**—PHAEDRUS
ROMAN WRITER AND FABULIST**

Definition of a Project

To put projects into perspective, you need a definition—a common starting point. All too often people call any work they have to do a "project." Projects actually have a very specific definition. If a set of tasks or work to be done does not meet the strict definition, then it cannot be called a project. To use the project management techniques presented in this book, you must first have a project.

A *project* is a sequence of unique, complex, and connected activities having one goal or purpose and that must be completed by a specific time, within budget, and according to specification.

This definition tells us quite a bit about a project. To appreciate just what constitutes a project let's look at each part of the definition.

Sequence of Activities

A project comprises a number of activities that must be completed in some specified order, or *sequence*. An activity is a defined chunk of work. We'll expand on this informal definition of an activity later in Chapter 7, "Identify Project Activities."

The sequence of the activities is based on technical requirements, not on management prerogatives. To determine the sequence, it is helpful to think in terms of inputs and outputs. What is needed as input in order to begin working on this activity? What activities produce those as output? The output of one activity or set of activities becomes the input to another activity or set of activities.

Specifying sequence based on resource constraints or statements such as "Pete will work on activity B as soon as he finishes working on activity A" should be avoided because it establishes an artificial relationship between activities. What if Pete wasn't available at all? Resource constraints aren't ignored when we actually schedule activities. The decision of what resources to use and when to use them will come later in the project planning activities.

Unique Activities

The activities in a project must be *unique*. A project has never happened before, and it will never happen again under the same conditions. Something will always be different each time the activities of a project are repeated. Usually the variations will be random in nature—for example, a part is delayed, someone is sick, a power failure occurs. These are random events that can happen, but we never are sure of when, how, and with what impact on the schedule. These random variations are the challenge for the project manager.

Complex Activities

The activities that make up the project are not simple, repetitive acts, such as mowing the lawn, painting the house, washing the car, or loading the delivery truck. They are *complex*. For example, designing an intuitive user interface to an application system is a complex activity.

Connected Activities

Connectedness implies that there is a logical or technical relationship between pairs of activities. In general, the rooms of a house can be painted in any order. There is no technical relationship between rooms or their painting. There is an order to the sequence in which the activities that make up the project must be completed. They are considered *connected* because the output from one activity is the input to another. For example, we must design the computer program before we can program it.

You could have a list of unconnected activities that must all be complete in order to complete the project. For example, consider painting the interior rooms of a house. With some exceptions, the rooms can be painted in any order. The interior of a house is not completely painted until all its rooms have been painted, but they may be painted in any order. Painting the house is a collection of activities, but it is not considered a project according to the definition.

One Goal

Projects must have a single *goal*, for example, to design an inner-city playground for ADC families. Very large or complex projects may be divided into several *subprojects*, each of which is a project in its own right. This division makes for better management control. For example, subprojects can be defined at the department, division, or geographic level.

This artificial decomposition of a complex project into subprojects often simplifies the scheduling of resources and reduces the need for inter-departmental communications while a specific activity is worked on. The downside is that the projects are now interdependent. Even though interdependency adds another layer of complexity and communication, it can be handled.

Specified Time

Projects have a specified *completion date*. This date can be self-imposed by management or externally specified by a customer or government agency. The deadline is beyond the control of anyone working on the project. The project is over whether or not the project work has been completed.

Within Budget

Projects also have *resource limits*, such as a limited amount of people, money, or machines that are dedicated to the project. While these resources can be adjusted up or down by management, they are considered fixed resources to the project manager. For example, suppose a company only has one Web designer at the moment. That is the fixed resource that is available to project managers. Senior management can change the number of resources, but that luxury is not available to the project manager. If the one Web designer is fully scheduled, the project manager has a resource conflict that he or she cannot resolve.

We'll cover resource limits in more detail in Chapter 10, "Finalize the Schedule Based on Resource Availability."

According to Specification

The customer, or the recipient of the project's deliverables, expects a certain level of functionality and quality from the project. These expectations can be self-imposed, such as the specification of the project completion date, or customer-specified, such as producing the sales report on a weekly basis.

Although the project manager treats the specifications as fixed, the reality of the situation is that any number of factors can cause the specification to change. For example, the customer may not have defined the requirements completely, or the business situation may have changed (this happens in long projects). It is unrealistic to expect the specification to remain fixed through the life of the project. Systems specifications can and will change, thereby presenting special challenges to the project manager. We will show you how to handle them effectively in Chapter 13, "Monitor and Control Progress."

What Is a Program?

A *program* is a collection of projects. The projects must be completed in a specific order for the program to be considered complete. Because programs comprise multiple projects, they are larger in scope than a single project. For example, the United States government has a space program that includes several projects such as the Challenger project. A construction company contracts a program to build an industrial technology park with several separate projects.

Unlike projects, programs can have many goals. The NASA space program is such that every launch of a new mission includes several dozen projects in the form of scientific experiments. Except for the fact that they are all aboard the same space craft, the experiments are independent of one another and together define a program.

Project Parameters

Five constraints operate on every project:
- Scope
- Quality
- Cost
- Time
- Resources

These constraints are an interdependent set; a change in one can cause a change in another constraint to restore the equilibrium of the project. In this context, the set of five parameters form a system that must remain in balance for the project to be in balance. Because they are so important to the success or failure of the project, let's discuss them individually.

Scope

Scope is a statement that defines the boundaries of the project. It tells not only what will be done but also what will not be done. In the information systems industry, scope is often referred to as a *functional specification*. In the engineering profession, it is generally called a *statement of work*. Scope may also be referred to as a document of understanding, a scoping statement, a project initiation document, and a project request form.

This document is the foundation for all project work to follow. It is critical that scope be correct. We spend considerable time discussing exactly how that should happen in Chapter 6, "Scope the Project," where we talk about Conditions of Satisfaction.

Beginning a project on the right foot is important, and so is staying on the right foot. It is no secret that scope can change. We do not know how or when, but it will change. Detecting that change and deciding how to accommodate it in the project plan are major challenges for the project manager. We discuss scope management in Chapter 13 and offer a strategy for dealing with it in a timely and professional manner.

Quality

Two types of quality are part of every project. The first is *product quality*. This refers to the quality of the deliverable from the project. The traditional tools of quality control, discussed in Chapter 5, "What Is Project Management?", are used to ensure product quality. The second type of quality is *process quality*, which is the quality of the project management process itself. The focus is on how well the project management process works and how can it be improved. Continuous quality improvement and process quality management are the tools used to measure process quality. These are discussed in Chapter 5.

A sound quality management program with processes in place that monitor the work in a project is a good investment. Not only does it contribute to customer satisfaction, it helps organizations use their resources more effectively and efficiently by reducing waste and rework. This is one area that should not be compromised. The payoff is a higher probability of successfully completing the project and satisfying the customer.

Cost

The dollar cost of doing the project is another variable that defines the project. It is best thought of as the budget that has been established for the project. This is particularly important for projects that create deliverables that are sold either commercially or to an external customer.

Cost is a major consideration throughout the project management life cycle. The first consideration occurs at an early and informal stage in the life of a project. The customer can simply offer a figure about equal to what he or she had in mind for the project. Depending on how much thought the customer put into it, the number could be fairly close to or wide of the actual cost for the project. Consultants often encounter situations in which the customer is willing to spend only a certain amount for the work. In these situations, you do what you can with what you have. In more formal situations, the project manager prepares a proposal for the projected work. That proposal includes an estimate (perhaps even a quote) of the total cost of the project. Even if a preliminary figure had been supplied by the project manager, the proposal allows the customer to base his or her go/no-go decision on better estimates.

Time

The customer specifies a timeframe or deadline date within which the project must be completed. To a certain extent, cost and time are inversely related to one another. The time a project takes to be completed can be reduced, but cost increases as a result.

Time is an interesting resource. It can't be inventoried. It is consumed whether we use it or not. The objective for the project manager is to use the future time allotted to the project in the most effective and productive ways possible. Future time (time that has not yet occurred) can be a resource to be traded within a project or across projects. Once a project has begun, the prime resource available to the project manager to keep the project on schedule or get it back on schedule is time. A good project manager realizes this and will protect the future time resource jealously. We cover this in more detail in Chapter 8, "Estimate Activity Duration, Resource Requirements, and Cost," Chapter 9, "Construct and Analyze the Project Network Diagram," and Chapter 10 when we talk about scheduling project activities.

Resources

Resources are assets, such as people, equipment, physical facilities, or inventory, that have limited availabilities, can be scheduled, or can be leased from an outside party. Some are fixed, others are variable only in the long term. In any case, they are central to the scheduling of project activities and the orderly completion of the project.

For systems development projects, people are the major resource. Another valuable resource for systems projects is the availability of computer processing time (mostly for testing purposes), which can present significant problems to the project manager when it comes to project scheduling.

The Scope Triangle: Time, Cost, and Resource Availability

Projects are dynamic systems that must be kept in equilibrium. Not an easy task, as we shall see! Figure 4.1 illustrates the dynamics of the situation. The geographic area inside the triangle represents the scope and quality of the project. Lines representing time, cost, and resource availability bound scope and quality. Time is the window of time within which the project must be completed. Cost is the dollar budget available

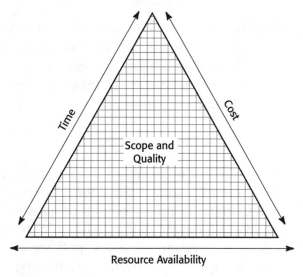

Figure 4.1 The scope triangle.

to complete the project. Resources are any consumables used on the project. People, equipment availability, and facilities are examples. While the accountants will tell us that everything can be reduced to dollars, and they are right, we will separate resources as defined here. They are controllable by the project manager and need to be separately identified for that reason.

The project plan will have identified the time, cost, and resource availability needed to deliver the scope and quality of a project. In other words, the project is in equilibrium at the completion of the project planning session and approval of the commitment of resources and dollars to the project. That will not last too long, however. Change is waiting around the corner.

The scope triangle offers a number of insights into the changes that can occur in the life of the project. For example, the triangle represents a system in balance before any project work has been done. The sides are long enough to encompass the area generated by the scope and quality statements. Not long after work begins, something is sure to change. Perhaps the customer calls with an additional requirement for a feature that was not envisioned during the planning sessions. Perhaps the market opportunities have changed, and it is necessary to reschedule the deliverables to an earlier date, or a key team member leaves the company and will be difficult to replace. Any one of these changes throws the system out of balance.

The project manager controls resource utilization and work schedules. Management controls cost and resource level. The customer controls scope, quality, and delivery dates. This suggests a hierarchy for the project manager as solutions to accommodate the changes are sought. We return to this topic in greater detail in Chapter 13.

Scope Creep

Scope creep is the term that has come to mean any change in the project that was not in the original plan. Change is constant. To expect otherwise is simply unrealistic. Changes occur for several reasons that have nothing to do with the ability or foresight of the customer or the project manager. Market conditions are dynamic. The competition can introduce or announce that they are going to introduce a new version of its product. Your management might decide that getting to the market before the competition is necessary.

Your job as project manager is to figure out how these changes can be accommodated. Tough job, but somebody has to do it! Regardless of how the scope change occurs, it is your job as project manager to figure out how, if at all, you can accommodate the change.

Hope Creep

Hope creep is the result of a project team member's getting behind schedule but reporting that he or she is on schedule and hoping to get back on schedule at the next report date. Hope creep is a real problem for the project manager. There will be several activity managers within your project, team members who manage a hunk of work. They do not want to give you bad news, and so they are prone to telling you that their work is proceeding according to schedule when, in fact, it is not. It is their hope that they will catch up by the next report period, so they mislead you into thinking that they are on schedule. Shame on you if you do not periodically check the accuracy of their status reports! In any case, the activity managers hope that they will catch up by completing some work ahead of schedule to make up the slippage. The project manager must be able to verify the accuracy of the status reports received from the team members. This does not mean that the project manager has to check into the details of every status report. Random checks can be used effectively.

Effort Creep

Effort creep is the result of the team member's working but not making progress proportionate to the work expended. Every one of us has worked on a project that always seems to be 95 percent complete no matter how much effort is expended to complete it. Each week the status report records progress, but the amount of work remaining doesn't seem to decrease proportionately. Other than random checks, the only effective thing that the project manager can do is to increase the frequency of status reporting by those team members who seem to suffer from effort creep.

Feature Creep

Closely related to scope creep is *feature creep*. Feature creep results when the team members arbitrarily adds features and functions to the deliverable that they think the customer would want to have. The problem is that the customer didn't specify the feature, probably for good reason. If the team member has strong feelings about the need for this new feature, formal change management procedures can be employed. The change management process is discussed in Chapter 13.

An example illustrates the point. The programmer is busy coding a particular module in the system. He or she gets an idea that the customer might appreciate having another option included. The systems requirements document does not mention this option. It seems so trivial that the programmer decides to include it rather than go through the lengthy change process.

While this approach may seem rather innocent, let's look at some possible consequences. First of all, because the feature is not in the system requirements document, it is also not in the acceptance test procedure, the systems documentation, the user documentation, and the user training program. What will happen if something goes wrong with the new option? How will another programmer know what to do? What will happen when the user discovers the option and asks for some modification of it? You can see the consequences of such an innocent attempt to please. The message here is that a formal change request must be filed, and if it is approved, the project plan and all related activities will be appropriately modified.

Project Classifications

In Chapter 2, "How To Become a World-Class Project Manger," we classified projects by technical and business complexity for the purposes of determining the skills and competencies of the project manager required to manage the project. In this section, we characterize projects in terms of a more detailed set of variables. The value of these variables will be used to determine which parts of the project management methodology must be used and which parts are left to the discretion of the project manager to use as he or she sees fit.

Many organizations have chosen to define a classification of projects based on such project characteristics as these:

- Risk
- Business value
- Length

- Complexity
- Cost

The project profile determines the classification of the project. The classification defines the extent to which the project management methodology is to be used.

We strongly advocate this approach because it adapts the methodology to the project. "One size fits all" does not work in project management. In the final analysis, we defer to the judgement of the project manager. Apart from the parts required by the organization, the project manager should adopt whatever parts of the methodology he or she feels will improve his or her ability to help successfully manage the project. Period.

Type A projects. Projects of Type A are the high-business-value, high-complexity projects. They are the most challenging projects the organization will undertake. Type A projects use the latest technology, which, when coupled with high complexity, causes risk to be high also. To maximize the probability of success, the organization will require that these projects utilize all the methods and tools available in their project management methodology. An example of a Type A project would be the introduction of a new technology into an existing product that has been very profitable for the company.

Type B projects. Type B projects are shorter in length, yet they still are significant projects for the organization. All of the methods and tools in the project management process will probably be required. The projects generally will have good business value and be technologically challenging. Many product development projects fall in this category.

Type C Projects. Type C projects are the projects occurring most frequently in an organization. They are short by comparison and use established technology. Many will be projects that deal with the infrastructure of the organization. A typical project team will consist of five people, the project will last six months, and the project will be based on a less-than-adequate scope statement. Many of the methods and tools will not be required for these projects. The project manager will use those tools, which are optional, if he or she sees value in their use.

Type D Projects. Projects of Type D just meet the definition of a project and may require only a scope statement and a few scheduling pieces of information. A typical Type D project could involve making a minor change in an existing process or procedure or revising a course in the training curriculum.

Table 4.1 Example Project Classes and Definitions

CLASS	DURATION	RISK	COMPLEXITY	TECHNOLOGY	LIKELIHOOD OF PROBLEMS
Type A	> 18 months	High	High	Breakthrough	Certain
Type B	9–18 months	Medium	Medium	Current	Likely
Type C	3–9 months	Low	Low	Best of breed	Some
Type D	< 3 months	Very low	Very low	Practical	None

Table 4.1 gives a hypothetical example of a classification rule.

These four types of projects might use the parts of the methodology shown in Figure 4.2. The figure lists the methods and tools that are required and optional given the type of project.

Now that we have defined the project, we turn our attention to defining project management. That is the topic of the next chapter.

Project Management Process	Project Classification			
	A	B	C	D
Define				
Conditions of Satisfaction	R	R	O	O
Project Overview Statement	R	R	R	R
Approval of Request	R	R	R	R
Plan				
Conduct Planning Session	R	R	O	O
Prepare Project Proposal	R	R	R	R
Approval of Proposal	R	R	R	R
Launch				
Kick-off Meeting	R	R	O	O
Activity Schedule	R	R	R	R
Resource Assignments	R	R	R	O
Statements of Work	R	O	O	O
Monitor/Control				
Status Reporting	R	R	R	R
Project Team Meetings	R	R	O	O
Approval of Deliverables	R	R	R	R
Close				
Post-Implementation Audit	R	R	R	R
Project Notebook	R	R	O	O

R = Required O = Optional

Figure 4.2 The use of required and optional parts of the methodology by type of project.

What Is Project Management?

A manager . . . sets objectives, . . . organizes, . . . motivates, . . . communicates, . . . measures, . . . and develops people. Every manager does these things—knowingly or not. A manager may do them well or may do them wretchedly but always does them.

—PETER DRUCKER

Principles of Project Management

When we think of the principles of management we usually associate them with the management of people. The management of people includes defining what the business unit will do, planning for the number and type of staff who will do it, organizing the staff, monitoring their performance of the tasks assigned them, and finally bringing a close to their efforts. Those same principles also apply to projects.

Project management is a method and a set of techniques based on the accepted principles of management used for planning, estimating, and controlling work activities to reach a desired end result on time—within budget and according to specification. The following sections investigate how these management principles apply to the phases of a project.

Defining

One of the first tasks for project managers is to define the work that needs to be done in their area of responsibility. Exactly the same task applies to people management. In project management, however, the defining phase is very formal while in people management it can often be informal.

There is a parallel in project management. For the project manager, defining the tasks to do is a preliminary phase of the project life cycle and an important one. In this phase, the requestor (also known as the customer) and the project manager come to an agreement about several important aspects of the project. Regardless of the format used, every good defining phase answers five basic questions:

- What is the problem or opportunity to be addressed?
- What is the goal of the project?
- What objectives must be met to accomplish the goal?
- How will we determine if the project has been successful?
- Are there any assumptions, risks, or obstacles that may affect project success?

The defining phase sets the scope of the project. It forms the basis for deciding if a particular function or feature is within the scope of the project.

Even the best of intentions to define project scope will fall short of the mark. The scope of the project can change for a variety of reasons, which we investigate in Chapter 13, "Monitor and Control Progress"—sometimes far more frequently than the project manager would prefer. As mentioned in the previous chapter, these changes are called *scope creep*; they are a way of life in today's organizations. Scope creep can be the bane of the project manager if it is not dealt with effectively. Scope creep occurs for a variety of reasons, from something the client forgot to include in the business requirements document to a change in business priorities that must be reflected in the project.

The project manager must respond to scope creep by documenting the alternative courses of action and their respective consequences on the project plan. A good project manager will have a formal change management process in place to address scope creep. We have much more to say on this later in Chapter 13.

Planning

How often have you heard it said that planning is a waste of time? No sooner is the plan completed than someone comes along to change it. These same naysayers would also argue that the plan, once completed, is disregarded and merely put on the shelf so the team can get down to doing some real work. In people management, the planning activity involves deciding on the types of people resources that will be needed to discharge the responsibilities of the department. That means identifying the types of skills needed and the number of people possessing those skills.

The project plan is indispensable. Not only is it a roadmap to how the work will be performed, but it is also a tool for decision making. The plan suggests alternative approaches, schedules, and resource requirements from which the project manager can select the best alternative.

Understand that a project plan is *dynamic*. We expect it to change. A complete plan will clearly state the tasks that need to be done, why they are necessary, who will do what, when it will be completed, what resources will be needed, and what criteria must be met in order for the project to be declared complete and successful.

There are three benefits to developing a project plan:

Planning reduces uncertainty. Even though we would never expect the project work to occur exactly as planned, planning the work allows us to consider the likely outcomes and to put the necessary corrective measures in place.

Planning increases understanding. The mere act of planning gives us a better understanding of the goals and objectives of the project. Even if we were to discard the plan, we would still benefit from having done the exercise.

Planning improves efficiency. Once we have defined the project plan and the necessary resources to carry out the plan, we can schedule the work to take advantage of resource availability. We also can schedule work in parallel; that is, we can do tasks concurrently, rather than in series. By doing tasks concurrently we can shorten the total duration of the project. We can maximize our use of resources and complete the project work in less time than by taking other approaches.

Just as Alice needed to know where in Wonderland she was going, so does the project manager. Not knowing the parameters of a project prevents measurement of progress and results in never knowing when the project is complete. The plan also provides a basis for measuring work planned against work performed.

Executing

Executing the project plan is equivalent to authorizing your staff to perform the tasks that define their respective jobs. Each staff member knows what is expected of him or her, how to accomplish the work, and when to have it completed.

Executing the project plan involves four steps. In addition to organizing the people who will work on the project, a project manager also needs to do the following:

1. Identify the specific resources (person power, materials, and money) that will be required to accomplish the work defined in the plan.

2. Assign workers to activities.

3. Schedule activities with specific start and end dates.

4. Launch the plan.

The final specification of the project schedule brings together all the variables associated with the project. To facilitate this exercise, we introduce a number of tools and techniques that we have developed and religiously use in our consulting practice. These are explained and illustrated in Chapters 6 through 13.

Controlling

As part of the planning process, an initial schedule is created. The schedule lists the following:

- What must be accomplished in the project
- When each task must be accomplished
- Who is responsible for completing each task
- What deliverables are expected as a result of completing the project

No matter how attentive the team is when creating the plan, the project work will not go according to plan. Schedules slip—this is the reality of project management. The project manager must have a system in place that constantly monitors the project progress, or lack thereof. The monitoring system summarizes the completed work measured against the plan and also looks ahead to forewarn of potential problems. Problem-escalation procedures and a formal change management process, which we discuss in Chapter 13, are essential to effective project control.

Closing

Closing a project is a formal means of signaling the completion of the project work and the delivery of the results to the customer. In managing people, the equivalent action is to signal the end of a task with some sign of completion and assign the individual to another task.

The closing phase evaluates what occurred during the project and provides historical information for use in planning and executing later projects. This historical information is best kept in a document called a *project notebook*. To be useful, the notebook should be in an electronic form so that it is easy to retrieve and summarize project information for use in projects currently being planned. Every good closing provides answers to the following questions:

- Do the project deliverables meet the expectations of the requestor?
- Do the project deliverables meet the expectations of the project manager?

- Did the project team complete the project according to plan?
- What information was collected that will help with later projects?
- How well did the project management methodology work and how well did the project team follow it?
- What lessons have we learned from this project?

The closing phase is very important to project management, but unfortunately it is the part that is most often neglected or omitted by management. Rather than spending time in the closing phase of this project, the project manager is under pressure to get started on the next project. Often the next project is already behind schedule and work hasn't yet begun. It is easy for management to skip the closing phase because it is perceived as an overhead expense, is easily overlooked, and delays getting the next project underway.

Project Management Life Cycle

Over the years that we have consulted and offered training in project management, we observed a number of project management methodologies that, on first look, seem to differ from one another. On closer examination, we actually found that there are a number of underlying principles that are present in the more successful methodologies. From them, we fashioned a project management life cycle that was first published by Weiss and Wysocki.[1]

Since that publication, we continue to compare this life cycle with client methodologies. The results confirm our assumptions that features reoccur in successful methodologies. More recently the Project Management Institute published its Project Management Body of Knowledge (PMBOK), which has an underlying life cycle that is remarkably similar to the one we adopted in our consulting practice. The one we present in this book parallels PMBOK. If your organization has a methodology in place, compare it to the model given here. If you map your methodology to this life cycle, you may discover that you already do bits and pieces of project management without realizing it. You may not be referring to each phase by the

[1]Joseph W. Weiss and Robert K. Wysocki, *5-Phase Project Management: A Practical Planning and Implementation Guide* (Reading, MA: Perseus Books, 1992), ISBN 0-201-56316-9.

same names as we do, but the actions in that phase are probably what you've been doing all these years. Take comfort, for project management can be defined as nothing more than *organized common sense.* In fact, if it were not common sense, we would have a difficult time gaining any converts!

Phases of Project Management

There are five phases of the project management life cycle, each of which contains five steps:

1. Scope the project
   - State the problem/opportunity.
   - Establish the project goal.
   - Define the project objectives.
   - Identify the success criteria.
   - List assumptions, risks, obstacles.

2. Develop the project plan
   - Identify project activities.
   - Estimate activity duration.
   - Determine resource requirements.
   - Construct/analyze the project network.
   - Prepare the project proposal.

3. Launch the plan
   - Recruit and organize the project team.
   - Establish team operating rules.
   - Level project resources.
   - Schedule work packages.
   - Document work packages.

4. Monitor/control project progress
   - Establish progress reporting system.
   - Install change control tools/process.
   - Define problem-escalation process.
   - Monitor project progress versus plan.
   - Revise project plans.

5. Close out the project
   - Obtain client acceptance.
   - Install project deliverables.
   - Complete project documentation.
   - Complete post-implementation audit
   - Issue final project report.

The five phases are performed in sequence, with one feedback loop from the monitor/control progress phase to the develop detailed plan phase. This model is adapted from the PMI PMBOK and from an earlier work of one of the authors (Weiss and Wysocki).[2] Figure 5.1 shows the project management life cycle. The following sections walk you through the five phases of the project management life cycle. Please refer to this figure as you read the following sections.

Scope the Project

The first phase of the project management life cycle is the scoping phase. This phase is the one most often given the least attention. The scoping phase plans the project.

Planning—or rather, effective planning—is painful. For many people, planning doesn't seem like real work. Projects are always behind schedule, so we are tempted to skip planning so that we can get down to the real work of the project. Experience has shown that good planning can actually decrease the time required to complete a project, even taking the planning time into account. Planning reduces risk and, in the experience of the authors, can increase productivity by as much as 50 percent. We find it interesting that project teams do not have time to plan, but they do have time to do work over again. What insanity!

Every project has one goal. The goal is an agreement between the requestor and the project manager about the deliverable—what is to be accomplished in the project. The goal tells the project developers where they are going so that, when the project is completed, they know it. Ideally, the scoping phase begins with an exchange of information between a requestor and a provider (usually the project manager). The information exchange usually involves a conversation between the two parties

[2]Joseph W. Weiss and Robert K. Wysocki, *5-Phase Project Management: A Practical Planning and Implementation Guide* (Reading, MA: Perseus Books, 1992), ISBN 0-201-56316-9.

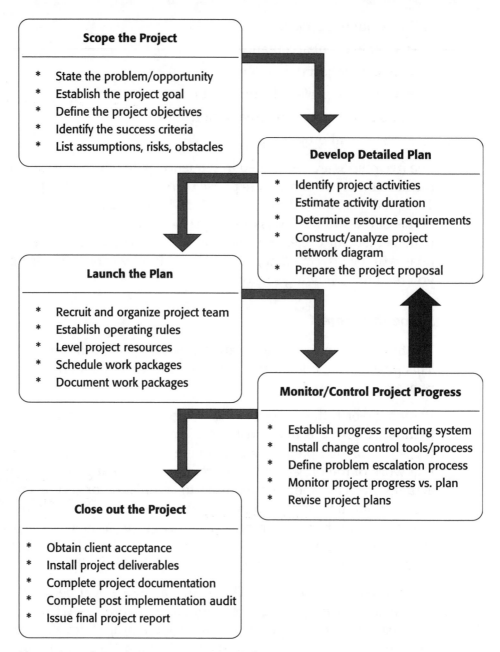

Figure 5.1 The project management life cycle.

to assure one another that the request is clearly understood and the response, in the form of deliverables, is also clearly understood.

In our project management life cycle, the goal is bounded by a number of objective statements. These objective statements clarify the fuzziness of the goal statement. Taken as a pair, the goal and objective statements scope the project. They are the framework within which the entire project planning process can be successfully conducted.

Once the scope is complete, it is documented in the form of the Project Overview Statement (POS). The POS is a brief document (usually one page) that describes, in the language of the business, the following:

- What problem or opportunity is addressed by the project?
- What are the project's goal and objectives?
- How will success will be measured?
- What assumptions, risks, and obstacles may affect the project that you wish to call to the attention of senior management?

The POS, or some form of it, is in wide use. We can trace the early history of the POS back to Texas Instruments in the early 1960s. TI used the POS to allow anyone in the organization to submit an idea for a project. It was the company's version of a project initiation form. The POS is also referred to as Document of Understanding, Scope Statement, Initial Project Definition, and Statement of Work. In our consulting practice, we have encountered organizations that require risk analysis, cost/benefit analysis, return on investment calculations, internal rate of return estimates, and break-even analysis as attachments to the POS. This information is used to decide whether the project should go forward to the detailed planning phase. If the project, as described in the POS, is approved, it moves to the detailed plan phase.

Develop the Detailed Plan

The second phase of the project management life cycle is to develop the project plan. In this phase, the details about the project are determined. This may be an exercise for one or two individuals, but it is often takes place in a formal planning session attended by those who will impact or be impacted by the project. We cover this planning session in more detail in Chapter 11, "Organize and Conduct the Joint Project Planning Session."

The deliverable from this planning session is the project proposal. This document includes the following:

- A detailed description of each work activity
- The resources required to complete the activity
- The scheduled start and end date of each activity
- The estimated cost and completion date of the project

In some organizations there can be any number of attachments, such as feasibility studies, environmental impact statements, or best-of-breed analysis.

The project plan is a description of the events to come. In that sense, it is a model of the project. As events occur in the project, the model is affected and can change to describe how future events in the project are likely to occur.

Because the project plan is a model, we can use it to test alternative strategies for redirecting future events. As project work begins, the nature of the project changes—sometimes radically. Activities can get behind or ahead of schedule; team members can be reassigned, leave the company, or get sick. Market situations can change, rendering all or some of the project objectives obsolete. These events can occur one at a time or in clumps, and the project manager must be ready to analyze, decide, and act. You should already have an appreciation for the complexity of the project plan and work. There are, in fact, several dimensions to consider when trying to formulate a going-forward strategy. Here are just a few:

- If a project activity finishes earlier or later than the schedule date, can the resource schedule for later activities be adjusted accordingly?
- If one or more project activities finish late, can other resources assigned to the project be reallocated to restore the project to its original schedule?
- How can the project manager simultaneously compress the project schedule while avoiding unresolvable resource scheduling conflicts?
- What resources can be reallocated from one project to another without adversely affecting each project's schedule?

Any one of these decision situations involves a number of interdependent variables. It is unlikely that any project manager could process these variables and all of the possible variations without the aid of a computer-based project model and the supporting software, such as Microsoft Project 2000, ABT Workbench, Open Plan, or any one of several other software packages.

Once the project proposal is approved, the project enters the next phase of the project management life cycle, in which the final details of the work schedule are completed and project work begins.

Launch the Plan

The third phase of the project management life cycle is to launch the plan. In this phase, the project team is specified. It is important to eliminate the notion that an individual is solely responsible for the success (or failure) of the project. It is true that you can point to examples in which the efforts of an individual brought the project to successful completion, but these events are rare. Although some of the specific team members could have been identified earlier in the life cycle, additional members are identified during this stage. In contemporary organizations, the project team is often cross-functional and can span other organizational boundaries. We discuss the special problems that arise in these situations in later chapters.

In addition to identifying the team, the exact work schedules are determined, and detailed descriptions of the tasks in the project are developed. Team operating rules, reporting requirements, and project status meetings are also established at this time.

The completion of this final planning activity signals the beginning of the monitoring phase.

Monitor/Control Project Progress

As soon as project work commences, the project enters the monitoring phase. A number of project status reports will have been defined in the previous phase and are used to monitor the project's progress. Some of these reports will be used only by the project team while others will be distributed to management and the customer.

Change management is a big part of this phase, and procedures will have been installed as part of the launch phase to process change requests. Change requests will always cause some amount of project replanning. When the requests are received, the feedback loop is activated, and the project manager revisits the project plan to identify ways to accommodate the change request. Problems also can occur as work finishes ahead of or behind schedule. A problem-escalation procedure will have been defined during the launch phase to handle these situations.

Close Out the Project

The final phase of the project management life cycle begins when the customer says the project is finished. The "doneness criteria" will have been specified and agreed to by the customer as part of the project plan. A number of activities occur to close out the project:

- Install the deliverables.
- File final reports and documentation.
- Perform a post-implementation audit.
- Celebrate!

Levels of Project Management

There are three variations to the project management life cycle. Which cycle you use in a given project depends on what management needs you are trying to meet.

Defining, planning, organizing. This first and simplest of the three cycles is concerned with getting the project going. There is no follow-up on performance against plan. We have encountered a number of situations in which one person will be solely responsible for completing all project activities. In such cases there is value in planning the project, but limited value in implementing the control and close phases. Here the project manager and client are often the same person and the interest is only in laying out a strategy for doing the work. Often the project following this cycle will have to be planned in conjunction with one or more other projects. The intent is to set a timeline for completing the project in conjunction with others underway. This cycle is closely related to good time-management practices. If you keep a to-do list, you will find your habits are quite comparable to this three-part cycle.

most common **Defining, planning, organizing, controlling.** The second cycle is most often thought of as project management. Getting the project started is only half (or actually much less than half) of the effort. The more people, the more activities, and the more resources involved, the more likely the project manager will need to follow with the control function. Things will go wrong—you can bet on it! A mechanism needs to be in place to identify problems early on and do something to keep the project moving ahead as planned.

Defining, planning, organizing, controlling, closing. The astute project manager will want to learn from the project that follows this cycle. Several questions can be answered from an audit of the records from completed projects. Chapter 14, "Close Out the Project," focuses on the closing activities.

Quality Management

In order to meet customer requirements, and do so on time and within budget, the project manager must incorporate sound quality management practices. He or she will be concerned with the quality of the following:

- The product/service/process that is the deliverable from the project
- The project management process itself

Countless books have been written on the product side of quality; we will not repeat those presentations here. Others have done a far better job than we could hope to achieve in this book. The bibliography lists some publications that may be of interest to you.

In this section we focus on the process of project management. Our emphasis is on the two tools and techniques that we have successfully integrated and used in our consulting practice to improve the process of project management: the continuous quality management model and the process quality management model.

Continuous quality management is a procedure that a company can use to improve its business processes. It is a way of life in those organizations that want to attain and sustain a competitive position in fast-paced information-age industries. As shown in Figure 5.2, continuous quality management begins with a definition of vision, mission-critical success factors, and business processes.

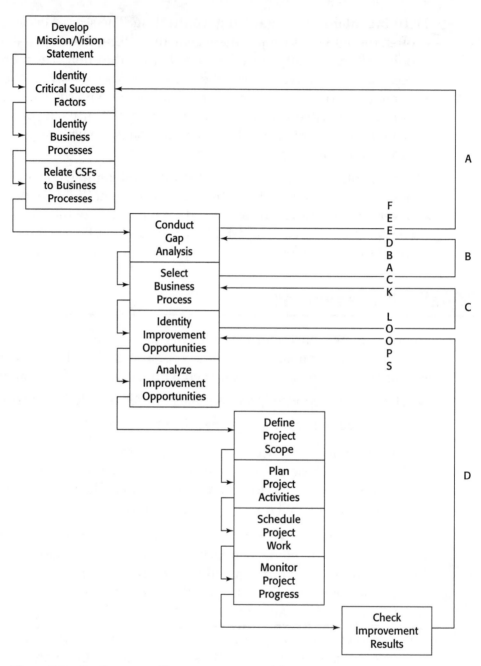

Figure 5.2 Continuous quality management model.

A second tool is integrated after the definition steps. This tool, *process quality management*, is used to relate critical success factors to business processes. This establishes the foundation on which the continuous quality management model proceeds to conduct a gap analysis that identifies processes and steps within processes where improvement opportunities might be made. Any number of improvement projects can be undertaken, and the resulting improvements are checked against targeted improvements and further projects commissioned. Because new improvement opportunities always present themselves, a series of feedback loops, shown in Figure 5.2, continues the process.

Continuous Quality Management Model

Continuous quality management is most evident in those organizations that are customer driven. Levi Strauss, Motorola, and Xerox are but a few. The companies that have applied for or won the coveted Baldrige Award, an award recognizing exemplary quality management within the company, are also on the list.

The continuous quality management model shown in Figure 5.2 is cyclical, as depicted by the feedback loops. A feedback loop occurs when there have been significant process changes and the relationship between critical success factors (CSF) and process may have changed. Feedback loop B occurs when a business process may have changed and affected the gap analysis. Feedback loop C simply continues the priority scheme defined earlier and selects another business process for improvement. Feedback loop D usually involves continued improvement efforts on the same business process. The results of the current project may not have been as expected, or new improvement ideas arose while conducting the current project. That is, the project management phase of the model is adaptive. Scope changes will often result from lessons learned during project execution.

Process Quality Management Model

Figure 5.3 is a schematic of the process quality management model (PQMM). We have used this model successfully in our project management engagements that involve quality improvement programs. The model is based on the assumption that the enterprise has documented its mission, vision, and critical success factors (CSFs). With these in

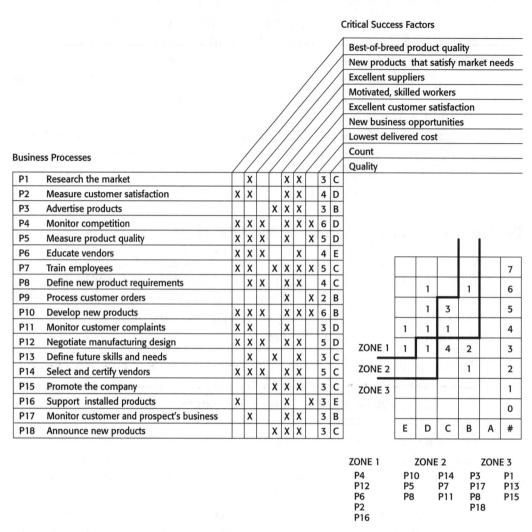

Figure 5.3 The process quality management matrix.

place, the processes that drive the business are identified and related to the CSFs using a grading system in which each business process is assigned a grade of A (excellent) through E (embryonic).

The next step is to identify which business processes affect which CSFs and mark each with an "X," as shown in Figure 5.3. The number of CSFs that have been related to each business process is counted, and the results are tabulated into the zone map. For example, in Figure 5.3 there are three business processes (P5, P7, and P14) that were given a grade of C and that are related to 5 CSFs. That is reflected by the 3 in the cell that lies at the intersection of the column labeled "C" and the row labeled "5" in the zone map.

By taking into account the process grade and the number of CSFs affected by the process, business processes can be ranked according to the priority needs for improvement programs. Those cells that lie in Zone 1 will contain data points that identify business processes that are strong candidates for improvement. In this example, P2, P4, P5, P6, P12, and P16 are business processes whose combination of grade and number of related CSFs identify them as processes where improvement efforts should be focused. The results are analyzed to identify and prioritize improvement opportunities for a given process. A project idea emerges out of this analysis, and the project management life cycle begins.

An Overview of Risk Management

A *risk* is some future happening that results in a change in the environment. It has associated with it a loss that can be estimated, a probability that the event will occur, which can be estimated, and a choice on the project manager's part as to what to do, if anything, to mitigate the risk and reduce the loss that will occur.

Risk management is a broad and deep topic, and we are only able to brush the surface in this book. A number of reference books on the topic are available. The bibliography lists some specific titles you can use as a reference. The risk analysis and management process that we briefly describe answers the following questions:

- What are the risks?
- What is the probability of loss that results from them?
- How much are the losses likely to cost?
- What might the losses be if the worst happens?
- What are the alternatives?
- How can the losses be reduced or eliminated?
- Will the alternatives produce other risks?

The business decision is to assess how the expected loss compares to the cost of defraying all or some of the loss and then taking the appropriate action.

Throughout the project management life cycle several issues give rise to increased risk of project failure. In a 1995 study, the Standish Group surveyed more than 1000 IT managers on reasons why projects fail. The top 10 reasons, according to this survey, are these:

1. Incomplete requirements
2. Lack of user involvement
3. Lack of resources
4. Unrealistic expectations
5. Lack of executive support
6. Changing requirements and specifications
7. Lack of planning
8. Elimination of need for the project
9. Lack of IT management
10. Technology illiteracy

To increase the likelihood of project success, the project team must put in place a program that addresses these risks. This program can include the following steps:

1. Identify risk areas and the constituent risk factors in each area.
2. Assess the risk factors identified and the probability of occurrence and potential damage.
3. Assign appropriate resources to reduce the risk factors.
4. Identify and analyze the alternatives available for reducing the risk factors.
5. Select the most promising alternatives for each risk factor.
6. Plan implementation of the selected alternatives for each risk factor.
7. Obtain feedback to determine the success of the risk-reducing action for each risk factor.

Risk Analysis Example

You can use several tools to conduct risk analysis and perform risk management. They range from very mathematical to paper-and-pencil tools. The tool that is described in the example that follows is the one we use in our consulting practice. We chose it because of its ease of use and versatility.

The first step is to identify the risk drivers that may be operative on a given project. These are the conditions or situations that may unfavorably affect project success. This is a candidate list from which the list of risk drivers that are appropriate for a given project is chosen. The list we start with is shown in Figure 5.4.

The second step is to pick the 10 top risk drivers for your project and rank them from most likely to impact the project to least likely to impact the project. Label them A (most likely) through J (least likely) and array the data as shown in Figure 5.5.

The data given in the worksheet is from a hypothetical project. The columns are the top 10 risk drivers that were identified from the candidate list, and the rows are steps in a process. For the sake of an example, we chose steps from a hypothetical systems development life cycle. Any collection of process steps may be used, and so the tool has broad application to a variety of contexts. A score of 1 is given to those risk

---

Candidate Risk Drivers

Find and prioritize (from A to J) the top 10 risk drivers for a specific project.

_____ Overambitious schedule
_____ Overambitious performance
_____ Underambitious budget
_____ Unrealistic expectations
_____ Misunderstood contract obligations
_____ Unfamiliar technology or processes
_____ Inadequate software sizing estimate
_____ Unsuitable development model
_____ Unfamiliar new hardware
_____ Poorly defined requirements
_____ Inadequately skilled personnel
_____ Continuous requirements changes
_____ Inadequate software development plan
_____ Unsuitable organizational structure
_____ Overambitious reliability requirements
_____ Poor software engineering methods
_____ Lack of adequate automation support
_____ Lack of political support/need for project
_____ Inadequate risk analysis or management

Figure 5.4   Candidate list of risk drivers.

Project Activity	A	B	C	D	E	F	G	H	I	J	Score
Rqmnts Anlys	2	3	3	2	3	3	2	2	1	1	22
Specifications	2	1	3	2	2	2	1	2	2	3	20
Prel Design	1	1	2	2	2	2	1	2	2	2	17
Design	2	1	2	2	2	3	1	2	2	1	18
Implement	1	2	2	3	3	2	1	2	2	1	19
Test	2	2	2	2	2	3	2	2	2	2	21
Integration	3	2	3	3	3	3	2	3	3	2	27
Checkout	1	2	2	3	3	3	2	3	2	2	23
Operation	2	2	3	3	3	3	3	3	1	1	24
Score	16	16	22	22	23	24	15	21	17	15	191

Maximum score is 270. Risk level for this project is 191/270 = 71%.

Figure 5.5 Risk analysis worksheet.

drivers that have a weak relationship to the process step; 2 for a medium relationship, and 3 for a strong relationship. Actually, any numeric scale may be used. The row and column totals are evaluated relative to one another and to scores from similar projects. These totals tell the story. High column totals suggest a risk driver that is operative across a number of steps in the process. High row totals suggest a process step that is affected by several risk drivers. Finally, the total for the whole worksheet gives us a percentage figure that can be used to compare this project against similar completed projects. The percentage is relative, but it may suggest a rule that gives an early warning of projects that are high risk overall.

To analyze the resulting scores, first examine column totals that are large relative to other column totals. In the example, we should focus on the risk drivers associated with columns C, D, E, and F. Because their column totals are high, they can potentially affect several process steps. The project team should identify strategies for either reducing the probability of the risk occurring or mitigating its impact, or both, should the event associated with that risk occur. The row totals can be analyzed in the same fashion. In the example, integration has the highest row total (27). That indicates that several risk drivers are related to integration. The project team should pay attention to the work associated with integration and look for ways to improve or better manage it. For example, the team might choose to have more skilled personnel work on integration than would otherwise be the practice.

Relationship between Project Management and Other Methodologies

Project management methods are very robust. They can be applied to a variety of situations. We can use the methods to plan a picnic or a trip to Mars. Regardless of the application the same steps apply. To illustrate exactly what we mean, let's look at the relationship between the typical project management methodology and two other methodologies.

Software development life cycle. Those of you who are systems development professionals will have recognized many similarities between the project management life cycle and the systems development life cycle. The two do, in fact, have many things in common. Many organizations that claim to be practicing project management have basically adapted their systems development methodology to a pseudo-project management methodology. Although this may work, in our experience several problems arise because of the lack of specificity in some parts of the systems development methodology. We also find that most systems development methodologies do not give enough how-to details to support good project management practices. Figure 5.6 shows the commonality that exists between the project management life cycle and a typical systems development life cycle. For each phase of the project management methodology note the corresponding phase in the systems development life cycle.

New product development life cycle. New product development can benefit from a well-defined project management methodology. Just as there is a similarity between systems development and project management, there also is a similarity between the product development life cycle and project management. To see this, consider Figure 5.7, which shows the parallelism between the two. Note that each phase of the project management methodology has a corresponding phase in new product development.

Time to market is a critical success factor in new product development. In Chapter 9, "Construct and Analyze the Project Network Diagram," and in Chapter 10, "Finalize the Schedule Based on Resource Availability," we explain several project management tools and techniques that can be used to reduce time to market. For the project manager, that means that the time side of the triangle is fixed and resource efficiency is not a binding constraint. Much of what we have taught

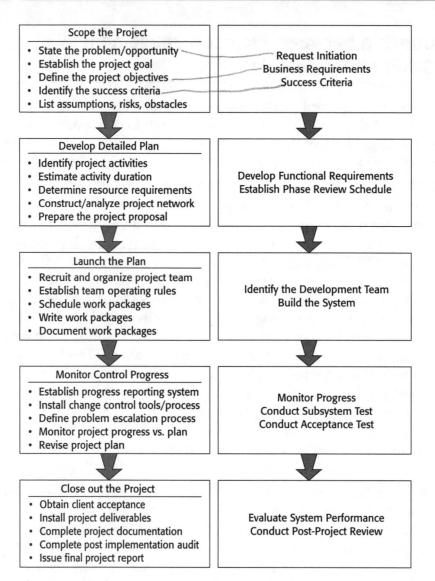

Figure 5.6   Project management and systems development.

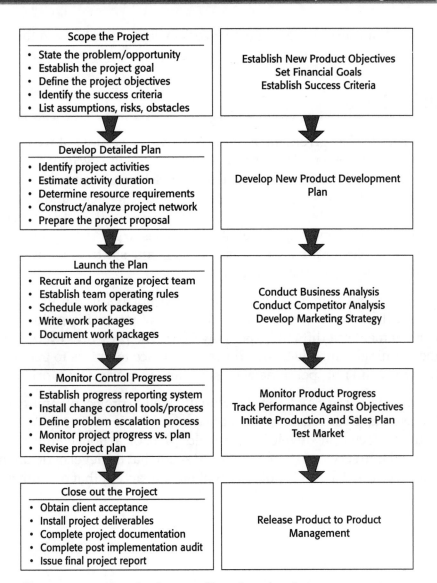

Figure 5.7 Product development life cycle and project management.

you about project management works very comfortably in the product development arena.

The Pain Curve

This chapter has given you a high-level overview of what we mean by project management. We introduced you to the life cycle of the project and discussed quality management and risk management as integral parts of project management. Beginning with Chapter 6 and extending through Chapter 14, we explore the five phases of the project management methodology in great detail. Our goal is to give you enough practical examples and case exercises to get you started on the road to world-class project management.

We would be remiss, however, if we did not warn you of what lies ahead. It is easy to talk about the benefits of practicing sound project management but difficult to actually do it. The pressures of the job and the seemingly unrealistic deadlines we all face tempt us to get on with the work and not spend the necessary time preparing for work.

Pay me now or pay me later applies equally well to project planning. When the team and your management are anxious for work to begin, it is difficult to focus on developing a solid plan of action before you are pressed into service. At times it would seem that the level of detail in the plan is overkill, but it is not. You will have to accept that on faith at this

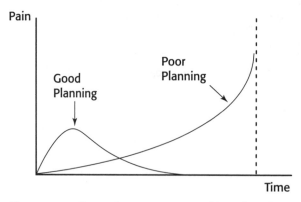

Figure 5.8 The project management life cycle pain curve.

point in your learning. The project manager must resist the pressure to start project work and instead spend the time up front generating a detailed project plan. It has been demonstrated that a poor planning effort takes its toll later in the project as schedules slip, quality suffers, and expectations are not met.

The *pain curve* (see Figure 5.8) tells us that proper planning is painful but pays off in less pain later in the project. To not plan is to expose yourself to significant pain as the project commences. In fact, that pain usually continues to increase. It would continue to increase indefinitely except that someone usually pulls the plug on the project once the pain reaches unbearable levels. The next chapters give you the skills you need to make project planning less painful.

PART THREE

Planning

Planning a project involves answering several questions:

What work is to be completed?

What conditions will determine that the work has been completed as agreed?

In what order should the work be completed?

How long will it take to complete each item of work?

What resources are needed to complete each item of work?

How can the work be scheduled to meet the requested deadlines?

The answers are certainly not independent of one another. Our minds, however, cannot absorb these six dimensions simultaneously, so we will consider them one at a time. That work will be done through the Joint Project Planning (JPP) Session, which is discussed in part in Chapters 6 through 10. Chapter 11, "Organize and Conduct the Joint Project Planning Session," brings all of the planning discussion from the previous five chapters together and describes the logistics of planning, conducting, and reporting the deliverables from the Joint Project Planning Session.

Chapter 6, "Scope the Project," discusses how to determine the boundaries of the project, and define through goal and objective statements what is to be done to meet the deliverables negotiated between the requestor and the provider. Once the scope has been approved, the items of work (labeled *activities* in this book) are defined to meet the requestor's requirements.

Some authors and project management software packages use the term *task* to describe the items of work. In Chapter 7, "Identify Project Activites," you'll learn why we've chosen to use the term activity, and the difference between activity, task, and work packages.

In Chapter 8, "Estimate Activity Duration, Resource Requirements, and Cost," you learn how to estimate the clock time needed to complete each activity (labeled *activity duration* in this book).

Chapter 9, "Construct and Analyze the Project Network Diagram," teaches you how to construct a graphical representation of the project work. An analysis of the project network provides an estimate of when the project will be completed.

In Chapter 10, "Finalize the Schedule Based on Resource Availability," the final schedule details are completed for the project.

Finally, in Chapter 11, "Organize and Conduct the Joint Project Planning Session," all of the planning tools and methods are brought together. This chapter discusses how to plan and conduct the Joint Project Planning Session. Chapter 11 closes with a brief discussion of the project proposal, which is the deliverable from the Joint Project Planning Session. This proposal is submitted to senior management for final approval, which acts as the authorization to proceed with the project work.

CHAPTER 6

Scope the Project

Chapter Learning Objectives

After reading this chapter, you will be able to:

- ✔ Explain the Conditions of Satisfaction development process
- ✔ Develop the Conditions of Satisfaction document
- ✔ Recognize the importance of maintaining the Conditions of Satisfaction throughout the entire project life cycle
- ✔ Define the basic parts and function of the Project Overview Statement
- ✔ Write a saleable Project Overview Statement for your project idea using the language of your business
- ✔ Understand the role of the Project Overview Statement in the project management life cycle
- ✔ Write clear goal and objective statements
- ✔ Establish measurable criteria for project success
- ✔ Identify relevant assumptions, risks, and obstacles
- ✔ Discuss attachments to the Project Overview Statement and their role in project approval
- ✔ Create a Project Definition Statement
- ✔ Understand the approval process for the Project Overview Statement

Prediction is very difficult, especially about the future.

—NEILS BOHR

Define the problem before you pursue a solution.

—JOHN WILLIAMS
CEO, SPENCE CORP.

Define the Project

If you don't know where you are going, how will you know when and if you ever get there? So many times we have seen projects get off to a terrible start simply because there never was a clear understanding of exactly what was to be done. This chapter gets you started on the right foot with a series of activities that lead to a clearly defined and understood definition of what the project is all about. We begin with a communications tool called Conditions of Satisfaction.

You may have observed from our discussion of the Standish Group's report of why projects fail that people-to-people communication is the cause of at least 7 of the 10 reasons for project failure. Our fix for that is the Conditions of Satisfaction.

The deliverable from the Conditions of Satisfaction will be a one-page document (with attachments) called the Project Overview Statement. The Project Overview Statement clearly states what is to be done. It is signed by the parties who completed the Conditions of Satisfaction exercise. Once the Project Overview Statement is approved, the scoping phase is complete.

Develop Conditions of Satisfaction

If we had to pick one area where a project could run into trouble it would be at the very beginning. For some reason, we have a difficult time understanding what we are saying to one another. How often do you find yourself thinking about what you are going to say while the other party is talking? If you are going to be a successful project manager, you must stop that kind of behavior. An essential skill that project managers need to cultivate is good listening skills.

Good listening skills are important in two critical stages of the project planning phase. The first, and the ideal one, occurs when a client makes a request for a project. At this point, two parties are brought together to define exactly what the request is and what kind of response is appropriate. The deliverable from this conversation is a *Conditions of Satisfaction document*.

The second, and the more likely situation, occurs when you inherit what we call the "watercooler project." As the name suggests, these are the projects that are assigned to you when you accidentally meet your manager at the watercooler. Up to that point, you probably had not heard of such a project, but you now need to find out all about it ASAP. The Conditions of Satisfaction document is the result of your investigation. This section describes the process for developing the Conditions of Satisfaction.

The conversations and negotiations that eventually lead to an agreed-on Conditions of Satisfaction have several dimensions. The process of developing the Conditions of Satisfaction involves four parts:

Request. A request is made.

Clarification. The provider explains what he or she heard as the request. This conversation continues until the requestor is satisfied that the provider clearly understands the request. Both parties have now established a clear understanding of the request.

Response. The provider states what he or she is capable of doing to satisfy the request.

Agreement. The requestor restates what he or she understands that the provider will provide. The conversation continues until the provider is satisfied that the requestor clearly understands what is being provided. At this point both parties have established a clear understanding of what is being provided.

Let's walk through an example. Suppose you want a certain model of widgets in forest green to ship to your warehouse by July 1, 2000. You call the manufacturer to make this request. The conversation would go something like this:

Requestor: *I would like you to build five prototypes of the new forest green widgets and ship them to my warehouse on July 1, 2000.*

Provider: *You are asking if we can get five green widget prototypes into your warehouse by July 1, 2000?*

Requestor: *Actually, if you can get them shipped by July 1, 2000 that will be acceptable. But remember, they have to be forest green.*

Provider:	So if on July 1, 2000 I can ship five forest green widgets to your warehouse, you will be satisfied.
Requestor:	Yes, but they must be the new model, not the old model.
Provider:	The new model?
Requestor:	The new model.
Provider:	I believe I understand what you have asked for.
Requestor:	Yes, I believe you do.
Provider:	Because of my current production schedule and the fact that I have to change paint colors, I can ship two forest green widgets on June 25, 2000 and the remaining three on July 8, 2000.
Requestor:	If I understand you correctly, I will get five prototypes of the new forest green widgets in two shipments—two prototypes on June 25 and three on July 8. Is that correct?
Provider:	Not exactly. You won't receive them on those dates. I will ship them to your warehouse on those dates.
Requestor:	So, let me summarize to make sure I understand what you are able to do for me. You will build a total of five prototypes of the new forest green widgets for me and ship two of them on June 25 and the remaining three on July 8?
Provider:	That is correct.

By the time you hang up the phone, both you and the manufacturer have stated your positions and know that the other party understands your position. While the example is simple, it does establish a language between you and the provider, and both of you understand the situation. The seeds have been planted for a continuing dialog. As the project work progresses, there will be changes that can be dealt with effectively because the effort has been made up front to understand each other.

The next step in the Conditions of Satisfaction process is to negotiate to closure on exactly what will be done to meet the request. Obviously, some type of compromise will be negotiated. The final agreement is documented in the Project Overview Statement.

Our example was fairly simple. More than likely, the parties will not come to an agreement on the first pass. This process repeats itself, as shown in Figure 6.1, until there is an agreed-to request that is satisfied by an agreed-to response. As part of this agreement there will be a statement, called success criteria, in the Project Overview Statement that specifies when and how the request will be satisfied. It is important that this statement be very specific. Do not leave whether the conditions have been met up to interpretation. An ideal statement will have only two results—the criteria were met or the criteria were not met. There can be no in-between answer here. The doneness criteria will become part of the *Project Overview Statement.* The result is documented as the Conditions of Satisfaction and becomes input to the POS.

This early step is very important to the success of the project. It is difficult to do a thorough job of establishing and agreeing to what will be done, especially when everyone is anxious to get to work on the project. It is also a painful process. People can be impatient; tempers may flare. You may be inclined to skip this step. Remember, pain me now or pain me later. You choose what you are willing to live with. We would like to leave one final thought with you. Even if the request seems straightforward, do not assume that you understand what the requestor has asked or that the requestor understands what you will provide, even if the request seems straightforward. Always use the Conditions of Satisfaction to ensure that you both understand what is expected.

The Conditions of Satisfaction is not a static document that is written and then filed. It is a *dynamic* document that becomes part of the continual project monitoring process. Situations change throughout the project life cycle, and so will the needs of the customer. That means that Conditions

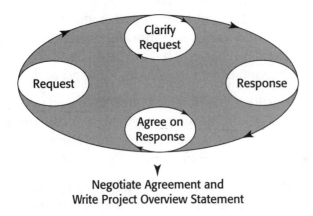

Negotiate Agreement and
Write Project Overview Statement

Figure 6.1   Establishing the Conditions of Satisfaction.

of Satisfaction will change. At every major project status review and project milestone, review the Conditions of Satisfaction. Do they still make sense? If not, change them and adjust the project plan accordingly.

Once a negotiated agreement has been reached, it must be documented in a Project Overview Statement.

Create the Project Overview Statement

The Conditions of Satisfaction statement provides the input you need to generate the POS. The POS is a short document (ideally one page) that concisely states what is to be done in the project, why it is to be done, and what business value it will provide to the enterprise when completed.

The main purpose of the POS is to secure senior management approval and the resources needed to develop a detailed project plan. It will be reviewed by the managers who are responsible for setting priorities and deciding what projects to support. It is also a general statement that can be read by any interested party in the enterprise. For this reason, the POS cannot contain any technical jargon that generally would not be used across the enterprise. Once approved, the POS becomes the foundation for future planning and execution of the project. It becomes the reference document for questions or conflicts regarding project scope and purpose.

The POS serves other purposes, as well.

Inheriting the project? There will be situations in which you will inherit the project. In these instances, the project has been defined and scoped; a budget, staff resources, and completion date also have been determined. In this scenario, do you write a POS? Yes!

There are several reasons to write a POS when you inherit a project. The first is to become familiar with and understand the project and the customer's and management's expectations. We can't stress enough how important it is for requestor and provider to ensure that what will be delivered is what the customer expects.

The second reason is that the POS will become the referent for the planning team. It is the foundation on which the project plan will be built. The project team can use the POS as the tie breaker or referent, to resolve any misunderstandings. In this case, the project scope has been determined, and it is up to the planning team to ensure that the resulting project plan is within the scope of the project, as defined in the POS.

Unsolicited individual initiative. Many organizations use the POS as a method for anyone in the organization to suggest an idea for increasing efficiency, improving productivity, or seizing a business opportunity. Because the POS can be drafted rather quickly by one person, it acts as a way to capture a brief statement of the nature of the idea. Senior management can react to the proposed idea without spending too much time. If the idea has merit, the proposer will be asked to provide a detailed plan. The idea may be conditionally accepted, pending a little more justification by the proposer. Again, the idea is pursued further if it has merit. Otherwise, it is rejected at this early stage, before too much time and too many resources are spent on needless planning.

A reference for the team. An equally important reason for writing a POS is to give your team briefing information on the project. Besides reaching a consensus with your customer on what will be done, the team members need to have an understanding of the project at their level of involvement. Think of this as a Conditions of Satisfaction for the team. Here the focus is on ensuring that the project manager and the team have a common understanding of the project. The POS serves as a good briefing tool for staff members who are added after the project commences. It helps them get up to speed with their understanding of the project.

Parts of the POS

The POS has five component parts:

1. Problem/opportunity
2. Project goal
3. Project objectives ·
4. Success criteria
5. Assumptions, risks, obstacles

Its structure is designed to lead senior managers from a statement of fact (problem/opportunity) to a statement of what this project will address (project goal). Given that senior management is interested in the project goal and that it addresses a concern of sufficiently high priority, they will read more detail on exactly what the project includes (project objectives). The business value is expressed as quantitative business outcomes (success criteria). Finally, a summary of conditions that may hinder project success are identified (assumptions, risks, obstacles). Let's take a look at each of these sections more closely.

State the Problem/Opportunity

The first part of the POS is a statement of the problem or opportunity that the project addresses. This statement is fact—it does not need to be defined or defended. Everyone in the organization will accept it as true. This is critical because it provides a basis for the rest of the document. The POS may not have the benefit of the project manager's being present to explain what is written or to defend the reason for proposing the project to the management. A problem or opportunity statement that is known and accepted by the organization is the foundation on which to build a rationale for the project. It also sets the priority with which management will view what follows. If you are addressing a high-priority area or high-business-value area, your idea will get more attention and senior management will read on.

There are several examples of situations that will lead to a statement of the problem or opportunity that has given rise to this POS:

Known problem/opportunity area. Every organization has a collection of known problems. Several attempts to alleviate part of or the entire problem may have already been made. The POS gives proposers a way to relate their idea to a known problem and to offer a full or partial solution. If the problem is serious enough and if the proposed solution is feasible, further action will be taken. In this case, senior managers will request a more detailed solution plan from the requestor.

With the business world changing and redefining itself continuously, opportunities for new or enhanced products and services present themselves constantly. Organizations must be able to take advantage of them quickly because the window of opportunity is not wide and is itself constantly moving. The POS offers an easy way to seize these opportunities.

Customer request. Internal or external customers make requests for products or services, and their requests are represented in the Conditions of Satisfaction. The POS is an excellent vehicle for capturing the request and forwarding it to senior management for resolution. More recently, with the empowerment of the worker, workers not only receive the request but have the authority to act on the request. The POS, coupled with the Conditions of Satisfaction, establishes an excellent and well-defined starting point for any project.

Corporate initiative. Proposals to address new corporate initiatives should begin with the POS. There will be several ideas coming from the employees, and the POS provides a standardized approach and document from which senior management can prioritize proposals and select those that merit further planning. A standard documentation method for corporate initiatives simplifies senior management's decision-making process for authorizing new projects.

Mandated requirements. There will be several instances in which a project must be undertaken because of a mandated requirement. These could arise from market changes, customer requirements, and federal legislation as well as other sources. The POS is a vehicle for establishing an agreement between the provider and the decision maker about the result of the project. The POS clarifies for all interested parties exactly how the organization has decided to respond to the mandate.

Establish the Project Goal

The second section of the POS states the goal of the project—what you intend to do to address the problem or opportunity identified in the problem/opportunity section. The purpose of the goal statement is to get senior management to value the idea enough to read on. In other words, they should think enough of the idea to conclude that it warrants further attention and consideration. Several submissions may propose the same issue. Because yours will not be the only one submitted, you want it to stand out among the crowd.

A project has one goal. The goal gives purpose and direction to the project. It defines the final deliverable or outcome of the project so that everyone understands what is to be accomplished in clear terms. The goal statement will be used as a continual point of reference for any questions that arise regarding scope or purpose.

The goal statement must not contain any language or terminology that might not be understandable to anyone having occasion to read it. In other words, no techie talk allowed. It is written in the language of the business so that anyone who reads it will understand it without further explanation from the proposer. Under all circumstances avoid jargon.

Just like the problem or opportunity statement, the goal statement is short and to the point. Remember, the more you write, the more you increase the risk that someone will find fault with something you have said. The goal statement does not include any information that might commit the project to dates or deliverables that are not practical. Remember, you do not have much detail about the project at this point.

Unfortunately, we have a habit of accepting as cast in stone any number that we see in writing, regardless of the origin of the number. The goal statement should not include a specific completion date. (Easier said than done, we realize.) If you expect management to ask for a date, estimate the date to the nearest quarter, month, or week as appropriate, but with the caveat that the delivery date will improve as you learn more about project specifics. It is important that management understand just how some of the early numbers are estimated, and that there is a great deal of variability in those early estimates. Assure them that better estimates will be provided as the project plan is built and as the project work is undertaken. Leave the specific dates for the detailed planning session when a more informed decision can be made.

Doran's S.M.A.R.T. characteristics provide the criteria for a goal statement:[1]

Specific. Be specific in targeting an objective.

Measurable. Establish a measurable indicator(s) of progress.

Assignable. Make the object assignable to one person for completion.

Realistic. State what can realistically be done with available resources.

Time-related. State when the objective can be achieved; that is, duration.

In practice we have incorporated the SMART characteristics into both the POS and the project plan. The specific characteristic can be found in the problem/opportunity statement, the goal statement, and the objective statements discussed later in this chapter. The measureable characteristic is incorporated into the success criteria, discussed later in the

[1]George T. Doran, "There's a S.M.A.R.T. Way to Write Management Goals and Objectives," *Management Review* (November 1981): 35–36.

chapter. The assignable, realistic, and time-related characteristics are part of the project plan and are discussed in Chapters 7 through 11.

Define the Project Objectives

The third section of the POS is the project objectives. Think of objective statements as a more detailed version of the goal statements. The purpose of the objective statements is to clarify the exact boundaries of the goal statement and define the boundaries or the scope of your project. In fact, the objective statements you write for a specific goal statement are nothing more than a decomposition of the goal statement into a set of necessary and sufficient objective statements. That is, every objective must be accomplished in order to reach the goal, and no objective is superfluous.

A good exercise to test the validity of the objective statements is to ask if it is clear what is in and what is not in the project. Statements of objectives should specify a future state, rather than be activity based. We like to think of them as statements that clarify the goal by providing details about the goal. Think of them as subgoals and you will not be far off the mark.

It is also important to keep in mind that these are the *current* objective statements. They may change during the course of planning the project. This will happen as the details of the project work are defined. We all have the tendency to put more on our plates than we need. The result is to include project activities and tasks that extend beyond the boundaries defined in the POS. When this occurs, stop the planning session and ask whether the activity is outside the scope of the project, and if so, should you adjust the scope to include the new activity or should you delete the new activity from the project plan. You will find that all through the project planning activities discussed in this book, there will be occasions to stop and reaffirm project boundaries. Boundary clarification questions will continually come up. Adopting this questioning approach is sound project management.

An objective statement should contain four parts:

An outcome. A statement of what is to be accomplished.

A time frame. The expected completion date.

A measure. Metrics that will measure success.

An action. How the objective will be met.

In many cases the complete objective statement will be spread across the POS rather than collected under the heading of "Objectives." This is especially true for the time frame and measures of success.

Identify Success Criteria

The fourth section of the POS answers the question, Why do we want to do this project? It is the measurable business value that will result from doing this project. It sells the project to senior management.

Whatever criteria is used, it must answer the question, What must happen for us and the customer to say the project was a success? The Conditions of Satisfaction will contain the beginnings of a statement of success criteria. Phrased another way, success criteria is a statement of *doneness*. It is also a statement of the business value to be achieved, and therefore it provides a basis for senior management to authorize the resources to do detailed planning. It is essential that the criteria be quantifiable and measurable, and if possible, expressed in terms of business value. Remember that you are trying to sell your idea to the decision makers.

In some cases, it can take some creativity to identify the success criteria. For example, customer satisfaction may have to be measured by some pre- and post-surveys. In other cases, a surrogate might be acceptable if directly measuring the business value of the project is impossible. Be careful, however, and make sure that the decision maker buys into your surrogate measure. Also be careful of traps such as this one: We haven't been getting any customer complaint calls; therefore, the customer must be satisfied. Did you ever consider the possibility that the lack of complaint calls may be the direct result of your lack of action responding to complaints? Customers may feel that it does no good to complain because nothing happens to settle their complaint.

The best choice for success criteria is to state clearly the *bottom-line impact* of the project. This is expressed in terms such as increased margins, higher net revenues, reduced turnaround time, improved productivity, reduced cost of manufacture or sales, and so on. Because you want senior management approval of your proposal, you should express the benefits in the terms with which they routinely work.

While you recognize bottom-line impact as the best success criteria, that may not be possible. As an alternative consider *quantifiable statements* about the impact your project will have on efficiency and effectiveness, error rates, reduced turnaround time to service a customer request, reduced cost of providing service, quality, or improved customer satisfaction. Management deals in deliverables, so always try to express your success criteria in quantitative terms. By doing this you avoid any possibility of disagreement as to whether the success criteria were met and the project was successful.

Senior management also will look at your success criteria and assign business value to your project. In the absence of other criteria this will be the basis for their decision whether to commit resources to complete the detailed plan. The success criteria are another place to sell the value of your project. For example, one success criteria can be as follows:

> *This reengineering project is expected to reduce order entry to order fulfillment cycle time by 6 percent.*

Management may conclude from this number:

> *If that is all you expect to gain from this project, we cannot finance the venture.*

Alternatively, they may respond:

> *If you can get 6 percent improvement from our current process, that will be a remarkable feat, so remarkable, in fact, that we would like more detail on how you expect to get that result. Can you provide an analysis to substantiate your claim?*

Subjective measures of success will not do the job. You must speak quantitatively about tangible business benefits. This may require some creativity on your part. For example, when proposing a project that will have an impact on customer satisfaction, you will need to be particularly creative. There may be some surrogates for customer satisfaction. A popular approach to such situations is to construct a pre- and post-survey. The change will measure the value of the project.

List Assumptions, Risks, and Obstacles

The fifth section of the POS identifies any factors that can affect the outcome of the project and that we want bring to the attention of senior management. These factors can affect deliverables, the realization of the success criteria, the ability of the project team to complete the project as planned, or any other environmental or organizational conditions that are relevant to the project. You want to record anything that can go wrong. Be careful, however, to put in the POS only those items that you want senior management to know about and in which they will be interested. Save for the *Project Definition Statement* (PDS) those items that are quite specific and too detailed to be of interest to senior managers. The PDS list may be extensive. It will generate good input for the risk analysis discussed in Chapter 5, "What Is Project Management?"

The project manager uses the assumptions, risks, and obstacles section to alert management to any factors that may interfere with the project work or compromise the contribution that the project can make to the organization. Management may be able to neutralize their impact. On the other hand, the project manager will include in the project plan whatever contingencies can help reduce the probable impact and its effect on project success.

Do not assume that everyone knows what the risks and perils to the project will be. Planning is a process of discovery—discovery about the project and those hidden perils that cause embarrassment for the team. Document them and discuss them.

There are several areas where the project can be exposed to factors that may inhibit project success. These are described in the following.

Technological. The company may not have much or any experience with new technology, whether it is new to the company or new to the industry. The same can be said for rapidly changing technology. Who can say whether the present design and technology will still be current in three months or six months?

Environmental. The environment in which the project work is to be done can also be an important determinant. An unstable or changing management structure can change a high-priority project to a low-priority project overnight. If your project sponsor leaves, will there be a new sponsor? And if so, how will he or she view the project? Will the project's priority be affected? High staff turnover will also present problems. The project team cannot get up on the learning curve because of high turnover. A related problem stems from the skill requirements of the project. The higher the skill level required, the higher the risk associated with the project.

Interpersonal. Relationships between project team members are critical to project success. You don't have to be friends, but you do have to be coworkers and team players. If sound working relationships are not present among the project team or stakeholders, there will be problems. These interpersonal problems should be called to the attention of senior management.

Cultural. How does the project fit with the enterprise? Is it consistent with the way the enterprise functions, or will it require a significant change to be successful? For example, if the deliverable from the project is a new process that takes away decision-making authority from staff who are used to making more of their own decisions, you can expect development, implementation, and support problems to occur.

Causal relationships. We all like to think that what we are proposing will correct the situation addressed. Assumptions about cause-and-effect relationships are inevitable. The proposer assumes that the solution will, in fact, solve the problem. If this is the case, these assumptions need to be clearly stated in the Project Overview Statement. Remember that the rest of the world does not stand still waiting for your solution. Things continue to change, and it is a fair question to ask whether your solution depends on all other things remaining equal.

Attachments

Even though we strongly recommend a one-page POS, there will be instances in which a longer document is necessary. As part of their initial approval of the resources to do detailed project planning, senior management may want some measure of the economic value of the proposed project. They recognize that many of the estimates are little more than a guess, but they will nevertheless ask for this information. In our experience, we have seen two types of analyses requested frequently:

- Risk analysis
- Financial analysis

The following sections briefly discuss these types of analysis. Check the bibliography for sources where you can find more information about these topics.

Risk Analysis

Risk analysis is the most frequently used attachment to the POS, in our experience. In some cases, this analysis is a very cursory treatment. In others, it is a mathematically rigorous exercise. Many business-decision models depend on quantifying risks, expected loss if the risk materializes, and the probability that the risk will occur. All of these are quantified, and the resulting analysis guides management in its project approval decisions.

In the high-technology industries, risk analysis is becoming the rule rather than the exception. Formal procedures are established as part of the initial definition of a project and continue through the life of the project. These analyses typically contain the identification of risk factors, the likelihood of their occurrence, the damage they will cause, and containment actions to reduce their likelihood or their potential damage. The cost of the containment program is compared with the expected loss as a basis for deciding which containment strategies to put in place.

Financial Analyses

Some organizations require a preliminary financial analysis of the project before granting approval to perform the detailed planning. Although such analyses are very rough because not enough information is known about the project at this time, they will offer a tripwire for project planning approval. In some instances, they also offer a criteria for prioritizing all of the POSs senior management will be reviewing. Some of the possible analyses are as follows:

Feasibility studies. The methodology to conduct a feasibility study is remarkably similar to the problem-solving method, or scientific method if you prefer:

1. Clearly define the problem.
2. Describe the boundary of the problem; that is, what is in the problem scope and what is outside the problem scope.
3. Define the features and functions of a good solution.
4. Identify alternative solutions.
5. Rank alternative solutions.
6. State the recommendations along with the rationale for the choice.
7. Provide a rough estimate of the timetable and expected costs.

   The project manager will be asked to provide the feasibility study when senior management wants to review the thinking that led to the proposed solution. The more thoroughly researched solution can help build credibility for the project manager.

Cost/benefit analysis. These analyses are always difficult to do because you need to include intangible benefits in the decision situation. Things such as improved customer satisfaction cannot be easily quantified. You could argue that improved customer satisfaction reduces customer turnover, which in turn increases revenues, but how do you put a number on that? In many cases, senior management will take these inferences into account, but they still want to see hard dollar comparisons. Opt for the direct and measurable benefits to compare against the cost of doing the project and the cost of operating the new process. If the benefits outweigh the costs over the expected life of the project deliverables, senior management may be willing to support the project.

Break-even analysis. This is a timeline that shows the cumulative cost of the project against the cumulative revenue or savings from the project. Wherever the cumulative revenue or savings line crosses the cumulative cost line is that point where the project recoups its costs. Usually senior management looks for an elapsed time less than some threshold number. If the project meets that deadline date, it may be worthy of support. The targeted breakeven date is getting shorter and shorter because of more frequent changes in the business and its markets.

Return on investment. This section analyzes the total costs as compared with the increased revenue that will accrue over the life of the project deliverables. Here senior management finds a common basis for comparing one project against another. They look for the high ROI projects or the projects that at least meet some minimum ROI.

Many books provide more detailed explanations of each of these analyses. The bibliography contains some suggested titles.

Using the Joint Project Planning Session to Develop the POS

The Joint Project Planning Session (JPP) is the tool we recommend for developing the project plan. We will not discuss the full project planning exercise until Chapter 11, "Organize and Conduct the Joint Project Planning Session." In this section, we'll briefly discuss how it could be used to draft the POS. In fact, there will be situations where you will want to convene a planning session to draft the POS.

Whenever a Conditions of Satisfaction exercise has not been completed and the project manager was given the project assignment (remember the watercooler example?), the first step should be to convene a pre-planning session to draft a POS. This will involve the customer or his or her representative, the project manager, and, if they have been identified, key members of the project team.

Drafting the POS is the first part of the JPP. It may have to be completed in two parts. The first part drafts the POS; the second part completes the detailed plan after having received approval of the POS.

The first order of business is to agree on the request and the response to the request. These are the Conditions of Satisfaction and become the problem/opportunity, goal, objectives, and success criteria parts of the POS. You are almost done.

Next you conduct a sanity check with those who were not party to developing the Conditions of Satisfaction. Discussion should follow until all parties are satisfied with the request and the response. Expect to add to the Conditions of Satisfaction in reaching consensus.

The last item is to complete the assumptions, risks, and obstacles portion. Here the planning participants will be able to offer a number of points to consider.

Beginning with the POS, the planning team will often begin the planning session by spending some time discussing the POS in greater detail. This will bring the team to a greater understanding of the scope of the project. This understanding should be documented using the PDS, which we discuss later in this chapter.

Approval Process

Once the POS is complete, it is submitted to management for approval. The approval process is far from a formality. It is a deliberate decision on the part of senior management that the project as presented does indeed have business value and that it is worth proceeding to the detailed planning phase. As part of the approval process, senior management asks several questions regarding the information presented. Remember, they are trying to make good business decisions and need to test your thinking along the way. Our best advice is to remember that the document must stand on its own. You will not be present to explain what you meant. Write in the language of the business, and anticipate questions as you review the content of the POS.

During this process, you should expect several iterations. Despite your best efforts to make the POS stand on its own, you will not be successful at first. Senior management always has questions. For example, they can question the scope of the project and may ask you to consider expanding or contracting it. They may ask for backup on how you arrived at the results that you claim in your success criteria. If financial analyses are attached, you may have to provide additional justification or explanation of the attachments.

The approved POS serves three audiences. The first is senior management. Their approval is their statement that the project makes enough business sense to move to the detailed planning stage. The second audience is the customer. The customer's approval is his or her concurrence that the project has been correctly described and he or she is in agreement with the solution being offered. For the team, the approved POS is their message from senior management and the customer that the project has been clearly defined at this high level of detail.

Approval of the POS commits the resources required to complete a detailed plan for the project. It is *not* the approval to do the project. Approval to proceed with the project is the result of an approval of the detailed plan. At this early stage, not too much is known about the project. Rough estimates of time or cost variables are often requested from the project manager and the project team (or WAGs, wild a** guesses, if you prefer; SWAGs are the scientific version) as well as what will be done and of what value it is to the enterprise. More meaningful estimates of time and cost are part of the detailed plan.

Gaining management approval of the POS is a significant event in the life of a project. The approving manager questions the project manager, and the answers are scrutinized very carefully. While the POS does not have a lot of detailed analysis supporting it, it is still valuable to test the thinking of the proposer and the validity of the proposed project. It is not unusual to have the project manager return to the drawing board several times for more analysis and thought as a prerequisite to management approval. As senior managers review the POS you can anticipate the following review questions:

- How important is the problem or opportunity to the enterprise?
- How is the project related to our critical success factors (CSFs)?
- Does the goal statement relate directly to the problem or opportunity?
- Are the objectives clear representations of the goal statement?
- Is there sufficient business value as measured by the success criteria to warrant further expenditures on this project?
- Is the relationship between the project objectives and the success criteria clearly established?
- Are the risks too high and the business value too low?
- Can senior management mitigate the identified risks?

The approval of the POS is not a perfunctory or ceremonial approval. By approving the document, professionals and managers are saying that, based on what they understand the project to involve and its business value, it demonstrates good business sense to go to the next level, that is, to commit the resources needed to develop a detailed project plan.

Participants in the Approval Process

Several managers and professionals participate in the approval process.

Core project team. At the preliminary stages of the project, a core project team may have been identified. These will be the managers, professionals, and perhaps the customer who will remain on the project team from the beginning to the very end of the project. They may participate in developing the POS and reach consensus on what it contains.

Project team. Some potential members of the project team are usually known beforehand. Their subject matter expertise and ideas should be considered as the POS is developed. At the least, you should have them review the POS before submission.

Project manager. Ideally the project manager will have been identified at the start and can participate in drafting the POS. Since he or she will manage the project, he or she should have a major role to play in its definition and its approval.

Resource managers. Those who will be asked to provide the skills needed at the times when they will be needed are certainly important in the initial definition of the project and later its detailed planning. There is little point in proposing a project if the resources are not or cannot be made available to the project.

Function/process managers. Project deliverables don't exist in a vacuum. Several units will provide input to or receive output from the project products/or services. Their advice should be sought. Give them an early chance to buy into your project.

Customer. Our project management methodology includes a significant role for the customer. We have discussed the Conditions of Satisfaction as a prerequisite to, or a concurrent exercise in developing, the POS. Many professionals are not skilled in interpersonal communications. Developing the Conditions of Satisfaction is a difficult task.

In some situations the customer is the project manager—for example, if the development of a product or service affects only one department or in projects whose customer is very comfortable with project management practices. In these situations, we encourage the customer to be the project manager. The benefits to the organization are several: buy-in, lower risk of failure, better implementation success, deliverables more likely to meet the needs of the customer, to name a few. Commitment and buy-in are always difficult to get. Having the customer as project manager solves that problem. For this approach to work, the technical members of the project team take on the role of advisor and consultant. It is their job to keep the feasible alternatives, and only the feasible alternatives, in front of the project manager. Decision making will be a little more difficult and time-consuming. By engaging the customer as project manager, the customer not only appreciates the problems that are encountered but also gains some skill in resolving them. We have seen marvelous learning curve effects that have their payoff in later projects with the same customer.

Senior management. Senior management support is a critical factor in successful projects and successful implementation of the deliverables. Their approval says "Go and do detailed planning, we are authorizing the needed resources."

The Project Definition Statement

Just as the customer and the project manager benefit from the POS, the project manager and the project team can benefit from a closely related document, which we call the *Project Definition Statement (PDS)*. The PDS uses the same form as the POS but incorporates considerably more detail. The detailed information provided in the PDS is for the use of the project manager and the project team:

- As a basis for planning
- To capture an idea
- To obtain an agreement from the customer to move forward
- To clarify the project for management
- As a reference that keeps the team focused in the right direction
- As an orientation for new team members
- As a method for discovery by the team

In most cases the PDS expands on two sections of the POS:

Project objectives. In the POS the project objectives are written so that they can be understood by anyone who might have reason to read them. In the PDS, the situation is somewhat different. The PDS is not circulated outside the project team; therefore, the language can be technical and the development more detailed. Project objectives take on more of the look of a functional requirements or functional specification document. The purpose is to provide a description that the project team can relate to.

Assumptions, risks, and obstacles. The POS contains statements of assumptions, risks, and obstacles that will be of interest to senior management. For the PDS, the list will be of interest to the project team. For that reason it will be much longer and more detailed. In our experience, this list is built during the Joint Project Planning Session, whereas the POS list was built as part of the scoping activity of the project.

The PDS is a new document and is discussed for the first time in this edition. More recent consulting engagements have suggested that we create a document that can be used by the team to help them understand the project at their level of detail. The POS did not satisfy this need, so we developed the PDS. It is simply a variant of the POS designed specifically for the team. In implementing the PDS, we did feel that it could further clarify the communications problems that often arise in the project as team members come and go. In the limited use we have made of it, it has proven to be of value to the team; we suspect that it in time it will reduce the risk of project failure.

Case Exercise: Developing the POS and the PDS

For this exercise, you will need to go to the file called GOLD.PDF on the companion CD-ROM. You will find a Table of Contents. Select "Developing the POS" and follow the instructions for how to run the exercise.

You are provided with a copy of the Overview of the Business Situation for O'Neill & Preigh and the introduction to the Gold Medallion Organ project as covered in Chapter 3, "Case Study: O'Neill & Preigh."

The first part of this exercise is to create a one-page Project Overview Statement. With the somewhat limited background information of the company and the project provided, you'll have lots of latitude. Be creative; you may want to try several examples. Print out the blank form, shown in Figure 6.2, and use it to create your POS. Our version of the POS is available on the CD-ROM, so you can check your answer. Try doing it yourself before taking a look at it.

The second part of this exercise is to create the Project Definition Statement. The PDS looks much like the POS, but it includes far more detail. Use the blank form, shown in Figure 6.3, to create your own. You'll notice the expanded detail in the areas of assumptions, risks, and obstacles and the success criteria. If projects are assigned to you rather than initiated by you, try creating the PDS version with its expanded detail.

(continued)

PROJECT OVERVIEW STATEMENT	Project Name	Project No.	Project Manager
Problem/Opportunity			
Goal			
Objectives			
Success Criteria			
Assumptions, Risks, Obstacles			

Prepared by	Date	Approved By	Date

Figure 6.2 POS form.

PROJECT DESCRIPTION STATEMENT	Project Name	Project No.	Project Manager
Problem/Opportunity			
Goal			
Objectives			
Success Criteria			
Assumptions, Risks, Obstacles			

Prepared by	Date	Approved By	Date

Figure 6.3   PDS form.

At this point, you have documented the project through the POS and received approval from senior management to go forward with detailed project planning. The next four chapters are devoted to the second phase of the project management life cycle, discussed earlier in Chapter 5: developing the detailed project plan.

Identify Project Activities

Chapter Learning Objectives

After reading this chapter, you will be able to:

✔ Recognize the difference between activities and tasks
✔ Understand the importance of the completeness criteria to your ability to manage the work of the project
✔ Explain the approaches to building the Work Breakdown Structure
✔ Determine which of the approaches to use for generating the Work Breakdown Structure for a given project
✔ Generate a complete Work Breakdown Structure
✔ Use a Joint Project Planning session to generate a Work Breakdown Structure
✔ Understand top-down versus bottom-up processes for building the Work Breakdown Structure in the Joint Project Planning session
✔ Use the Work Breakdown Structure as a planning tool
✔ Use the Work Breakdown Structure as a reporting tool

Any plan is bad which is not susceptible to change.

—BARTOLOMMEO DE SAN CONCORDIO
FLORENTINE PAINTER

Let all things be done decently and in order.

—I CORINTHIANS 14:40

The Work Breakdown Structure

The *Work Breakdown Structure* (WBS) is a hierarchical description of the work that must be done to complete the project as defined in the Project Overview Statement (POS). Several processes can be used to create this hierarchy, which we discuss in this chapter. An example of the WBS is shown in Figure 7.1.

To begin our discussion of the WBS, you need to be familiar with the terms introduced in Figure 7.1. The first term is *activity*. An activity is simply a chunk of work. Later in this chapter in the section *Six Criteria to Test for Completeness in the WBS*, we'll expand on this definition. The second term is *task*. Note that in Figure 7.1, activities turn to tasks at some level in the hierarchy. A *task* is a smaller chunk of work. While these definitions seem a bit informal, the difference between an activity and a task will become clearer shortly.

The terms *activity* and *task* have been used interchangeably. Some would use the convention that activities are made up of tasks, while others would say that tasks are made up of activities, and still others would use one term to represent both concepts. In this book, we refer to higher-level work as activities, which are made up of tasks.

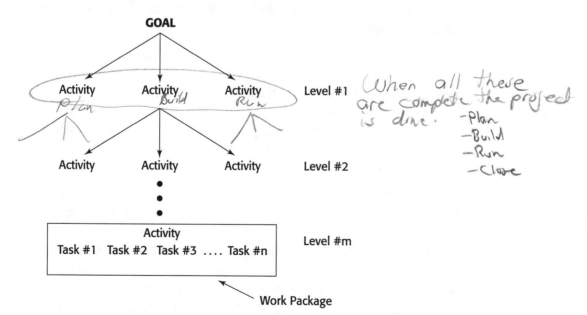

Figure 7.1 Hierarchical visualization of the Work Breakdown Structure.

We also use the term *work package*. A work package is a complete description of how the tasks that make up an activity will actually be done. It includes a description of the what, who, when, and how of the work. We'll describe work packages in more detail later in this chapter.

Breaking down work into a hierarchy of activities, tasks, and work packages is called *decomposition*. For example, take a look at the top of the WBS in Figure 7.1. Notice that the goal statement from the POS is defined as a *Level 0* activity in the WBS. The next level, *Level 1*, is a decomposition of the *Level 0* activity into a set of activities defined as *Level 1* activities. These *Level 1* activities are major chunks of work. When the work associated with each *Level 1* activity is complete, the *Level 0* activity is complete. For this example, that means that the project is complete. As a general rule, when an activity at *Level* n is decomposed into a set of activities at *Level n+1* and the work associated with those activities is complete, the activity at *Level n*, from which they were defined, is complete.

Decomposition is important to the overall project plan because it allows you to estimate the duration of the project, determine the required resources, and schedule the work. The complete decomposition will be developed by using the completeness criteria discussed later in this chapter. By following those criteria, the activities at the lowest levels of decompostion will possess known properties that allow us to meet planning and scheduling needs.

This process of decomposition is analogous to the process we all used in grammar school to prepare a detailed outline of a research paper we were going to write. Despite the teacher's extolling the value of preparing the outline before we wrote the paper, we chose to do it the other way around—by writing the paper first and extracting the outline from it. That won't work in project planning. We have to define the work before we set out to do the work!

Those who have experience in systems development should see the similarity between the hierarchical decomposition and functional decomposition. In principle, there is no difference between a WBS and a functional decomposition of a system. Our approach to generating a WBS departs from the generation of a functional decomposition in that we follow a specific process with a stopping rule for completing the WBS. We are not aware of a similar process being reported for generating the functional decomposition of a system. Veterans of system development might even see some similarity to stepwise refinement or pseudo-code. These tools do, in fact, have a great deal in common with the techniques we use to generate the WBS.

Uses for the WBS

There are four uses for the WBS:

Thought process tool. First and maybe foremost, the WBS is a thought process. As a thought process it is a design and planning tool. It helps the project manager and the project team visualize exactly how the work of the project can be defined and managed effectively. It would not be unusual to consider alternative ways of decomposing the work until an alternative is found with which the project manager is comfortable.

Architectural design tool. When all is said and done, the WBS is a picture of the work of the project and how the items of work are related to one another. It must make sense; in that context it is a design tool.

Planning tool. In the planning phase, the WBS gives the project team a detailed representation of the project as a collection of activities that must be completed in order for the project to be completed. It is at the lowest activity level of WBS that we will estimate effort, elapsed time, and resource requirements; build a schedule of when the work will be completed; and estimate deliverable dates and project completion.

Project status reporting tool. The WBS is used as a structure for reporting project status. The project activities are consolidated (that is, rolled up) from the bottom as lower-level activities are completed. As work is completed, activities will be completed. Completion of lower-level activities causes higher-level activities to be partially complete. Some of these higher-level activities may represent significant progress whose completion will be milestone events in the course of the project. Thus, the WBS defines milestone events that can be reported to senior management and to the customer.

Trying to find a happy compromise between a WBS architecture that lends itself well to the planning thought process and the rolling up of information for summary reporting can be difficult. It is best to have input from all the parties that may be using the WBS before settling on a design. There is no one right way to do it; it's subjective. You will get better with practice.

In the final analysis, it is the project manager who will decide on the architecture of the WBS and the level of detail required. This is important because the project manager is accountable for the success of the project. The WBS must be defined so that the project manager can manage the project. That means that the approach and detail in the WBS might not be the way others would have approached it. Apart from any senior management requirements for reporting or organizational requirements for documentation or process, the project manager is free to develop the WBS according to his or her needs and those of management. Because of this requirement, the WBS is not unique. That should not bother you because all that is required is a WBS that defines the project work so that you, the project manager, can manage it. "Beauty is in the eyes of the beholder" applies equally well to the WBS.

Generating the WBS

The best way to generate the WBS is as part of the Joint Project Planning (JPP) session. We will describe the steps as we look at two different approaches to building the WBS. Before we discuss those approaches, let us recall where we are in the planning process and then offer a few general comments about procedures we have followed in our practice regardless of the approach taken.

One of two simple decomposition processes is used to identify the activities that must be performed from the beginning to the completion of the project. These activities are the lowest level of managed work for the project manager. At this point in the planning process, you should have completed the Project Overview Statement. You may have to go back and reconsider the Project Overview Statement as a result of further planning activities, but for now let's assume the POS is complete. Our technique for generating the WBS will reduce even the most complex project to a set of clearly defined activities. The WBS will be the document that guides the remainder of the planning activities.

Noting that there may be as many as 10 to 20 participants, gathering around a computer screen won't do the job. Neither will projecting the screen on an overhead projector. The only way we have found that works consistently is to use Post-It notes, marking pens, and plenty of whiteboard space. In the absence of whiteboard space you might wallpaper the planning room with flip chart or butcher paper. You cannot have too much writing space. We have even used butcher paper and filled the four walls of the planning room and several feet of hallway outside the planning room. It is sloppy, but it gets the job done.

Two approaches can be used to identify the project activities. The first is the top-down approach; the second is the bottom-up approach.

Top-Down Approach

The *top-down approach* begins at the goal level and successively partitions work down to lower levels of definition until the participants are satisfied that the work has been sufficiently defined. The completion criteria discussed later in this chapter structure the partitioning exercise for this approach.

Once the project activities have been defined using the top-down approach, they will be defined at a sufficient level of detail to allow you to estimate time, cost, and resource requirements first at the activity level and then aggregate to the project level. Because the activities are defined to this level of detail, project time, cost, and resource requirements are estimated much more accurately.

Once the activities are described, you can sequence the project work so that as many activities as possible are performed in parallel, rather than in sequence. In other words, the list of activities can be sequenced so that the project duration (clock time needed to complete all project work) will be much less than the sum of all the times needed to complete each activity.

We recommend two variations of the top-down approach. We have used both in our consulting practices.

Team Approach

The team approach, while it requires more time to complete than the sub-team approach discussed next, is the better of the two. In this approach the entire team works on all parts of the WBS. For each Level 1 activity, appoint the most knowledgeable member of the planning team to facilitate the further decomposition of that part of the WBS. Continue with similar appointments until the WBS is complete. This approach allows all members of the planning team to pay particular attention to the WBS as it is developed, noting discrepancies and commenting on them in real time.

Subteam Approach

When time is at a premium, the planning facilitator will prefer the sub-team approach. The first step is to divide the planning team into as many subteams as there are activities at Level 1 of the WBS. Then follow these steps:

1. The planning team agrees on the approach to building the first level of the Work Breakdown Structure.

2. The planning team creates the Level 1 activities.

3. A subject matter expert leads the team in further decomposition of the WBS for his or her area of expertise.

4. The team suggests decomposition ideas for the expert until each activity within the Level 1 activities meets the WBS completion criteria.

Note that the entire planning team decides on the approach for the first-level breakdown. After that the group is partitioned into teams, with each team having some expertise for that part of the WBS. It is hoped that they will have all the expertise they need to develop their part of the WBS. If not, outside help may be brought in as needed. Be careful not to clutter the team with too many people.

The important thing is to pay close attention to each presentation and ask yourself these questions: Is there something in the WBS that I did not expect to see? Or is there something not there that I expected to see? The focus here is to strive for a complete WBS. In cases where the WBS will be used for reporting purposes, the project manager must be careful to attach lower-level activities to higher-level activities to preserve the integrity of the status reports that will be generated.

As the discussion continues and activities are added and deleted from the WBS, questions about agreement between the WBS and the POS will occur. Throughout the exercise the POS should be posted on flip chart paper and hung on the walls of the planning room. Each participant should compare the scope of the project as described in the POS with the scope as presented in the WBS. If something in the WBS appears out of scope, challenge it. Either redefine the scope or discard the appropriate WBS activities. Similarly, look for complete coverage of the scope as described in the WBS with the POS. This is the time to be critical and carefully define the scope and work to accomplish it. Mistakes found now, before any work is done, are far less costly and disruptive than they will be if found late in the project.

The dynamic at work here is one of changing project boundaries. The boundaries of the project are never clearly defined at the outset. There will always be reason to question what is in and what is not in the project. That is all right! Just remember that the project boundaries have not yet been formally set. That will happen once the project has been approved to begin. Until then we are still in the planning mode, and nothing is set in concrete.

Bottom-Up Approach — avoid

Another approach to identifying the activities in the project is to take a *bottom-up approach*. This approach is more like a brainstorming session than an organized approach to building the WBS.

The bottom-up approach works as follows. The first steps are the same as those for the top-down approach. Namely, the entire planning team agrees to the first-level breakdown. The planning team is then divided into as many groups as there are first-level activities. Each group then makes a list of the activities that must be completed in order to complete the first-level activity. To do this they proceed as follows. Someone in the group identifies an activity and tells it to the group. If the group agrees, then the activity is written on a slip of paper and put in the middle of the table. The process repeats itself until no new ideas are forthcoming. The group then sorts the slips into activities that seem to be related to one another. This grouping activity should help the planning team add missing activities or remove redundant ones. Once the team is satisfied it has completed the activity list for the first-level breakdown, the members are finished. Each group then reports to the entire planning team the results of its work. Final critiques are given, missing activities added, redundant activities removed.

While this approach has worked well in many cases, there is the danger of not defining all activities or defining activities at too high or low a level of granularity. The completeness criteria that we define later in the chapter are not ensured through this process. Our caution then is that you may not have as manageable a project as you would if you followed the top-down approach. Obviously, risk is associated with the bottom-up approach; if you do not have to take the risk, why expose yourself to it voluntarily? Unless there is a compelling reason to the contrary, we recommend the top-down approach. In our experience there is less danger of missing part of the project work using the top-down approach.

WBS for Small Projects

While we have advocated a whiteboard and marker pen approach to building the WBS, we would be remiss if we did not make you aware of some automated tools that you might want to consider for small projects. Small projects are those where the team might be you or you and only one or two others. While the approaches described previously could certainly be used, you might want to consider modifying the approach taken to incorporate some help from available software. We have used a technique called *mindmapping*.

Mindmapping has been popularized by Joyce Wycoff[1] and Tony Buzan.[2] The technique is best described as a graphic dump of your brain. It is a nonsequential approach to recording your thoughts about things that must be done or considered in completing a certain task. Figure 7.2 is an example output from a software package called MindMan, which was developed and is sold through the Buzan Centre.[3]

Intermediate WBS for Large Projects

For very large projects you may be tempted to modify the top-down approach. While we prefer to avoid modification, difficulty in scheduling people for the planning meeting may necessitate some modification. We offer here not another approach but rather a modification to the top-down approach.

As project size increases, it becomes unwieldy to build the entire WBS with the entire planning team assembled. When the size of the project forces you into this situation, begin by decomposing the WBS down to Level 3. At that point, develop intermediate estimates of time, resources,

[1]Joyce Wycoff, *Mindmapping* (New York, NY: Berkley Books, 1991) ISBN 0-425-12780-X.

[2]Tony Buzan, *The Mind Map Book* (New York, NY: Penguin Group, 1996) ISBN 0-452-27322-6.

[3]The Buzan Centre's U.S. distribution center can be contacted at (561) 881-0188 or BuzanCentres@Buzan.co.uk.

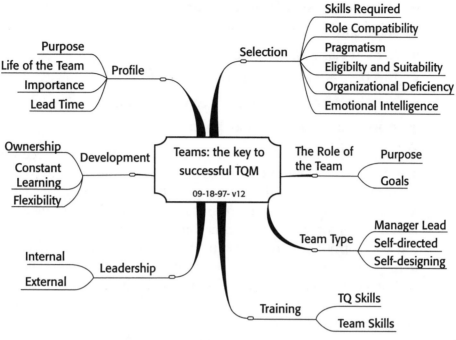

Figure 7.2 A typical mindmap generated by MindMan.

and dependencies for all Level 3 activities. The planning session is adjourned, and the Level 3 activity managers are charged with completing the WBS for their part of the project. They will convene a JPP session to complete that work. The JPP facilitator may choose to consolidate these Level 3 WBSs into the WBS for the entire project. The full JPP team can be reassembled and the planning process continue from that point.

In many large projects the project manager may manage only down to the Level 3 activities and leave it to the Level 3 activity managers to manage their part of the project according to the schedule developed at Level 3.

Six Criteria to Test for Completeness in the WBS

Developing the WBS is the most critical part of the JPP. If we do this part right, the rest is comparatively easy. How do you know that you've done this right? Each activity must possess six characteristics to be considered complete—that is, completely decomposed. The six characteristics are as follows:

- Status/completion is measurable.
- Start/end events are clearly defined.
- Activity has a deliverable.
- Time/cost is easily estimated.
- Activity duration is within acceptable limits.
- Work assignments are independent.

If the activity does not possess these six characteristics, decompose the activity and ask the questions again. As soon as an activity possesses the six characteristics, there is no need to further decompose it. As soon as every activity in the WBS possesses these six characteristics, the WBS is defined as complete. An earlier four-criteria version of this completion test was introduced in Weiss and Wysocki (1991).[4] We have continued to refine the criteria and present an updated version here. The following sections look at each of these characteristics in more detail.

Measurable Status

The project manager can ask for the status of an activity at any point in time during the project. If the activity has been defined properly, that question is answered easily. For example, if a system's documentation is estimated to be about 300 pages long and requires approximately four months of full-time work to write, here are some possible reports that your activity manager could provide regarding the status:

1. Let's see, the activity is supposed to take four months of full-time work. I've been working on it for two months full time. I guess I must be 50 percent complete.

2. I've written 150 pages, so I guess I am 50 percent complete.

3. I've written, and had approved, 150 pages and estimate that the remaining work will require two more months. I am 50 percent complete.

No one would buy the first answer, but how many times is that the information we get? Even worse, how many times do we accept it as a valid statement of progress? Although the second answer is a little better, it doesn't say anything about the quality of the 150 pages that have

[4]Joseph W. Weiss, and Robert K. Wysocki, *5-Phase Project Management: A Practical Planning and Implementation Guide* (Reading, MA: Perseus Publishing Company, 1991).

been written nor does it say anything about the reestimate of the remaining work. And so we see that an acceptable answer must state what has been actually completed (approved, not just written, in our example) and what remains to be done, along with an estimate to completion. ETC Remember, you always know more tomorrow than you do today. After working through about half of the activity, the activity manager should be able to give a very accurate estimate of the time required to complete the remaining work.

A simple metric that has met with some success is to compute the proportion of tasks completed as a percentage of all the tasks that make up the activity. For example, suppose the activity has six tasks associated with it and four of the tasks are complete; the ratio of tasks complete to total tasks is 4/6. That is, the activity is 66 percent complete. Even if work had been done on the fifth task in this activity, because the task is not complete on the report date, it cannot be counted in the ratio. This is certainly a very objective measure. Although it may seem somewhat inaccurate, it is a good technique. Best of all, it is quick. Project manager and activity manager do not have to sit around mired in detail about the percentage complete. This same approach can be used to measure the earned value of an activity. We define and discuss earned value in Chapter 13, "Monitor and Control Progress."

Bounded

Each activity should have a clearly defined start and end event. Once the start event has occurred, work can begin on the activity. The deliverable is most likely the end event that signals work is closed on the activity. For example, using the systems documentation example, the start event might be notification to the team member who will manage the creation of the systems documentation that the final acceptance tests of the system are complete. The end event would be notification to the project manager that the customer has approved the system documentation.

Deliverable

The result of completing the work that makes up the activity is the production of a deliverable. The deliverable is a visible sign that the activity is complete. This could be an approving manager's signature, a physical product or document, the authorization to proceed to the next activity, or some other sign of completion.

Cost/Time Estimate

Each activity should have an estimated time and cost of completion. Being able to do this at the lowest level of decomposition in the WBS allows you to aggregate to higher levels and estimate the total project cost and the completion date. By successively decomposing activities to finer levels of granularity, you are likely to encounter primitive activities that you have performed before. This experience at lower levels of definition gives you a stronger base on which to estimate activity cost and duration for similar activities. We cover activity duration estimation in more detail in the next chapter.

activity duration = < 2 calendar week

Acceptable Duration Limits

While there is no fixed rule for the duration of an activity, we recommend that activities have a duration of less than two calendar weeks. This seems to be a common practice in many organizations. Even for long projects where contractors may be responsible for major pieces of work, they will generate plans that decompose their work to activities having this activity duration. There will be exceptions when the activity defines process work, such as will occur in many manufacturing situations. There will be exceptions, especially for those activities whose work is repetitive and simple. For example, if we are going to build 500 widgets and it takes 10 weeks to complete this activity, we are not going to decompose the activity into 5 activities with each one building 100 widgets. There is no need to break the 500-widget activity down further. If we can estimate the time to check one document then it does not make much difference if the activity requires 2 months to check 400 documents or 4 two-week periods to check 100 documents per period. The danger you avoid is longer-duration activities whose delay can create a serious project-scheduling problem.

Activity Independence

It is important that each activity be independent. Once work has begun on the activity, it can continue reasonably without interruption and without the need of additional input or information until the activity is complete. The work effort could be contiguous, but it can be scheduled otherwise for a variety of reasons. You can choose to schedule it in parts

Status weekly.

because of resource availability, but you could have scheduled it as one continuous stream of work.

Related to activity independence is the temptation to micro-manage an activity. Best practices suggest that you manage an individual's work down to units of one week. For example, Harry is going to work on an activity that will require 10 hours of effort. The activity is scheduled to begin on Monday morning and be completed by Friday afternoon. Harry has agreed that he can accommodate the 10 hours within the week given his other commitments during that same week. Now, Harry's manager (or the project manager) could ask Harry to report exactly when during the week he will be working on this 10-hour activity and then hold him to that plan. What a waste of everyone's time that would be! Why not give Harry credit for enough intelligence to make his commitments at the one-week level? No need to drill down into the work week and burden Harry with a micro-plan and his manager with the burden of managing to that micro-plan. The bottom line may, in fact, be to increase the time to complete the activity because it has been burdened with unnecessary management overhead.

Approaches to Building the WBS

There are many ways to build the WBS. Even though we might like the choice to be a personal one that the project manager makes (after all, he or she is charged with managing the project, so why not allow him or her to choose the architecture that makes that task the easiest), unfortunately that will not work in many cases. The choice of approach must take into consideration the uses to which the WBS will be put. What may be the best choice for defining the work to be done may not be the best choice for status reporting.

There is no one correct way to create the WBS. Hypothetically, if we put each member of the JPP session in a different room and asked that person to develop the project WBS, they might all come back with different renditions. That's all right—there is no single best answer. The choice is subjective and based more on the project manager's preference than on any other requirements. In practice we have tried to follow one approach only to find that it was making the project work more confusing rather than simpler. In such cases our advice is simply to throw away the work you have done and start all over again with a fresh approach.

There are three general approaches to building the WBS:

Noun-type approaches. Noun-type approaches define the deliverable of the project work in terms of the components (physical or functional) that make up the deliverable.

Verb-type approaches. Verb-type approaches define the deliverable of the project work in terms of the actions that must be done to produce the deliverable. These include the design-build-test-implement and project objectives approaches.

Organizational approaches. Organizational approaches define the deliverable of the project work in terms of the organizational units that will work on the project. This type of approach includes the department, process, and geographic location approaches.

We have seen these approaches used in practice to create the WBS. Let's take a look at each of these approaches in more detail.

Noun-Type Approaches

There are two noun-type approaches:

Physical decomposition. In projects that involve building products, it is tempting to follow the physical decomposition approach. Take a mountain bike, for example. Its physical components include a frame, wheels, suspension, gears, and brakes. If each component is to be manufactured, this approach might produce a simple WBS. As mentioned previously, though, you have to keep in mind the concern of summary reporting.

As an example, think about rolling up all the tasks related to gears. If you were to create a Gantt chart for reporting at the summary level, the bar for the gears summary activity would start at the project start date. A Gantt Chart is a simple graphical representation of the work to be done and the schedule for completing it. The Gantt Chart consists of a number of rectangular bars—each one representing an activity in the project. The length of each bar corresponds to the estimated time it will take to complete the activity. These bars are arranged across a horizontal time scale with the left edge of the bar lined up with the scheduled start of the activity. The bars are arranged vertically in the order of scheduled start date. The resulting picture forms a descending stair-step pattern. That is, after all, where the detail tasks of doing design work would occur. The finish of the bar would occur at about the project completion date. That is where testing and documentation for the gears occurs. Using the summary Gantt chart as a status reporting tool for the gears doesn't have much use. The bar extends from beginning to end of the time line. The same is true of all the other nouns mentioned. Showing all of them on a summary Gantt chart would simply look like the stripes on a prison uniform.

This type of WBS is initially attractive because it looks similar and, in fact, could be identical to a company's financial chart of accounts (CoA). CoAs are noun-oriented because they account for the cost of developing things such as gears and brakes. A CoA should not be confused with the WBS. The WBS is a breakdown of work; the CoA is a breakdown of costs. Most popular project management software products provide code fields that can be used to link project task costs with accounting CoA categories.

Functional decomposition. Using the bicycle example, we can build the WBS using the functional components of the bicycle. The functional components include the steering system, gear-shifting system, braking system, and pedaling system. The same cautions that apply to the physical decomposition approach apply here as well.

Verb-Type Approaches

There are two verb-type approaches.

Design-build-test–implement. The design-build-test-implement approach is commonly used in those projects that involve a methodology. Application systems development is an obvious situation. Using our bicycle example again, a variation on the classic waterfall categories could be used. The categories are design, build, test, document, and implement. If we were to use this architecture for our WBS, then the bars on the Gantt Chart would all have lengths that correspond to the duration of each of the design, build, test, and implement activities and hence would be shorter than the bar representing the entire project. Most, if not all, would have differing start and end dates. Arranged on the chart, they would cascade in a stair-step manner, hence the name waterfall. These are just representative categories; yours may be different. The point is that when the detail-level activity schedules are summarized up to them, they present a display of meaningful information to the recipient of the report.

Remember, the WBS activities, at the lowest levels of granularity, must always be expressed in verb form. After all, we are talking about work, and that implies action, and that implies verbs.

Objectives. The objectives approach is similar to the design-build-test-implement approach and is used when progress reports at various stages of project completion are prepared for senior management. Reporting project completion by objectives gives a good indication of the deliverables that have been produced by the project team. Objectives will almost always relate to business value and will be well received by senior management and the customer as well. There is a caveat, however. This approach can cause some difficulty because objectives often overlap. Their boundaries can be fuzzy. You'll have to give more attention to eliminating redundancies and discovering gaps in the defined work.

Other Approaches

The deployment of project work across geographic or organizational boundaries often suggests a WBS that parallels the organization. The project manager would not choose to use this approach but rather would use it out of necessity. In other words, the project manager had no other reasonable choice. These approaches offer no real advantages and tend to create more problems than they solve. We list them here only because they are additional approaches to building the WBS.

Geographic. If project work is geographically dispersed (our space program, for example), it may make sense from a coordination and communications perspective to partition the project work first by geographic location and then by some other approach at each location.

Departmental. On the other hand, departmental boundaries and politics being what they are, we may benefit from partitioning the project first by department and then within department by whatever approach makes sense. We benefit from this structure in that a major portion of the project work is under the organizational control of a single manager. Resource allocation is simplified this way. On the other hand, we add increased needs for communication and coordination across organizational boundaries in this approach.

Business Function. Finally, breaking the project down first by business process, then by some other method for each process may make sense. This has the same advantages and disadvantages as the departmental approach but the added complication that integration of the deliverables from each process can be more difficult than in the former case.

Again, no single approach can be judged to be best for a given project. Our advice is to consider each at the outset of the JPP session and pick the one that seems to bring clarity to defining the project work.

Representing the WBS

Whatever approach you use, the WBS can be generically represented, as shown in Figure 7.1. The goal statement represents the reason for doing the project. The Level 1 partitioning into some number of activities (also known as chunks of work) is a necessary and sufficient set of activities. That is, when all of these first-level activities are complete, the project is complete. For any activity that does not possess the six characteristics, we partition it into a set of necessary and sufficient activities at Level 2. The process continues until all activities have met the six criteria. This defines a set of activities that will each have an activity manager, someone who is responsible for completing the activity.

The lowest-level activities are defined by a work package. A work package is simply the list of things to do to complete the activity. The work package may be very simple, such as getting management to sign off on a deliverable. On the other hand, a work package may be a mini-project and may consist of all the properties of any other project except that the activity defining this project possesses the six criteria and need not be further partitioned. We will return to the work package later in this book.

Some examples will help clarify. Figure 7.3 is a partial WBS for building a house, and Figure 7.4 is the indented outline version (for those of you who prefer an outline format to a hierarchical graph). Both convey exactly the same information.

Figure 7.5 shows the WBS for the traditional waterfall systems development methodology. For our systems readers this format could become a template for all your systems development projects. It is a good way to introduce standardization into your systems development methodology.

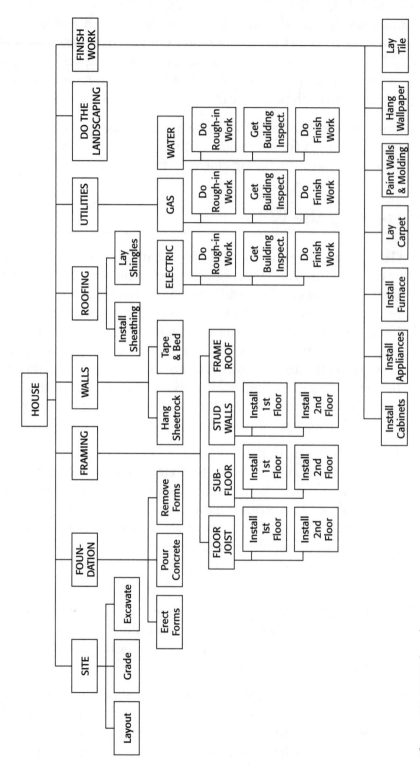

Figure 7.3 WBS for a house.

1. SITE PREPARATION
   1.1. Layout
   1.2. Grading
   1.3. Excavation

2. FOUNDATION
   2.1. Erect Forms
   2.2. Pour Concrete
   2.3. Remove Forms

3. FRAMING
   3.1. Floor Joists
      3.1.1. Install first-floor joists
      3.1.2. Install second-floor joists
   3.2. Subflooring
      3.2.1. Install first-floor subflooring
      3.2.2. Install second-floor subflooring
   3.3. Stud Walls
      3.3.1. Erect first-floor stud walls
      3.3.2. Erect second-floor stud walls
   3.4. Frame the roof

4. UTILITIES
   4.1. Electrical
      4.1.1. Do Rough-in Work
      4.1.2. Get Building Inspection
      4.1.3. Do Finish Work
   4.2. Gas
      4.2.1. Do Rough-in Work
      4.2.2. Get Building Inspection
      4.2.3. Do Finish Work
   4.3. Water
      4.3.1. Do Rough-in Work
      4.3.2. Get Building Inspection
      4.3.3. Do Finish Work

5. WALLS
   5.1. Hang Sheetrock
   5.2. Tape and Bed

6. ROOFING
   6.1. Install Sheathing
   6.2. Lay Shingles

7. FINISH WORK
   7.1. Install Cabinets
   7.2. Install Appliances
   7.3. Install Furnace
   7.4. Lay Carpet
   7.5. Paint Walls and Molding
   7.6. Hang Wallpaper
   7.7. Lay Tile

8. LANDSCAPING

Figure 7.4   Indented outline WBS for a house.

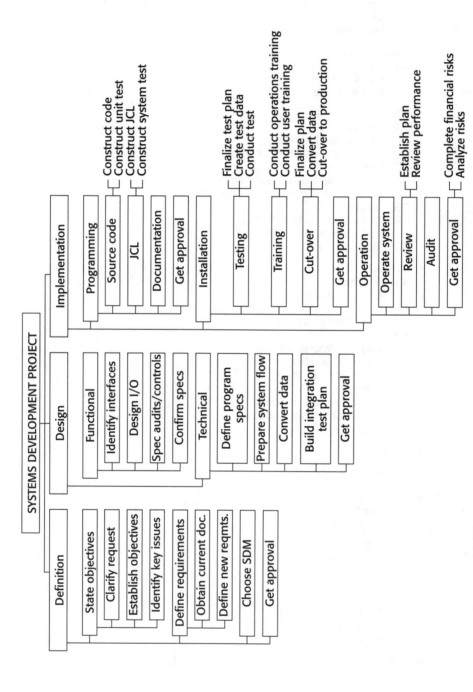

Figure 7.5 WBS for a waterfall systems development methodology.

Case Exercise: Develop a WBS

For this exercise, you will need to go to the file called GOLD.PDF on the companion CD-ROM. You will find a Table of Contents. Select "Developing a WBS" and follow the instructions for how to run the exercise.

In this exercise, you have an opportunity to create a portion of the WBS for the Gold Medallion project. Level 1 has already been defined and consists of the following:

- Project management
- Product design and development
- Feasibility evaluation
- Marketing/product launch
- Customer sales and support training
- Product testing
- Select/sign up production vendors

The detail activities for most of the project have been created. You must develop the detail activities for select/sign up production vendors.

When you have developed your list of activities, compare your ideas to ours. Remember, creating a WBS is probably more art than science; your ideas and ours will vary. Yours may be a lot better than ours. We have kept the overall list of activities short in the Gold Medallion case for the sake of convenience. A real project of this nature would have a much larger WBS.

CHAPTER 8

Estimate Activity Duration, Resource Requirements, and Cost

Chapter Learning Objectives

After reading this chapter you will be able to:

- ✔ Understand the difference between effort and duration
- ✔ Explain the relationship between resource loading and activity duration
- ✔ List and explain the causes of variation in activity duration
- ✔ Use any one of six activity duration estimation methods
- ✔ Use a particular estimation technique
- ✔ Assign resources to meet project schedules
- ✔ Understand the process of creating cost estimates at the activity level
- ✔ Schedule people to project activities using a skill matrix
- ✔ Understand the process of determining resource requirements at the activity level

Round numbers are always false.

Figures are not always facts.

You get more control over estimation by learning from evolutionary early and frequent result deliveries than you will if you try to estimate in advance for a whole large project.

Duration

Before we can estimate duration, we need to make sure everyone is working from a common definition. The *duration* of a project is the elapsed time in business working days, not including weekends, holidays, or other nonwork days. Duration is different from *work effort*. Work effort is labor required to complete an activity. That labor can be consecutive or nonconsecutive hours.

Duration and work effort are not the same thing. For example, we had a client pose the following situation. The client had an activity that required him to send a document to his client's lawyer, where it would be reviewed, marked up, and then returned. He had done this on several previous occasions, and it normally took about 10 business days before the document was back in his office. He knew the client's lawyer took only about 30 minutes to review and mark up the document. His question was, what's the duration? The answer is 10 days. The work effort on the part of the lawyer is 30 minutes.

It is important to understand the difference between labor time and clock time. They are not the same. Let's say that an estimate has been provided that a certain task requires 10 hours of *focused* and *uninterrupted* labor to complete. Under normal working conditions, how many hours do you think it will really take? Something more than 10 for sure. To see why this is so, let's consider the data shown in Figure 8.1.

If a person could be focused 100 percent of the time on an activity, he or she could accomplish 10 hours of work in 10 hours. Such a person would

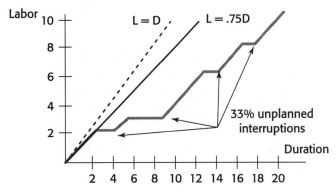

Figure 8.1   Elapsed time versus work time.

be unique, for what is more likely is that his or her work will be interrupted by e-mail, beepers, meetings, coffee breaks, and socializing. Several estimates for the percent of a person's day that he or she can devote to project activity work have been made. Past data that we have collected from information technology professionals indicates a range of 66 to 75 percent. More recently, among the same client base, we have seen a downward trend in this percentage *to* 50 to 65 percent. Using the 75 percent estimate means that a 10-hour task will require about 13 hours and 20 minutes to complete. That is without interruptions, which we know always happen.

For some professionals interruptions are frequent (technical support, for example); for others interruptions are infrequent. We polled the 17-person technical support unit of a midsized Information Services department and found that about one-third of their time was spent on unplanned interruptions. Unplanned interruptions might include a phone call with a question to be answered, a systems crash, power interrupts, random events of nature, the boss stopping in to visit on an unrelated matter, or a phone call from your golfing buddies. Using the 75 percent focus figure and the 33 percent on unplanned interruptions figure means that a 10-hour task will take approximately 20 hours to complete.

It is this elapsed time that we are interested in estimating for each activity in the project. It is the true duration of the activity. For costing purposes we are interested in the labor time (work) actually spent on an activity.

Resource Loading versus Activity Duration

The duration of an activity is influenced by the amount of resources scheduled to work on it. We say *influenced* because there is not necessarily a direct linear relationship between the amount of resource assigned to an activity and its duration.

Adding more resources to hold an activity duration within the planning limits can be effective. This is called *crashing the activity*. For example, suppose you are in a room where an ordinary size, four-legged chair is in the way. The door to the room is closed. You are asked to pick up the chair and take it out of the room into the hallway. You might try to do it without any help, in which case you would perform the following steps:

1. Pick up the chair.
2. Carry it to the door.

3. Set the chair down.

4. Open the door.

5. Hold the door open with your foot as you pick up the chair.

6. Carry the chair through the door.

7. Set the chair down in the hallway.

Suppose you double the resources. We'll get someone to help you by opening the door and holding it open while you pick up the chair and carry it out to the hallway. With two people working on the activity, you'd probably be willing to say it would reduce the time to move the chair out into the hall.

Doubling the resources sounds like a technology breakthrough in shortening duration. Let's try doubling them again and see what happens. Now, we've got four resources assigned to the activity. The activity would go something like this: First, you hold a committee meeting to decide roles and responsibilities. Each person would like to get equal credit, so each one grabs a leg of the chair and tries to go through the door, but they all get stuck in the door. (By the way, there's nobody left to open the door because each of the four resources is dedicated to one leg of the chair.)

The point of this silly example is to show that there are diminishing returns for adding more resources. You would probably agree that there is a maximum loading of resources on a task to minimize the activity duration, and that by adding another resource you will actually begin to increase the duration. You have reached the *crashpoint* of the activity. The crashpoint is that point where adding more resources will increase activity duration. There will be many occasions when the project manager will have to consider the optimum loading of a resource on a task.

A second consideration for the project manager is the amount of reduction in duration that results from adding resources. The relationship is not linear. Consider the chair example again. Does doubling the resource cut the duration in half? Can two people dig a hole twice as fast as one? Probably not. The explanation is simple. By adding the nth person to an activity, you create the need for n more communication links. Who is going to do what? How can the work of several persons be coordinated? There may be other considerations that actually add work. To assume that the amount of work remains constant as you add resources is simply not correct. New kinds of work will emerge from the addition of a resource to an activity. For example, adding another person adds the need to communicate with more people and increases the duration of the activity.

A third consideration for the project manager is the impact on risk that results from adding another resource. If we limit the resource to people, we must consider the possibility that two people will prefer to approach the activity in different ways, with different work habits, and with different levels of commitment. The more people working on an activity, the more likely one will be absent, the higher the likelihood of a mistake being made, and the more likely they will get in each other's way.

Variation in Activity Duration

Activity duration is a random variable. Because we cannot know what factors will be operative when work is underway on an activity, we cannot know exactly how long it will take. There will, of course, be varying estimates with varying precision for each activity. One of your goals in estimating activity duration is define the activity to a level of granularity so that your estimates have a narrow variance—that is, the estimate is as good as you can get it at the planning stages of the project. As project work is completed, you will be able to improve the earlier estimates of activities scheduled later in the project. There are several causes of variation in the actual activity duration:

Varying skill levels. Our strategy is to estimate activity duration based on using people of average skills assigned to work on the activity. In actuality, this may not happen. You may get a higher- or lower-skilled person assigned to the activity, causing the actual duration to vary from planned duration. These varying skill levels will be both a help and a hindrance to us.

Unexpected events. Murphy lives in the next cubicle and will surely make his presence known, but in what way, and at what time we do not know. Random acts of nature, vendor delays, incorrect shipments of materials, traffic jams, power failures, and sabotage are but a few of the possibilities.

Efficiency of work time. Every time a worker is interrupted it takes more time to get up to the level of productivity prior to the time of the interruption. You cannot control the frequency or time of interruptions, but you do know that they will happen. As to their effect on staff productivity, you can only guess. Some will be more affected than others.

Mistakes and misunderstandings. Despite all of your efforts to be complete and clear in describing the work to be performed, you simply will miss a few times. This will take its toll in rework or scrapping semi-completed work.

Six Methods for Estimating Activity Duration

Estimating activity duration is challenging. You can be on familiar ground for some activities and totally unfamiliar ground for others. Whatever the case, you must produce an estimate. It is important that senior management understand that the estimate can be little more than a WAG (wild a** guess). In many projects the estimate will be improved as you learn more about the deliverables from having completed some of the project work. Reestimation and replanning are common. In our consulting practice we have found six techniques to be quite suitable for initial planning estimates:

- Similarity to other activities
- Historical data
- Expert advice
- Delphi technique
- Three-point technique
- Wide-band Delphi technique

Let's take a look at each of these techniques in more detail.

Similarity to Other Activities

Some of the activities in your WBS may be similar to activities completed in other projects. Your or others' recollections of those activities and their duration can be used to estimate the present activity's duration. In some cases, this may require extrapolating from the other activity to this one, but in any case it does provide an estimate. In most cases, using the estimates from those activities provides estimates that are good enough.

Historical Data

Every good project management methodology contains a project notebook that records the estimated and actual activity duration. This historical record can be used on other projects. The recorded data becomes your knowledge base for estimating activity duration. This differs from the previous technique in that it uses a record, rather than depending on memory.

Historical data can be used in quite sophisticated ways. One of our clients has built an extensive database of activity duration history. They have recorded not only estimated and actual duration but also the characteristics of the activity, the skill set of the people working on it, and other variables that they found useful. When an activity duration estimate is needed they go to their database with a complete definition of the activity and, with some rather sophisticated regression models, estimate the activity duration. They build product for market, and it is very important to them to be able to estimate as accurately as possible. Again, our advice is that if there is value-added for a particular tool or technique, use it.

Expert Advice

When the project involves a breakthrough technology or a technology that is being used for the first time in the organization, there may not be any local experience or even professionals skilled in the technology within the organization. In these cases, you will have to appeal to outside authorities. Vendors may be a good source, as are noncompetitors who use that technology.

Delphi Technique

The Delphi technique can produce good estimates in the absence of expert advice. This is a group technique that extracts and summarizes the knowledge of the group to arrive at an estimate. After the group is briefed on the project and the nature of the activity, each individual in the group is asked to make his or her best guess of the activity duration. The results are tabulated and presented, as shown in Figure 8.2, to the group in a histogram labeled First Pass. Those participants whose estimates fall in the outer quartiles are asked to share the reason for their

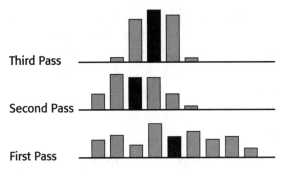

Figure 8.2 The Delphi technique.

guess. After listening to the arguments, each group member is asked to guess again. The results are presented as a histogram labeled Second Pass, and again the outer quartile estimates are defended. A third guess is made, and the histogram plotted is labeled Third Pass. Final adjustments are allowed. The average of the third guess is used as the group's estimate. Even though the technique seems rather simplistic it has been shown to be effective in the absence of expert advice.

We attended an IBM business partners' meeting several years ago. One of the sessions dealt with estimating software development time, and the presenter demonstrated the use of the Delphi technique with a rather intriguing example. She asked if anyone in the group had ever worked in a carnival as a weight-guessing expert. None had, and so she informed the group that they were going to use the Delphi technique to estimate the average weight of the 20 people who were in the room. She asked everyone to write his or her best guess as to his or her weight on a slip of paper. These were averaged by the facilitator and put aside. Each person took an initial guess as to the average weight, wrote it down, and passed it to the facilitator. She displayed the initial pass histogram and asked the individuals with the five high and five low guesses to share their thinking with the group; a second guess was taken and then a third. The average of the third guess became the group's estimate of the average body weight. Surprisingly, the estimate was just two pounds off from the reported average.

The approach the presenter used is actually a variation of the original Delphi technique. The original version used a small panel of experts (say five or six) who were asked for their estimate independently of one another. The results were tabulated and shared with the panel, who were then asked for a second estimate. A third estimate was solicited in the same manner. The average of the third estimate was the one chosen. Note that the original approach does not involve any discussion or collaboration between the panel members. In fact, they weren't even aware of who the other members were.

Three-Point Technique

Activity duration is a random variable. If it were possible to repeat the activity several times under identical circumstances, duration times would vary. That variation may be tightly grouped around a central value, or it might be widely dispersed. In the first case, you would have a considerable amount of information on that activity's duration as compared to the latter case, where you would have very little or none. In any given instance of the activity you would not know at which extreme the duration would likely fall, but you could make probabilistic statements about their likelihood in any case.

The three-point technique gives us a framework for doing just that. To use the method you need three estimates of activity duration: optimistic, pessimistic, and most likely. The optimistic time is defined as the shortest duration one has had or might expect to experience given that everything happens as expected. The pessimistic time is that duration that would be experienced (or has been experienced) if everything that could go wrong did go wrong and yet the activity was completed. Finally, the most likely time is that time usually experienced. For this method you are calling on the collective memory of professionals who have worked on similar activities but for which there is no recorded history. Figure 8.3 is a graphical representation of the three-point method.

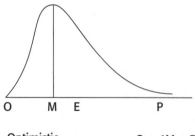

O: Optimistic
P: Pessimistic $E = \dfrac{O + 4M + P}{6}$
M: Most Likely

Figure 8.3   The three-point method.

Wide-Band Delphi Technique

Combining the Delphi and three-point methods results in the wide-band Delphi technique. It involves a panel, as in the Delphi technique. In place of a single estimate the panel members are asked, at each iteration, to give their optimistic, pessimistic, and most likely estimates for the duration of the chosen activity. The results are compiled, and any extreme estimates are removed. Averages are computed for each of the three estimates, and the averages are used as the optimistic, pessimistic, and most likely estimates of activity duration.

Estimation Precision

A word of advice on estimating is in order. Early estimates of activity duration will not be as good as later estimates. It's a simple fact that we get smarter as the project work commences. Estimates will always be subject to the vagaries of nature and other unforeseen events. We can only hope that we have gained some knowledge through the project to improve our estimates.

In our top-down project planning model, we start out with "roughly right" estimates with the intention of improving the precision of these estimates later in the project. Management and the customer must be aware of this approach. Most of us have the habit of assuming that a number, once written, is inviolate and absolutely correct regardless of the circumstances under which the number was determined.

Resources

By defining project activities according to the completion criteria, you should have reached a point of granularity with each activity so that it is familiar. You may have done the activity or something very similar to it in a past project. That recollection, that historical information, gives us the basis for estimating the resources you will need to complete the activities in the current project. In some cases it is a straightforward recollection; in others, the result of keeping a historical file of similar activities; in others, the advice of experts.

The importance of resources varies from project to project. The six estimation techniques discussed in the previous section can be used to estimate the resource requirements for any project.

Types of resources include the following:

People. In most cases the resources you will have to schedule are people resources. This is also the most difficult type of resource to schedule.

Facilities. Project work takes place in locations. Planning rooms, conference rooms, presentation rooms, and auditoriums are but a few examples of facilities that projects require. The exact specifications as well as the precise time at which they are needed are some of the variables that must be taken into account. The project plan can provide the detail required. The facility specification will also drive the project schedule based on availability.

Equipment. Equipment is treated exactly the same as facilities. What is needed and when drive the activity schedule based on availability.

Money. Accountants would tell us that everything is eventually reduced to dollars, and that is true. Project expenses typically include travel, room and meals, and supplies.

Materials. Parts to be used in the fabrication of products and other physical deliverables are often part of the project work, too. For example, the materials needed to build a bicycle might include nuts, bolts, washers, and spacers.

People as Resources

People are the most difficult type of resource to schedule because we plan the project by specifying the types of skills we need, when we need them, and in what amounts. Note that we do not specify by name the resource (that is, the individual) we need; this is where problems arise.

There are a few tools you can use to help you schedule people.

Skills Matrices

We find more and more of our clients are developing skills inventory matrices for staff and skill needs matrices for activities. The two matrices are used to assign staff to activities. The assignment could be based on activity characteristics such as risk, business value, criticality, or skill development. Figure 8.4 illustrates how the process can work.

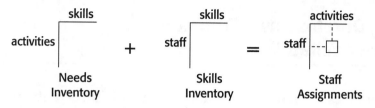

Figure 8.4   Assigning staff to activities.

This process involves gathering inventory data for two inventories. The first is an inventory of the demand for skills needed to perform the tasks associated with specific activities. This is represented as a matrix whose rows are the activities and whose columns are the skills. These are both current and long-term needs. The second is an inventory of the current skills among the professional staff. This is represented as a matrix whose rows identify the staff and whose columns are the skills. The columns of both matrices define the same set of skills. This gives us a way to link the two matrices and assign staff to activities. This approach can be used for on-the-job staff development. As an on-the-job development strategy, the manager would have previously met with the staff member, helped him or her define career goals, and translated those goals into skill development needs. That information can now be used to assign staff to activities, such that the work they will do on the activity will give them that on-the-job development.

Skill Categories

This part of the skill matrix is developed by looking at each activity that the unit must perform and describing the skills needed to perform the activity. Because skills may appear in unrelated activities, the list of possible skills must be standardized across the enterprise.

Skill Levels

A binary assessment—that is, you either have the skill or you don't—is certainly easier to administer, but it isn't sufficient for project management. Skills must be qualified with a statement of how much of the skill the person possesses. Various methods are available, and companies often develop their own skill-level system. We prefer to use Bloom's Taxonomy, as described in Chapter 2, "How to Become a World-Class Project Manager."

Estimating Duration as a Function of Resource Availability

Three variables influence the duration estimate of an activity, and all of them influence each other. They are as follows:

- The duration itself
- The total amount of work, as in person hours/days, that will be done on the activity by a resource
- The percent per day of his or her time that the resource can devote to working on it

Many project management software products today allow you to enter any two of these three variables and calculate the third for you. There is no one right way; it's a matter of what works best and is most consistent with the way you mentally approach estimating. There are four ways to approach the calculation of duration, total effort, and percent/day. Remember that two of them are specified and the third is calculated. The methods are listed here and described in the sections that follow.

- Assign as a total work and constant percent/day
- Assign as a duration and total work effort
- Assign as a duration and percent/day
- Assign as a profile

Assign as a Total Work and a Constant Percent/Day

If we know that the total "head down, focused" work effort required to do the activity is 40 hours but that the resource can only devote 50 percent of his or her typical day to doing project activity work, then the resulting duration is going to be 80 hours or 10 business days. The formula is simply:

40 hours / .50 = 80 hours

The duration becomes a calculated value based on the percent per day and the work. This is the method that most software products use as their default method. It's tempting to use a percent per day resource allocation value that's higher than it actually will be. We can be a bit squeamish about telling it like it really is. If that is done, the duration is shortened accordingly. The project completion date is then invalid because it is calculated using an overly optimistic duration.

Assign as a Duration and Total Work Effort

Alternatively, you could use your or someone else's experience and estimate the duration based on history. Then the total work could be averaged over that duration, yielding the percent per day value. Using the same values as above, the formula would look like:

5 person days / 10 days = .5

Here again we're making the assumption of an eight-hour day. In this case, the percent is calculated. Approaching the estimate from this direction (we're just running the numbers a different way) seems in practice to avoid the problem of squeamishness. You still need to do a sanity check on the resulting value; don't just blindly accept it. In our consulting we've found that this usually results in an estimated duration that come closer to matching the actual when all is said and done.

Assign as a Duration and Percent/Day

The third method is to estimate the duration as previously described and assign the percent per day. This will calculate the total work effort. The formula works like this:

10 days x .50 = 5 person days

Of the three methods this is the least used.

Assign as a Profile

The three duration estimating and resource assignment methods discussed here all presume that the resource is going to work at about the same percent per day for each day of the activity. In other words, they are flat loaded at a constant rate. There will be cases where the person cannot work at a constant rate because of other commitments. In such cases, the duration is estimated first and then the work is assigned at different percents over the 40-hour window. For example, we might assign the worker 75 percent for 20 hours and 50 percent for 20 hours. If you find yourself having to use this profiling of resource assignments capability on activities more than two or three times in a project, you may need to take your WBS to a lower level of detail. In doing that, the duration will be shorter and the resources can work in a contiguous manner for the entire activity.

Estimating Cost

Now that we have estimated activity duration and resource requirements we have the data we need to establish the cost of the project. This is our first look at the dollars involved in doing the project. We know the resources that will be required and the number of hours or volume of resources needed. Unit cost data can be applied to the amount of resource required to estimate cost.

Estimating cost begins at the activity level. Once costs at the activity level have been determined, they are aggregated to the project level. For the sake of simplicity, we categorize costs as either labor costs or material costs. We could be more detailed, but this approach is sufficient for this book. See the bibliography for more references.

Material costs are resources other than people resources. Materials will be priced on a per-use or per-time-unit basis. These will be standard costs that can be easily calculated for each activity.

Labor costs are people resources. These are classified according to their skills profile or standard job classification. In order to estimate people costs for an activity, you need to know the rate of pay for a time unit of labor. The time unit can be hourly or daily. Because you know the resource requirement by skill or job classification for an activity, you can easily calculate the total labor cost for an activity. The variable here is the activity duration over which the labor costs are accrued. This will be important when you calculate earned value for cost/schedule control purposes.

Case Exercise: Estimate Activity Durations and Resource Assignments

For this exercise, you will need to go to the file called GOLD.PDF on the companion CD-ROM. You will find a Table of Contents. Select "Estimating Activity Durations and Resource Assignments" and follow the instructions for how to run the exercise.

In this exercise, you will estimate the durations and resource assignments for a portion of the Gold Medallion project. You will continue to work with the "Select/Sign up Production Vendors" portion of the project. To maintain consistency in the exercises, work with our version of the WBS.

In the second part of this exercise, you will be provided with a list of resources that include both names and job titles. Using this information, assign the resource(s) that you feel are appropriate to each activity. The exercise asks you to assign the duration first and then the resource work using the three methods explained in this chapter. Remember that estimating the duration first and then the total amount of work (person hours/days) for each resource working on the activity provides the best results.

Using a JPP Session to Estimate Activity Duration and Resource Requirements

You have assembled the subject matter experts on your planning team, so you have all the information you need to estimate activity duration in the JPP session. The methodology is simple. During the WBS exercise ask each subteam to provide activity duration estimates as part of their presentation. The subteam's presentation will then include the activity duration estimates they determined. Any disagreement can be resolved during the presentation.

We have conducted many JPP sessions and have some advice for estimating activity duration during the JPP session.

Get it roughly right. Do not waste time deciding whether the duration is 9 days or 10 days. By the time the activity is open for work the team will have a lot more knowledge about the activity and will be able to provide an improved estimate—rendering the debate a waste of time. After some frustration with getting the planning team to move ahead quickly with estimates, someone once remarked, "Are you 70 percent sure you are 80 percent right? Good, let's move on."

Spend more effort on front-end activities than on back-end activities. As project work commences back-end activities may undergo change. In fact, some may be removed from the project altogether.

Consensus is all that is needed. If you have no serious objections to the estimate, let it stand. It is easy to get bogged down in minutia. The JPP session is trying enough on the participants. Let's not make it any more painful than needed. Save your energy for the really important parts of the plan—like the WBS.

Determining Resource Requirements

The planning team includes resource managers or their representatives. At the time the planning team is defining the WBS and estimating activity duration, they will also estimate resource requirements.

We have found the following practice effective: First, create a list of all the resources required for the project. For people resources, list only position title or skill level. Do not name specific people even if there is only one person with the requisite skills. Envision a person with the typical skill set and loading on the project activity. Activity duration estimates are based on workers of average skill level, and so should be resource requirements. You will worry about changing this relationship later in the planning session. Second, when the WBS is presented, resource requirements can be reported, too.

What If the Specific Resource Is Known?

Knowing the specific resource will occur quite often, and we are faced with the question: Should we put that person in the plan? If you do and if that person is not available when you need him or her, how will that affect your project plan? If he or she is very highly skilled and you used that information to estimate the duration of the activity that person was to work on, you may have a problem. If you cannot replace him or her with an equally skilled individual, will that create a slippage that dominoes through the project schedule? Take your choice.

We now have estimated the parameters needed to begin constructing the project schedule. The activity duration estimates provide input to planning the order and sequence of completing the work defined by the activities. Once the initial schedule is built, we can use the resource requirements and availability data to further modify the schedule.

Construct and Analyze the Project Network Diagram

Chapter Learning Objectives

After reading this chapter, you will be able to:

✔ Construct a network representation of the project activities
✔ Understand the four types of activity dependencies and when they are used
✔ Recognize the types of constraints that create activity sequences
✔ Compute the Early Start (ES), Early Finish (EF), Late Start (LS), and Late Finish (LF) times for every activity in the network
✔ Understand lag variables and their uses
✔ Identify the critical path in the project
✔ Understand the basic concepts of critical chains
✔ Define free slack and total slack and know their significance
✔ Analyze the network for possible schedule compression
✔ Use advanced network dependency relationships for improving the project schedule
✔ Understand and apply management reserve
✔ Use the critical path for planning, implementation, and control of the project activities

Structure is not organization.

—ROBERT H. WATERMAN
MANAGEMENT CONSULTANT

The man who goes alone can start today, but he who
travels with another must wait 'til that other is ready.

—HENRY DAVID THOREAU
AMERICAN NATURALIST

In every affair consider what precedes
and what follows, and then undertake it.

—EPICTETUS
GREEK PHILOSOPHER

Every moment spent planning saves three or four in execution.

—CRAWFORD GREENWALT
PRESIDENT, DUPONT

The Project Network Diagram

At this point in the project management lifecycle, you have identified the set of activities in the project as output from the WBS-building exercise and the activity duration for the project. The next task for the planning team is to determine the order in which these activities are to be performed.

The activities and the activity duration are the basic building blocks needed to construct a graphic picture of the project. This graphic picture provides you with two additional pieces of schedule information about the project:

- The earliest time at which work can begin on every activity that makes up the project
- The earliest expected completion date of the project

This is critical information for the project manager. Ideally, the required resources must be available at the times established in this plan. This is not very likely. Chapter 10, "Finalize the Schedule Based on Resource Availability," discusses how to deal with that problem. In this chapter, we focus on the first part of the problem—creating an initial project network diagram and the associated project schedule.

A *project network diagram* is a pictorial representation of the sequence in which the project work can be done. There are a few simple rules that you need to follow to build the project network diagram.

Recall from the definition of a project that a project is a sequence of interconnected activities. You could perform the activities one at a time until they are all complete. That is a simple approach, but in all but the most trivial projects, this approach would not result in an acceptable completion date. In fact, it results in the longest time to complete the project. Any ordering that allowed even one pair of activities to be worked on concurrently would result in a shorter project completion date.

Another approach is to establish a network of relationships between the activities. You can do this by looking forward through the project. What activities must be complete before another activity can begin? Or, you can take a set of activities and look backward through the project: Now that a set of activities is complete, what activity or activities come next? Both ways are valid. The one you use is a matter of personal preference.

Are you more comfortable looking backward in time or forward? Our advice is to look at the activities from both angles. One can be a check of the completeness of the other.

The relationships between the activities in the project are represented in a flow diagram called a *network diagram* or *logic diagram*.

Benefits to Network-Based Scheduling

There are two ways to build a project schedule:

- Gantt chart
- Network diagram

The *Gantt chart* is the oldest of the two and is used effectively in simple, short-duration types of projects. To build a Gantt chart the project manager begins by associating a rectangular bar with every activity. The length of the bar corresponds to the duration of the activity. He or she then places the bars horizontally along a timeline in the order in which the activities should be completed. There can be instances in which activities are located on the timeline so that they are worked on concurrently with other activities. The sequencing is often driven more by resource availability than any other consideration.

There are two drawbacks to using the Gantt chart. Because of its simplicity, the Gantt chart does not contain detailed information. It only reflects the order imposed by the manager and, in fact, hides much of that information. You see, the Gantt chart does not contain all of the sequencing information that exists. Unless you are intimately familiar with the project activities you cannot tell from the Gantt chart what comes before and after what.

Second, the Gantt chart does not tell the project manager whether the schedule that results from the Gantt chart completes the project in the shortest possible time or even uses the resources most effectively. The Gantt chart only reflects when the manager would like to have the work done.

Although a Gantt chart is easier to build and does not require the use of an automated tool, we recommend using the network diagram. The network diagram provides a visual layout of the sequence in which project work flows. It includes detailed information and serves as an analytical tool for project scheduling and resource management problems as they arise during the life of the project. In addition, the network diagram allows you to compute the earliest time at which the project can be completed. That information does not follow from a Gantt chart.

Network diagrams can be used for detailed project planning, during implementation as a tool for analyzing scheduling alternatives, and as a control tool.

Planning. Even for large projects, the project network gives a clear graphical picture of the relationship between project activities. It is, at the same time, a high-level and detailed-level view of the project. We have found that displaying the network diagram on the whiteboard or flip charts during the planning phase is beneficial. This way, all members of the planning team can use it for scheduling decisions. We explore using the network diagram in the JPP later in this chapter.

Implementation. For those project managers who use automated project management software tools, you will update the project file with activity status and estimate-to-completion data. The network diagram is then automatically updated and can be printed or viewed. The need for rescheduling and resource reallocation decisions can be determined from the network diagram, although some argue that this method is too cumbersome due to project size. Even a project of modest size, say 100 activities, produces a network diagram that is too large and awkward to be of much use. We cannot disagree, but we place the onus on software manufacturers to market products that do a better job of displaying network diagrams.

Control. While the updated network diagram will retain the status of all activities, the best graphical report for monitoring and controlling project work will be the Gantt chart view of the network diagram. This Gantt chart cannot be used for control purposes unless you have done network scheduling or incorporated the logic into the Gantt chart. Comparing the planned schedule with the actual schedule, the project manager will discover variances and, depending on their severity, will be able to put a get-well plan in place. In Chapter 13, "Monitor and Control Progress," we will examine this in more detail and provide additional reporting tools for analyzing project status.

Building the Network Diagram Using the PDM

One of the early methods for representing project activities as a network dates back to the early 1950s and the Polaris Missile Program. It is called the activity-on-the-arrow (AOA) method. As Figure 9.1 shows, an arrow

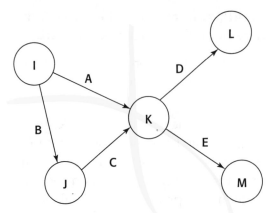

Figure 9.1   The activity-on-the-arrow method.

represents each activity. The node at the left edge of the arrow is the event "begin the activity" while the node at the right edge of the arrow is the event "end the activity." Every activity is represented by this configuration. Nodes are numbered sequentially and the sequential ordering had to be preserved, at least in the early versions. Due to the limitations of the AOA method, ghost activities had to be added to preserve network integrity. Only the simplest of dependency relationships could be used. This technique proved to be quite cumbersome as networking techniques progressed. One seldom sees this approach used today.

With the advent of the computer the AOA method lost its appeal, and a new method replaced it. Figure 9.2 shows the activity-on-the-node (AON) method. The term more commonly used to describe this approach is *precedence diagramming method (PDM)*.

The basic *unit of analysis* in a network diagram is the activity. Each activity in the network diagram is represented by a rectangle that is called an *activity node*. Arrows represent the predecessor/successor relationships between activities. Figure 9.2 shows an example network diagram. We'll take a more detailed look into how the PDM works later in this chapter.

Every activity in the project will have its own activity node (see Figure 9.3). The entries in the activity node describe the time-related properties of the activity. Some of the entries describe characteristics of the activity such as its expected duration (E), while others describe calculated val-

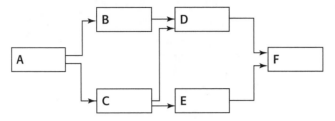

Figure 9.2   PDM format of a project network diagram.

ues (ES, EF, LS, LF) associated with that activity. We will define these terms shortly and give an example of their use.

In order to create the network diagram using the PDM, you need to determine the predecessors and successors for each activity. To do this, you ask "What activities must be complete before I can begin this activity?" Here, you are looking for the technical dependencies between activities. Once an activity is complete it will have produced an output, a deliverable, which becomes input to its successor activities. Work on the successor activities requires only the output from its predecessor activities. Later we will incorporate management constraints that may alter these dependency relationships. For now we prefer to delay consideration of the management constraints; they will only complicate the planning at this point. What is the next step? While the list of predecessors and successors to each activity contains all the information we need to proceed with the project, it does not represent the information in a format that tells the story of our project. Our goal will be to provide a graphical picture of the project; in order to do that we need to spell out a few rules first. Once we know the rules we can create the graphical image of the project. In this section we will teach you the few simple rules for constructing a project network diagram.

The network diagram is logically sequenced to be read from left to right. Every activity in the network, except the start and end activities, must

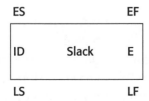

Figure 9.3   Activity node.

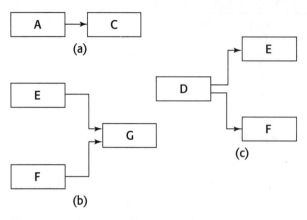

Figure 9.4 Diagramming conventions.

have at least one activity that comes before it (its immediate predecessor) and one activity that comes after it (its immediate successor). An activity begins when its predecessors have been completed. The start activity has no predecessor and the end activity has no successor. These networks are called *connected*. In this book we have adopted the practice of using connected networks. Figure 9.4 gives examples of how the variety of relationships that might exist between two or more activities can be diagrammed.

Dependencies

A dependency is simply a relationship that exists between pairs of activities. To say that activity A depends on activity B means that activity B produces a deliverable that is needed in order to do the work associated with activity A. There are four types of activity dependencies, illustrated in Figure 9.5:

Finish to start. The finish to start (FS) dependency says that activity A must be complete before activity B can begin. It is the simplest and most risk-averse of the four types. For example, activity A can represent the collection of data and activity B can represent entry of the data into the computer. To say that the dependency between A and B is finish to start means that once we have finished collecting the data we may begin entering the data. We recommend using FS dependency in the initial project planning session. The finish to start dependency is displayed with an arrow emanating from the right edge of the predecessor activity and leading to the left edge of the successor activity.

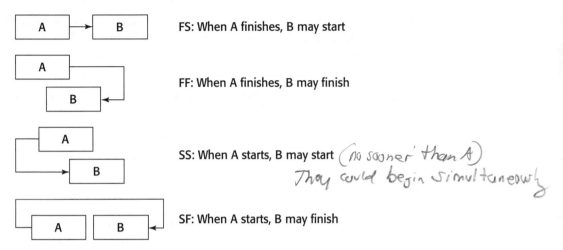

FS: When A finishes, B may start

FF: When A finishes, B may finish

SS: When A starts, B may start *(no sooner than A)* *They could begin simultaneously*

SF: When A starts, B may finish

Figure 9.5 Dependency relationships.

Start to start. The start to start (SS) dependency says that activity B may begin once activity A has begun. Note that there is a no-sooner-than relationship between activity A and activity B. Activity B may begin no sooner than activity A begins. In fact, they could both start at the same time. For example, we could alter the data collection and data entry dependency: As soon as we begin collecting data (activity A) we may begin entering data (activity B). In this case there is an SS dependency between activity A and B. The start to start dependency is displayed with an arrow emanating from the left edge of the predecessor (A) and leading to the left edge of the successor (B). We will use this dependency relationship in the section dealing with schedule compression strategies.

Start to finish. The start to finish (SF) dependency is a little more complex than the FS and SS dependencies. Here activity B can not be finished sooner than activity A has started. For example, suppose you have built a new information system. You don't want to eliminate the legacy system until the new system is operable. When the new system starts to work (activity A) the old system can be discontinued (activity B). The start to finish dependency is displayed with an arrow emanating from the left edge of activity A to the right edge of activity B. SF dependencies can be used for just-in-time scheduling between two tasks, but they rarely occur in practice.

Finish to finish. The finish to finish (FF) dependency states that activity B cannot finish sooner than activity A. For example, let's refer back to our data collection and entry example. Data entry (activity B) cannot finish until data collection (activity A) has finished. In this case, activity A and B have a finish to finish dependency. The finish to finish dependency is displayed with an arrow emanating from the right edge of activity A to the right edge of activity B. To preserve the connectedness property of the network diagram, the SS dependency on the front end of two activities should have an accompanying FF dependency on the back end.

Constraints

The type of dependency that describes the relationship between activities is determined as the result of *constraints* that exist between those activities. Each type of constraint can generate any one of the four dependency relationships. There are four types of constraints that will affect the sequencing of project activities and hence the dependency relations between activities:

- Technical constraints *can not be reversal*
- Management constraints *can be reversed*
- Interproject constraints
- Date constraints

Let's take a look at each of these in more detail.

Technical Constraints

Technical dependencies between activities are those that arise because one activity (the successor) requires output from another (the predecessor) before work can begin on it. In the simplest case, the predecessor must be completed before the successor can begin. We advise using FS relationships in the initial construction of the network diagram because it is the least complex and risk-prone dependency. If the project can be completed by the requested date using only FS dependencies, then there is no need to complicate the plan by introducing other, more complex and risk-prone dependency relationships. SS and FF dependencies will be used later when you analyze the network diagram for schedule improvements.

Within the category of technical constraints four related situations should be accounted for:

Discretionary constraints. Discretionary constraints are judgment calls by the project manager that result in the introduction of dependencies. These judgment calls may be merely a hunch or a risk-aversion strategy taken by the project manager. Through the sequencing activities the project manager gains a modicum of comfort with the project work. For example, let's revisit the data collection and data entry example. The project manager knows that a team of recent hires will be collecting the data and that the usual practice is to have them enter the data as they collect it (SS dependency). The project manager knows that this introduces some risk to the process, and because new hires will be doing the data collection and data entry, the project manager decides to use an FS rather than SS dependency between data collection and data entry.

Best-practices constraints. Best practices are past experiences that have worked well for the project manager or are known to the project manager based on the experiences of others in similar situations. The practices in place in an industry can be powerful influences here, especially in dealing with bleeding-edge technologies. In some cases, the dependencies that result from best practices constraints, which are added by the project manager, might be part of a risk-aversion strategy following the experiences of others. For example, consider the dependency between software design and software build activities. The safe approach has always been to complete design before beginning build. The current business environment, however, is one in which getting to the market faster has become the strategy for survival. In an effort to get to market faster many companies have introduced concurrency into the design-build scenario by changing the FS dependency between design and build to an SS dependency as follows. At some point in the design phase enough is known about the final configuration of the software to begin limited programming work. By introducing this concurrency between designing and building, the project manager can reduce the time to market for the new software. While the project manager knows that this SS dependency introduces risk (design changes made after programming has started may render the programming useless), the project manager will adopt this best-practices approach.

Logical constraints. Logical constraints are like discretionary constraints that arise from the project manager's way of thinking about the logical way to sequence a pair of activities. We feel that it is important for the project manager to be comfortable with the sequencing of work. After all, the project manager has to manage it! Based on past practices and common sense we prefer to sequence activities in a certain way. That's acceptable, but do not use this as an excuse to manufacture a sequence out of convenience. As long as there is a good, logical reason, that is sufficient justification. For example, in the design-build scenario, certainly several aspects of the software design lend themselves to some concurrency with the build activity. Part of the software design work, however, involves the use of a recently introduced technology with which the company has no experience. For that reason, the project manager decides that the part of the design that involves this new technology must be complete before any of the associated build activity can start.

Unique requirements. This constraint occurs in situations where a critical resource, say an irreplaceable expert or a one-of-a kind piece of equipment is involved on several project activities. For example, a new piece of test equipment will be used on the software development project. There is only one piece of this equipment, and it can be used on only one part of the software at a time. It will be used to test several different parts of the software. In order to ensure that there will be no scheduling conflicts with the new equipment, the project manager creates FS dependencies between every part of the software that will use this test equipment. Apart from any technical constraints, the project manager may impose such dependencies to ensure that no scheduling conflicts will arise from the use of scarce resources.

Management Constraints

A second type of dependency arises as the result of a management-imposed constraint. For example, suppose that the product manager on a software development project is aware that a competitor is soon to introduce a new product that will have similar features to theirs. Rather than following the concurrent design-build strategy, the product manager wants to ensure that the design of the new software will yield a product that can compete with the competitor's new product. He or she expects design changes in response to the competitor's new product and, rather than risk wasting the programmers' time, imposes the FS dependency between the design and build activities.

You'll see management constraints at work when you analyze the network diagram and as part of the scheduling decisions you make as project manager. They differ from technical dependencies in that they can be reversed while technical dependencies cannot. For example, the product manager finds out that the competitor has discovered a fatal flaw as a result of beta testing and has decided to indefinitely delay the new product introduction pending resolution of the flaw. The decision to follow the FS dependency between design and build now can be reversed, and the concurrent design-build strategy can be reinstituted. That is, management will have the project manager change the design-build dependency from FS to SS.

Interproject Constraints

Interproject constraints result when deliverables from one project are needed by another project. Such constraints result in dependencies between the activities that produce the deliverable in one project and the activities in the other project that require the use of those deliverables. For example, suppose the new piece of test equipment is being manufactured by the same company that is developing the software that will use the test equipment. In this case, the start of the testing activities in the software development project depends on the delivery of the manufactured test equipment from the other project. The dependencies that result are technical but exist between activities in two or more projects, rather than within a single project.

Interproject constraints arise when a very large project is decomposed into smaller, more manageable projects. For example, the construction of the Boeing 777 took place in a variety of geographically dispersed manufacturing facilities. Each manufacturing facility defined a project to produce its part. To assemble the final aircraft, the delivery of the parts from separate projects had to be coordinated with the final assembly project plan. Thus there were activities in the final assembly project that depended on deliverables from other subassembly projects.

These interproject constraints are common. Occasionally large projects are decomposed into smaller projects or divided into a number of projects that are defined along organizational or geographic boundaries. In all of these examples, projects are decomposed into smaller projects that are related to one another. This approach creates interproject constraints.

Although we would prefer to avoid such decomposition because it creates additional risk, it may be necessary at times.

Date Constraints

At the outset we want to make it clear that we do not approve of using date constraints. We avoid them in any way we can. In other words, "just say no" to typing dates into your project management software. If you have been in the habit of using date constraints, read on.

Date constraints impose start or finish dates on an activity that force it to occur according to a particular schedule. In our date-driven world it is tempting to use the requested date as the required delivery date. These constraints generally conflict with the schedule that is calculated and driven by the dependency relationships between activities.

Date constraints create unneeded complication in interpreting the project schedule.

Date constraints come in three types:

No earlier than. This date constraint specifies the earliest date on which an activity can be completed.

No later than. This date constraint specifies a date by which an activity must be completed.

On this date. This date constraint specifies the exact date on which an activity must be completed.

All of these date constraints can be used on the start or finish side of an activity. The most troublesome is the on-this-date constraint. It firmly sets a date and affects all activities that follow it. The result is the creation of a needless complication in the project schedule and later in reporting the status of the project. The next most troublesome is the no-later-than constraint. It will not allow an activity to occur beyond the specified date. Again, we are introducing complexity for no good reason. Both types can result in negative slack. If at all possible, do not use them. There are alternatives, which we will discuss in the next chapter. The least troublesome is the no-earlier-than constraint. At worst, it simply delays an activity's schedule and by itself cannot cause negative float.

The Use of the Lag Variable

Pauses or delays between activities are indicated in the network diagram through the use of *lag variables*. Lag variables are best defined by way of an example. Suppose that the data was being collected by mailing out a survey and entered as the surveys are returned. Imposing an SS dependency between mailing out the surveys and entering the data would not be correct unless we introduced some delay between mailing surveys and getting back the responses that could be entered. For the sake of the example, let's suppose that we wait 10 days from the date we mailed the surveys until we schedule entering the data from the surveys. Ten days is the time we think it will take for the surveys to arrive, for the recipients to answer the survey questions, and get the surveys back to us in the mail. In this case, we have defined an SS dependency with a lag of 10 days. Or, to put it another way, activity B (data entry) can start 10 days after activity A (mail the survey) has started.

Creating an Initial Project Network Schedule

As we mentioned, all activities in the network diagram have at least one predecessor and one successor activity, with the exception of the start and end activities. If this convention is followed, then the sequence is relatively straightforward to identify. If, however, the convention is not followed, or if date constraints are imposed on some activities, or if the resources follow different calendars, then understanding the sequence of activities that result from this initial scheduling exercise can be rather complex.

To establish the project schedule, you need to compute two schedules: the early schedule, which we calculate using the forward pass, and the late schedule, which we calculate using the backward pass.

The early schedule consists of the earliest times at which an activity can start and finish. These are calculated numbers that are derived from the dependencies between all the activities in the project. The late schedule consists of the latest times at which an activity can start and finish without delaying the completion date of the project. These are also calculated numbers that are derived from the dependencies between all of the activities in the project.

The combination of these two schedules gives us two additional pieces of information about the project schedule:

- The window of time within which each activity must be started and finished in order for the project to complete on schedule
- The sequence of activities that determine the project completion date

The sequence of activities that determine the project completion date is called the *critical path*. The critical path can be defined in several ways:

- It is the longest duration path in the network diagram.
- It is the sequence of activities whose early schedule and late schedule are the same.
- It is the sequence of activities with zero slack or float (we define these terms later in this chapter).

All of these definitions say the same thing: what sequence of activities must be completed on schedule in order for the project to be completed on schedule.

The activities that define the critical path are called *critical path activities*. Any delay in a critical path activity will delay the completion of the project by the amount of delay in that activity. This is a sequence of activities that will warrant the project manager's special attention.

The earliest start (ES) time for an activity is the earliest time at which all of its predecessor activities have been completed and the subject activity can begin. The ES time of an activity with no predecessor activities is arbitrarily set to 1, the first day on which the project is open for work. The ES time of activities with one predecessor activity is determined from the EF time of the predecessor activity. The ES time of activities having two or more predecessor activities is determined from the latest of the EF times of the predecessor activities. The earliest finish (EF) of an activity is calculated as ((ES + duration) - one time unit). The reason for subtracting the one time unit is to account for the fact that an activity starts at the beginning of a time unit (hour, day, and so forth) and finishes at the end of a time unit. In other words, a one-day activity, starting at the beginning of a day, begins and ends on the same day. For example, take a look at Figure 9.6. Note that activity E has only one predecessor, activity C. The EF for activity C is the end of day 3. Because it is the only predecessor of activity E, the ES of activity E is the beginning of day 4. On the other hand, activity D has two predecessors, activity B and activity C. When there are two or more predecessors, the ES of the successor, activity D in this case, is calculated based on the maximum of the EF dates of the predecessor activities. The EF dates of the predecessors are the end of day 4 and the end of day 3. The maximum of these is 4, and therefore the ES of activity D is the morning of day 5. The complete calculations of the early schedule are shown in Figure 9.6.

The latest start (LS) and latest finish (LF) times of an activity are the latest times at which the activity can start or finish without causing a delay in the completion of the project. Knowing these times is valuable for the project manager, who must make decisions on resource scheduling that can affect completion dates. The window of time between the ES and LF of an activity is the window within which the resource for the work must be scheduled or the project completion date will be delayed. To calculate these times, you work backward in the network diagram. First set the LF time of the last activity on the network to its calculated EF time. Its LS is calculated as ((LF – duration) + one time unit). Again, you add the one time unit to adjust for the start and finish of an activity within the same day. The LF time of all immediate predecessor activities is determined by the minimum of the LS, minus one time unit, times of all activities for which it is the predecessor. For example, let's calculate the late schedule for activity E. Its only successor, activity F, has an LS date of day 10. The LF date for its only predecessor, activity E, will therefore be the end of day 9. In other words, activity E must finish no later than the end of day 9 or it will delay the start of activity F and hence delay the completion date of the project. The LS date for activity E will be, using the formula, 9 – 2 + 1, or the beginning of day 7. On the other hand, consider activity C. It has two successor activities, activity D and activity E. The LS dates for them are day 5 and day 7, respectively. The minimum of those dates, day 5, is used to calculate the LF of activity C,

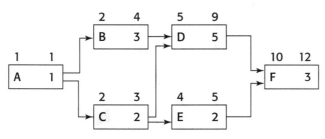

Figure 9.6 Forward pass calculations.

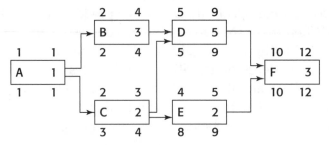

Figure 9.7 Backward pass calculations.

namely the end of day 4. The complete calculations for the late schedule are shown in Figure 9.7.

Critical Path Calculation

The *critical path* is the longest path or sequence of activities (in terms of activity duration) through the network diagram. The critical path drives the completion date of the project. Any delay in the completion of any one of the activities in the sequence will delay the completion of the project. The project manager pays particular attention to critical path activities. The critical path for the example problem we used to calculate the early schedule and the late schedule is shown in Figure 9.8.

One way to identify the critical path in the network diagram is to identify all possible paths through the network diagram and add up the durations of the activities that lie along those paths. The path with the longest duration time is the critical path. For projects of any size this method is not feasible, and we have to resort to the second method of finding the critical path—computing the slack time of an activity.

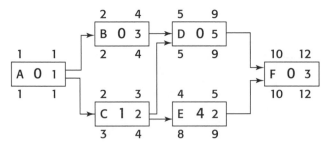

Figure 9.8 Critical path.

Slack

The second method of finding the critical path requires us to compute a quantity known as the activity *slack time*. Slack time (also called *float*) is the amount of delay expressed in units of time that could be tolerated in the starting time or completion time of an activity without causing a delay in the completion of the project. Slack time is a calculated number. It is the difference between the late finish and the early finish (LF – EF). If the result is greater than zero, then the activity has a range of time in which it can start and finish without delaying the project completion date, as shown in Figure 9.9.

As weekends, holidays, and other nonwork periods are not conventionally considered part of the slack, these must be subtracted from the period of slack.

There are two types of slack: free slack and total slack.

Free slack. This is the range of dates in which an activity can finish without causing a delay in the early schedule of any activities that are its immediate successors. Notice in Figure 9.8 that activity C has an ES of the beginning of day 2 and a LF of the end of day 4. Its duration is two days, and it has a day 3 window within which it must be completed without affecting the ES of any of its successor activities (activity D and activity E). Therefore, it has free slack of one day. Free slack can be equal to but never greater than total slack. When you choose to delay the start of an activity, possibly for resource scheduling reasons, first consider activities that have free slack associated with them. By definition, if an activity's completion stays within the free slack range,

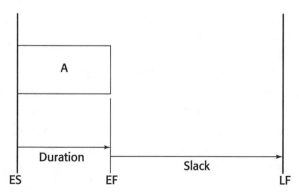

Figure 9.9   ES to LF window of an activity.

it can never delay the early start date of any other activity in the project.

Total slack. This is the range of dates in which an activity can finish without delaying the project completion date. Look at activity E in Figure 9.8. Activity E has a free float of four days as well as a total float of four days. In other words, if activity E were to be completed more than three days later than its EF date, it would delay completion of the project. We know that if an activity has zero slack, it determines the project completion date. In other words, all the activities on the critical path must be done on their earliest schedule or the project completion date will suffer. If an activity with total slack greater than zero were to be delayed beyond its late finish date, it would become a critical path activity and cause the completion date to be delayed.

Based on the method you used to compute the early and late schedules, the sequence of activities having zero slack is defined as the critical path. If an activity has been date constrained using the on-this-date type of constraint, it will also have zero slack. This usually gives a false indicator that an activity is on the critical path. Finally, in the general case, the critical path is the path that has minimum slack.

Near-Critical Path

Even though project managers are tempted to rivet their attention on critical path activities, other activities also require their attention. These are activities that we call *near-critical path*. The full treatment of near-critical activities is beyond the scope of this book. We introduce it here so that you are aware that there are paths other than critical paths that are worthy of attention. By way of a general example, suppose the critical path activities are activities in which the project team has considerable experience; duration estimates are based on historical data and are quite accurate in that the estimated duration will be very close to the actual duration. On the other hand, there is a sequence of activities not on the critical path for which the team has little experience. Duration estimates have large estimation variances. Suppose further that such activities lie on a path that has little total slack. It is very likely that this near-critical path may actually drive the project completion date even though the total path length is less than that of the critical path. This will happen if larger-than-estimated durations occur. Because of the large duration variances this is very likely. Obviously, this path cannot be ignored.

Analyzing the Initial Project Network Diagram

After you have created the initial project network diagram, one of two situations will be present. First, the initial project completion date meets the requested completion date. Usually this is not the case, but it does sometimes happen. The more likely situation is that the initial project completion date is later than the requested completion date. In other words, we have to find a way to squeeze some time out of the project schedule.

We will eventually need to address two considerations: the project completion date and resource availability under the revised project schedule. In this section we proceed under the assumption that resources will be available to meet this compressed schedule. In the next chapter we look at the resource-scheduling problem. The two are quite dependent on one another, but they must be treated separately.

Schedule Compression

Almost without exception, the initial project calculations will result in a project completion date beyond the required completion date. That means that the project team must find ways to reduce the total duration of the project to meet the required date.

To address this problem, you analyze the network diagram to identify areas where you can compress project duration. You look for pairs of activities that allow you to convert activities that are currently worked on in series into more parallel patterns of work. Work on the successor activity might begin once the predecessor activity has reached a certain stage of completion. In many cases some of the deliverables from the predecessor can be made available to the successor so that work might begin on it. The caution, however, is that project risk increases because we have created a potential rework situation if changes are made in the predecessor after work has started on the successor. Schedule compressions affect only the time frame in which work will be done; they do not reduce the amount of work to be done. The result is the need for more coordination and communication, especially between the activities affected by the dependency changes.

First you need to identify strategies for locating potential dependency changes. You focus your attention on critical path activities because these are the activities that determine the completion date of the project, the very thing we want to impact. You might be tempted to look at critical path activities that come early in the life of the project, thinking that you can get a jump on the scheduling problem, but this usually is not a good strategy for the following reason. At the early stages of a project the project team is little more than a group of people who have not worked together before (we refer to them as a herd of cats). Because you are going to make dependency changes (FS to SS) you are going to introduce risk into the project. Our herd of cats is not ready to assume risk early in the project. You should give them some time to become a real team before intentionally increasing the risk they will have to contend with. That means you should look downstream on the critical path for those compression opportunities.

A second factor to consider is to focus on activities that are *partitionable*. A partitionable activity is one whose work can be assigned to more than one individual working in parallel. For example, painting a room is partitionable. One person can be assigned to each wall. When one wall is finished a successor activity, like picture hanging, can be done on the completed wall. In that way you don't have to wait until the room is entirely painted before you can begin decorating the walls with pictures.

Writing a computer program may or may not be partitionable. If it is partitionable, then you could begin a successor activity like testing the completed parts before the entire program is complete. Whether a program is partitionable will depend on many factors, such as how the program is designed, whether the program is single function or multifunction, and other considerations. If an activity is partitionable, then it is a candidate for consideration. You could be able to partition it so that when some of it is finished you can begin working on successor activities that depend on the part that is complete. Once you have identified a candidate set of partitionable activities, you need to assess the extent to which the schedule might be compressed by starting the activity's successor activity earlier. There is not much to gain by considering activities with short duration times. We hope we have given you enough hints at a strategy that you will be able to find those opportunities. If you can't, don't worry. We have other suggestions for compressing the schedule in the next chapter.

Let's assume you have found one or more candidate activities to work with. Let's see what happens to the network diagram and the critical path as dependencies are adjusted. As you begin to replace series (SF dependencies) with parallel (SS dependencies) sequences of activities, the critical path may change to a new sequence of activities. This will happen if the length of the initial critical path, because of your compression decisions, is reduced to a duration less than that of some other path. The result is a new critical path. Figure 9.10 shows two iterations of the analysis.

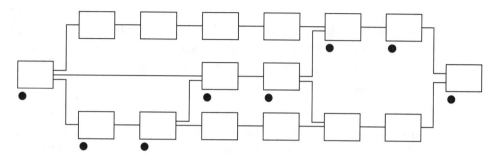

Original Critical path

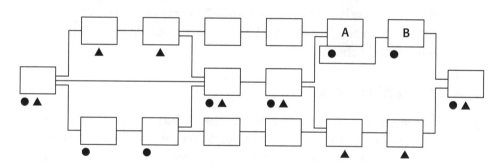

Critical path after changing AB from FS to SS

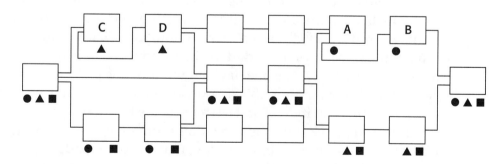

Critical path after changing CD from FS to SS

Figure 9.10   Schedule compression iterations.

The top diagram is the original critical path that results from constructing the initial network diagram using only FS dependencies. The critical path activities are identified with a filled dot.

The middle diagram in Figure 9.10 is the result of changing the dependency between activities A and B from FS to SS. Now, the critical path has changed to a new sequence of activities. The new critical path is shown in the middle diagram of Figure 9.10 by the activities with filled triangles. If you change the FS dependency between activities C and D, the critical path again moves to the sequence of activities identified by the filled squares.

Occasionally, some activities always remain on the critical path. For example, notice in the figure the set of activities that have a filled circle, triangle, and square. They have remained on the critical path through both changes. We label this set of activities a bottleneck. While further compression may result in this set of activities changing, it does identify a set of activities deserving of particular attention as the project commences. Because all critical paths generated to this point pass through this bottleneck we might want to take steps to ensure that these activities do not fall behind schedule.

Management Reserve

Management reserve is a topic associated with activity duration estimates, but it more appropriately belongs in this chapter because it should be a property of the project network more so than of the individual activities.

At the individual activity level, we are tempted to pad our estimates to have a better chance of finishing an activity on schedule. For example, we know that a particular activity will require three days of our time to complete, but we submit an estimate of four days just to make sure we can get the three days of work done in the four-day schedule we hope to get for the activity. The one day that we added is padding. First, let's agree that you will not do this. Parkinson's Law will surely strike you down, and the activity will, in fact, require the four days you estimated it would take. Stick with the three-day estimate and work to make it happen. That is a better strategy. Now that we know padding is bad at the activity level we are going to apparently contradict ourselves by saying that it is all right at the project level. There are some very good reasons for this.

Management reserve is nothing more than a contingency budget of time. The size of that contingency budget can be in the range of 5 to 10 percent of the total of all the activity durations in your project. The size might be closer to 5 percent for projects having few unknowns; it could range to 10 percent for projects using breakthrough technologies or that are otherwise very complex. Once you have determined the size of your management reserve, you create an activity whose duration is the size of management reserve and put that activity at the end of the project. It will be the last activity and its completion will signal the end of the project. This management reserve activity becomes the last one in your project plan, succeeded only by the project completion milestone.

So what is this management reserve used for? First, the project team should manage the project so that the reserve activity is not needed; in reality, though, this is rarely possible. The date promised to the customer is the one calculated by the completion of the reserve activity. The reserve activity's duration can be shortened as necessary. For example, if the critical path slips by two days, then the reserve activity's duration will be reduced by two days. This holds the project completion date constant.

This technique keeps the management reserve activity visible and allows you to manage the rate at which it's being used. If 35 percent of the overall project timeline has gone by and 50 percent of the reserve task has been used, you know you're heading for trouble.

Second, management reserve can be used as incentives for the project team. For example, many contracts include penalties for completing milestones later than planned as well as rewards for completing milestones ahead of schedule. Think of management reserve as a contingency fund that you do not want to spend. Every day that is left in the contingency fund at the completion of the project is a day ahead of schedule for which the customer should reward you. On the other hand, if you spend that contingency fund and still require more time to complete the project, this means that the project was completed later than planned. For every day that the project is late you should expect to pay a penalty.

Critical Chain Project Management

Closely related to the concept of management reserve is a relatively new approach to analyzing the project schedule called *critical chain project management* (CCPM). This approach was developed by Eliyahu M.

Goldratt[1,2] and is based on the systems thinking and the Theory of Constraints. Companies using it report project completions dramatically shorter than the traditional network-based project management techniques. We will introduce CCPM only at the concept level. An excellent source for a complete treatment can be found in *The Critical Chain Fieldbook*, a self-published work by Larry P. Leach, principal in the firm, Quality Systems.

In a recent article in the *Project Management Journal*, Larry Leach explains CCPM this way :

- It specifies the critical chain, rather than the critical path, as the project constraint. This path includes resource dependencies and does not change during project execution.

- It uses 50 percent probable activity times and aggregates allowances for uncertainty of estimates and activity performance into *buffers* at the end of activity chains.

- It uses the buffers as an immediate and direct measurement tool to control project schedule.

- It defines the constraint for multiple projects as the constraining company resource. It links projects through this resource, using buffers to account for activity duration variability.

- It seeks to change project team behavior; encouraging reporting early completion of activities and elimination of multitasking.[3]

The CCPM buffer is analogous to management reserve. Let's assume that we have estimated every activity duration using the three-point technique discussed in Chapter 8, "Estimate Activity Duration, Resource Requirements, and Cost." The point estimate of activity duration that you put in the project plan will be a value, for example, the 70 percent or 80 percent point, in the range of the three-point estimate. CCPM uses the 50 percent point instead and places the difference between that and the estimate you would have used in the buffer for the chain that contains that activity. These buffers are managed just as you would manage the management reserve.

[1]Eliyahu M. Goldratt, *The Goal*. (Croton-on-Hudson, NY: North River Press, 1984).

[2]Eliyahu M. Goldratt, *Critical Chain*. (Croton-on-Hudson, NY: North River Press, 1997).

[3]Larry P. Leach, "Critical Chain Project Management Improves Project Performance," *Project Management Journal* 30 (June 1999): 39-51.

Case Exercise: Construct a Project Network Diagram

For this exercise, you will need to go to the file called GOLD.PDF on the companion CD-ROM. You will find a Table of Contents. Select "Construct a Project Activity Network" and follow the instructions for how to run the exercise.

In this exercise, you will try to work out the network dependencies for just a portion of the project. This time, use the marketing portion of the WBS. Marketing offers a bit more in the way of complexity; the vendor activities are too linear in their schedule.

The appropriate activities are provided for you in a Microsoft Word file as small boxes that can be cut out and arranged in a logical dependency order. A second Word file contains the complete WBS. Because there are dependencies for the marketing activities, both predecessors and successors, that are outside that group, you'll need to use the full WBS to determine what they are.

If you want more information on CCPM, an excellent source is *The Critical Chain Fieldbook*, a self-published work by Larry P. Leach.

Using the JPP Session

We believe in using the appropriate technology and nowhere is that more obvious than in our approach to constructing and analyzing the project network. If you have tried to use automated tools for this planning exercise, you have probably experienced nothing short of complete frustration. Automated tools will do the job for small projects or one-person project teams, but for large projects they just get in the way.

For example, let's say your project has 100 activities (and that is not a large project). You can only see about 6 to 8 activity nodes on your computer screen at any time, and so any attempt to analyze the network diagram using the automated tool will do nothing but add confusion. You will require a tool that allows the planning team to see all the data at one time. How many people can you crowd around the computer screen and hope to get any meaningful work done? Even if you broadcast the computer screen to a larger screen you are still limited to 6 to 8 nodes per view.

The best way to explain our approach for generating the project network diagram, which is foolproof, by the way, is to discuss it step for step:

Start / end   milestones

1. **Enter activities and their durations in the software tool.** First enter all the activities and their durations into the software tool. Print the network diagram. Because no dependencies have been entered, the network diagram for most software tools will be a columnar report with one activity node per row—not a very informative network diagram, but it serves our purposes. Some software tools might display these nodes in formats other than columnar, and that will work just fine, too.

2. **Cut out each activity node and tape it to a Post-It note.** (Don't forget to create start and end node milestones.) We use 3" by 3" Post-It notes because they allow you to put the node at the top and write in large numbers the activity ID number on the bottom. This makes it possible for the project planning team to see the activity ID from anyplace in the planning room.

3. **Affix each Post-It note to the white board in order.** We recommend placing them at the rightmost edge of the white board space so that you have enough room to work. Ordering them by task ID number and/or WBS major category makes it easier to find them later.

4. **Place the start node at the left edge of the white board.** Ask the planning group to identify all activities that have no predecessors. As each activity is called out, the planning group should listen and voice any objections, such as they believe that one of the identified activities does, in fact, have a predecessor. The objection is settled, and the exercise continues. When there are no objections, place these activities on the left side of the white board and connect them to the start node with a black erasable marker pen. Continue this process until all the remaining activities have predecessors.

For each major part of the WBS there will be a corresponding set of activities that must be incorporated into the nodes already connected from the previous step. The most expert person on the planning team will facilitate the activity sequencing exercise for the activities that are in his or her area of expertise. This person will build his or her part of the network using a left-to-right build. That is, once an activity has been posted on the left side of the white board, what other activity or activities may now be worked on? The other members of the planning team will be responsible for critiquing and commenting as the expert completes his or her part of the activity sequencing. One expert at a time facilitates completing part of the activity sequencing until the network diagram is complete. The conclusion of this exercise is a great time for a break. The team has reached a significant milestone in the project plan, and they deserve a rest.

5. **Input the network diagram into the software tool.** While the planning team is on break, the network diagram is input into the software tool by the planning facilitator and his or her assistant, whom we call a technographer. As part of that exercise they can input the network sketch into the software tool and review the predecessor and successor data to make sure the network is fully connected and note and correct any discrepancies. If an activity does not have a logical successor activity, then it should be connected to the end activity. Remember, fully connected means that every activity (except the start and end activities) has at least one predecessor and one successor activity.

6. **Reassemble the planning team.** It is now time to find out if the first draft of the network meets the project delivery dates. If it does, consider yourself fortunate. Usually it does not meet the expected completion date, and you need to analyze the network diagram. You can use the automated tool to find activities on the critical path. Place a large red dot on the sequence of activities that identify the critical path. The real value of the white board and Post-It note approach is that it facilitates using the planning group to identify ways to reduce the time on the critical path. To compress the project schedule, look for opportunities to change FS relationships to SS relationships with perhaps some lag time introduced. Be careful not to get carried away with schedule compression because it will aggravate the resource-scheduling problem. Remember that you are cramming the project work into a shorter window of time, and that tends to increase the probability of creating scheduling conflicts. At each iteration, use the automated tool to check if the critical path has moved to a new sequence of activities. If it has, there may be other compression opportunities on the new critical path. When all of these types of schedule compression possibilities are exhausted,

this part of the compression exercise is finished. Further improvements will be discussed in the next chapter.

Now you've established a project schedule that meets the requested project completion date. The final step is to schedule the resources so as to complete the work according to the revised schedule.

Finalize the Schedule Based on Resource Availability

The hammer must be swung in cadence,
when more than one is hammering the iron.

—GIORDANO BRUNO
ITALIAN PHILOSOPHER

Behind an able man there are always other able men.

—CHINESE PROVERB

Rather than allowing them [subordinates] the autonomy to get involved
and do the work in their own ways, what happens all too often is the
manager wants the workers to do it the manager's way.

—EDWARD L. DECI
UNIVERSITY OF ROCHESTER

Work smarter, not harder.

—ANONYMOUS

Resources

The final step to putting together the project plan is to assign the resources according to the schedule developed in Chapter 9, "Construct and Analyze the Project Network Diagram." Up to this point, we have identified the activities in the project and developed a schedule that meets the expected end date of the project. Now, you need to determine if you can accomplish this schedule with the resources available. This chapter looks at tools and methods available to help you answer this question.

There could be cases where the resources are not available according to the project schedule. In those situations, the project manager will have to revert to the original project definition, budget, time, and resource allocations to resolve the scheduling problem. This may require additional time, budget, and/or resource allocation in order to comply with the requested deliverables and deliverable schedule.

Leveling Resources

Resource leveling is part of the broader topic of resource management. This is an area that has always created problems for organizations. Some of the situations that organizations have to deal with are these:

- Committing people to more than they can reasonably handle in the given time frame, reasoning that they will find a way to get it done

- Changing project priorities and not considering the impact on existing resource schedules

- The absence of a resource management function that can measure and monitor the capacity of the resource pool and the extent to which it is already committed to projects

- Employee turnover that is not reflected in the resource schedule

Any organization that does not have a way of effectively handling these situations will find itself in the situation analogous to the flow through a funnel, as depicted in Figure 10.1.

Figure 10.1 is a graphic portrayal of the resource scheduling problem. The diameter of the funnel represents the total of all the resources available for the project. Activities can pass through the funnel at a rate that

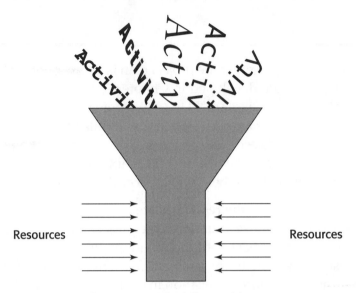

Figure 10.1   The resource scheduling problem.

is limited by the amount of work that can be completed by the available resources according to the schedule of the activities. You can try to force more into the funnel than it can accommodate, but doing so only results in turbulence in the funnel. You are familiar with the situation where managers try to force more work onto your already fully loaded schedule. The result is either schedule slippage or less-than-acceptable output. In the funnel example, it results in rupture due to overload (weekend time and long hours are the root cause of the rupture).

The core teamwork takes place at the center of the pipeline. This is where the activity flow through the funnel is the smoothest because it is based on a well-executed schedule. The work assigned to the contract team takes place along the edge of the funnel. According to the laws of flow in a pipeline there is more turbulence at the walls of the structure. The deliverables are the completed activity work. Because the diameter of the funnel is fixed, only so much completed work can flow from it. Too many organizations think that by simply adding more into the top, more will come out the bottom of the funnel. Their rationale is that people will work harder and more efficiently if they know that more is expected. While this may be true in a limited sense, it is not in the best interest of the project because it results in mistakes and compromised quality. Mistakes will be made as a direct result of the pressure of the overly ambitious schedule forced on people. In this chapter we develop resource leveling strategies that the project manager can adopt to avoid the situation depicted in the funnel example.

Let's take a step back for a moment. When you were creating the project network diagram, the critical path was the principal focal point for trying to finish the project by a specified date. Resource over- or under-allocation was not a consideration. We do this for a reason. It is important to focus your attention on planning one portion of the project at a time. If you can't hit the desired finish date based strictly on the logical order in which activities must be completed, why worry about whether resources are over- or under-allocated? You've got another problem to solve first. After the finish date has been accepted, you can address the problem of over-, and in some cases, under-allocation.

Resource leveling is a process that the project manager follows to schedule how each resource is allocated to activities in order to accomplish the work within the scheduled start and finish dates of the activity. Recall that the scheduled start and finish dates of every activity are constrained by the project plan to lie entirely within their ES-LF window. Were that not the case, the project would be delayed beyond its scheduled completion date. As resources are leveled, they must be constrained to the ES-LF window of the activities to which they are assigned, or the project manager must seek other alternatives to resolve the conflict between resource availability and project schedule.

The resource schedule needs to be leveled for two reasons. The first is to ensure that no resource is over-allocated. That is, we do not schedule a resource to more than 100 percent of its available time.

A second reason to level resources is that the project manager wants the number of resources (people in most cases) to follow a logical pattern throughout the life of the project. You would not want the number of people working on the project to fluctuate wildly from day to day or from week to week. That would impose too many management and coordination problems. Resource leveling avoids this by ensuring that the number of resources working on a project at any time are fairly constant. The ideal project would have the number of people resources relatively level over the planning phases, building gradually to a maximum during the project work phases, and decreasing through the closing phases. Such increases and decreases are manageable and expected in the life of a well-planned project.

Acceptably Leveled Schedule

As we begin this discussion of leveling resources, let's be clear on one point. It is very unlikely, perhaps impossible, that you will develop a resource schedule that simultaneously possesses all the desirable characteristics we discussed. Of course, you will do the best you can and hope for a resource schedule that is acceptable to management and to those who manage the resources employed on your project. When a resource schedule is leveled, the leveling process is done within the availability of the resource to that project. When we discussed activity estimating and resource assignments in Chapter 8, "Estimate Activity Duration, Resource Availability, and Cost," we said that resources are not available to work on an activity 100 percent of any given day. Our current observations show that this number ranges between 50 and 65 percent. This value, for a typical average day, is the *resources maximum availability*. Project management software products may also refer to it as *max availability* or *max units*. Some software applications allow this value to be varied by time period; others do not.

Ideally, we want to have a project in which all resource schedules can be accommodated within the resources maximum availability. On occasion this may not be possible, especially when project completion dates are paramount. This means that some overtime may be necessary. We're all familiar with this. Overtime should be your final "fall-back" option, however. Use it with discretion and only for short periods of time. If at all possible, don't start your project off with overtime as the norm. You'll probably need it somewhere along the line, so keep it as part of your management reserve (see the discussion on management reserve in Chapter 9).

Resource Leveling Strategies

You can use three approaches to level project resources:

- Slack
- Shifting the project finish date
- Smoothing

Let's take a look at each of these strategies in more detail.

Slack

Slack was defined in Chapter 9 as the amount of delay expressed in units of time that could be tolerated in the starting time or completion time of an activity without causing a delay in the completion of the project. Recall that slack is the difference between the ES-LF window of an activity and its duration. For example, if the ES-LF window is four days and the duration of the activity is three days, its slack is $4 - 3$, or one day.

Slack can be used to alleviate the over-allocation of resources. With this approach, one or more of the project activities are postponed to a date that is later than their early start date but no later than their late finish date. In other words, the activities are rescheduled but remain within their ES-LF window.

This is one of the times that having free slack can come in handy. Free slack, as mentioned in Chapter 9, is the amount of delay that can be tolerated in an activity without affecting the ES date of any of its successor activities. When you need to resolve the "stack up" of activities on the schedule, first look to see if any of the activities has free slack. If any of them do, and if rescheduling the activity to that later start date will solve the resource over-allocation problem, then you are done. If moving the start date of the activity does not resolve the over-allocation you have to use total slack, and at least one other activity will have its early start date delayed.

Shifting the Project Finish Date

Not all projects are driven by the completion date. For some, resource availability is their most severe constraint. On these projects, the critical path may have to be extended to achieve an acceptably resource-leveled schedule. This could very well mean that the parallel scheduling on the activity network diagram that moved the original finish date to an earlier one may need to be reversed. The Start to Start and Finish to Finish dependencies might need to be set back to the linear Finish to Start type.

In some cases, a project is of a low enough priority within the organization that it is used mostly for fill-in work. In that case, the completion date is not significant and doesn't have the urgency that it does in a *time-to-market* project. For most projects, however, moving the finish date to beyond a desired date is the least attractive alternative.

If you find yourself caught between over-allocated resources on a schedule that cannot be acceptably leveled and a firm fixed completion date, you may have to consider reducing the scope of the project. Consider delaying some of the features to the next release as one way of resolving the issue. In saying this, we're referring to the concepts introduced regarding the scope triangle in Chapter 4, "What Is a Project?"

Smoothing

Occasionally, limited overtime is required to accomplish the work within the scheduled start and finish dates of the activity. Overtime can help alleviate some resource over-allocation because it allows more work to be done within the same scheduled start and finish dates.

Alternative Methods of Scheduling Activities

Rather than treating the activity list as fixed and within that constraint leveling resources, you could resolve the leveling problem by considering further decomposition of one or more activities. One of the six characteristics of a complete WBS mentioned in Chapter 7, "Identify Project Activities," was activity independence. Activity independence means that once work has begun on an activity, work can continue without interruption until the activity is complete. Usually, you do not schedule the work to be continuous for a number of reasons, such as resource availability, but you could if you wanted. Other than for resource availability issues, the decision to do that may simply be a preference of the project manager.

Further Decomposition of Activities

Resource availability, or rather the lack of it, can require some creative activity scheduling on the part of the project manager. For example, suppose that an activity requires one person for three days within a five-day window. There are two days of slack in the schedule for that activity. In other words, the ES-LF window of the activity is five days and the activity duration is three days. The project manager would prefer to have the activity scheduled for its early start date, but the unavailability of the resource for three consecutive days beginning on the ES date will require scheduling the activity work to a longer period of time. One solution would be to have the resource work for three nonconsecutive days as early as possible in the five-day window. Continuing with the example, let's say that the resource is available for the first two days in the five-day window and for the last day in the five-day window. To simplify the scheduling of the resource the project manager could decompose the five-day activity into two activities—one two-day activity and one one-day activity. The two-day activity would then have an FS dependency on the one-day activity. The scheduled start and finish dates of the two activities would be set so that they fit the availability of the resource. There are other solutions to this scheduling problem, but we do not discuss them here. The one we have presented is the best approach to situations similar to the example.

Stretching Activities

Another alternative that preserves the continuity of the activity work is to stretch the work over a longer period of time by having the resource work on the activity *at a percent per day lower than was originally planned.* Let's modify the previous example to illustrate what we mean by stretching the activity. Suppose the resource is available 80 percent of each day in the five-day window and you need four days of work. The resource is therefore available for .80 times five days, or four days of work, over the five-day window. You need only four days of work from the resource, so how do you schedule the work in the five-day window to accomplish the four days of work you need? The solution is to stretch the activity from four days to five and schedule the resource to work on the activity for those five days. Because the resource can only work 80 percent of the time on the activity, the resource will accomplish four days of work in five days.

In this simple example the percentage was constant over the five days, but it might also follow some profile. For example, suppose you needed the resource for three days and the resource was available full-time for the first and second days but only half-time for the remaining three days of the five-day window. You could first split the activity into two activities—a two-day activity and a one-day activity. The two-day activity would fully use the resource and get two days of work completed. The second activity would be stretched to two days, and the resource would be assigned half-time for two days to complete the remaining day of work on the activity. In other words, you got the three days of work in four days—the first two days at full-time and the next two days at half-time. Resource availability can be the determining factor for how the activity can be stretched within its ES-LF window and still get the required amount of work from the resource.

Assigning Substitute Resources

Our estimate of activity duration was based on the assumption that a typically skilled resource will be available to work on the activity. That may not be possible, though, because of unavailability of the resource. This will be especially true in the case of scarce resources such as some of the newer technologies. The project manager needs to find some other strategy. One approach would be to use less-skilled resources and add to the total number of hours requested. Here, the thinking is that a less-skilled resource would require a longer period of time to complete the activity work. Be careful in using this tactic, however, because there will be additional risk in using a less-skilled person and it is not clear exactly what increase in activity duration is needed to account for the lesser skilled person. This strategy will work only for noncritical path activities. Using it for a critical path activity would extend the completion date of the project.

Work Packages *— tasks for each activity*

At this point, you have essentially completed all JPP session activities. The project work has been defined as a list of activities; activity duration and resource requirements are specified, the project network is built, the activity schedule is done, and resources have been scheduled. The JPP session attendees have reached a consensus! Whew, that's a lot—and you probably wondered if it would ever be finished. There is one more step to go before project work can commence—that is, to define the work to be done in each activity but at the task level. Recall from Chapter 7 that activities are made up of tasks. The work to be done within an activity is called a *work package*.

This is really the final test of the feasibility of the schedule and resource leveling decisions. The work package is a statement by each activity manager as to how he or she plans to complete the activity within the scheduled start and finish dates. It is like an insurance policy. For the project manager, the work package is a document that describes the work at a level of detail so that if the activity manager or anyone working on the activity were not available (if he or she were fired, hit by a bus on the way to work, or otherwise not available), someone else could use the work package to figure out how to continue the work of the activity with minimal lost time. This is especially important for critical path activities for which schedule delays are to be avoided.

A work package can consist of one or several tasks. They may be nothing more than a to-do list, which can be completed in any order. On the other hand, the work package can consist of tasks that take the form of a mini-project, with a network diagram that describes it. In this case, work packages are assigned to a single individual, who we call an activity manager or work package manager. This manager is responsible for completing the activity on time, within budget, and according to specification. Sounds like a project manager, doesn't it? That person has the authority and the access to the resources needed to complete the assignment.

Purpose of a Work Package

The work package becomes the bedrock for all project work. It describes in detail the tasks that need to be done to complete the work for an activity. In addition to the task descriptions, the package includes start and end dates for the activity.

The *work package manager* (or activity manager) may decide to include the start and end dates for each task in the package so that anyone who has occasion to use the work package will have a sense of how the plan to complete the work would be accomplished. Be careful if you adopt this approach because you encourage micro-management on the part of the project manager. The more you say, the more you encourage objections; the trade-off, though, is to protect the project schedule. There is always a trade-off between the need for detail and the need to spend work time accomplishing work, not shuffling papers.

The work package also can be adapted to status reporting. Tasks constitute the work to be done. Checking off completed tasks measures what percent of the activity is complete. Some organizations use the percent of tasks completed as the percent of activity completion. This is a simple yet effective metric that serves as the basis for earned value calculations. Earned value is discussed in detail in Chapter 13, "Monitor and Control Progress."

Format of a Work Package

We recommend two work package documents. The first is a very special type of telephone directory, called a *work package assignment sheet*. It is used as a ready reference for the project manager and contains some basic information about each work package and its manager. The second is a detailed description of the activity plan, called the *work package description report*. It contains much of the same information that is in found in a project plan but focuses on activities, not projects. It is therefore a much simpler document than a project plan even though it contains the same type of information as the project plan.

Work Package Assignment Sheet

The work package assignment sheet, shown in Figure 10.2, is a report for the project manager only. It includes the earliest start and latest finish times for each activity. This is one of the few resources available to the

WORK PACKAGE ASSIGNMENT SHEET	**Project Name**		**Project No.**		**Project Manager**	
Work Package			Schedule			
Number	Name		Early Start	Late Finish	Work Package Manager	Contact Information
A	DESIGN		03/01/00	04/01/00	ANNA LYST	
B	PROD. EVAL		04/02/00	07/02/00	HY ROWLER	
C1	PLACE.LOCATE.PT1		04/02/00	03/04/01	SY YONARA	
C2	PLACE.LOCATE.PT2		07/03/00	03/04/01	HY ROWLER	
D	PROD.FCAST		07/03/00	03/04/01	SY YONARA	
E	PROD.DELETE		03/05/01	06/02/01	HY ROWLER	
F	PROMO.REGION		03/05/01	07/06/01	TERRI TORY	
H	PRICE		08/04/01	02/05/02	HY ROWLER	
I	PLACE.DESIGN		06/05/01	08/03/02	HY ROWLER	
J	PROMO.SALES.LEAD		07/07/01	11/05/01	TERRI TORY	
G	PROMO.MEDIA		07/07/01	02/05/02	SY YONARA	
K	PROMO.SALES.RPT		10/07/01	02/05/02	TERRI TORY	
L	SYSTEM.TEST		02/08/02	05/10/02	ANNA LYST	
M	SYSTEM.ACCEPT		05/10/02	06/10/02	ANNA LYST	
Prepared by		Date	Approved by		Date	Sheet 1 of 1

Figure 10.2 Work package assignment sheet.

project manager and should not be made available to anyone other than the project manager. The project manager is unlikely to tell an activity manager that the activity is scheduled for completion on July 15, for example, but the activity manager really has until August 15 because of slack. Activity managers should be given only the scheduled start and end dates for their activities.

The work package assignment sheet has limited value in smaller projects but can be invaluable in larger ones. We were involved in a project that consisted of more than 4000 activities. Over the seven-year life of the project more than 10,000 activity managers were involved. This report became a phone directory that needed constant updating as team members came and went. Because of the complexity and personnel changes that accompany these large projects, the project manager needs an effective and efficient way of keeping up with the project team membership, who is assigned to what, and how will they accomplish their work.

Work Package Description Report   *Roles + responsibility*

A work package is a document prepared by the activity manager in which he or she describes the details of how he or she will accomplish the work of the activity. A very simple example of a work package, or statement of work, is shown in Figure 10.3.

Once the project plan has been approved, it is the activity manager's responsibility to generate the work package documentation. Not all activities will require or should require work package documentation. The documentation can be limited to critical path activities, near-critical path activities, high-risk activities, and activities that use very scarce or highly skilled staff. It is the project manager who will decide which activities need a work package description report.

The descriptions must be complete so that anyone could pick them up, read them, and understand what has to be done to complete the activity. Each task must be described so that the status of the work package can be determined easily. Ideally, the task list is a check-off list. Once all the tasks have been checked off as being completed, the activity is completed. Each task will also have a duration estimate attached to it. In some project planning sessions these estimates may have been supplied as a bottom-up method of estimating activity duration.

WORK PACKAGE DESCRIPTION			Project Name		Project No.		Project Manager		
Work Package Name			Work Package No.		Work Package Manager			Contact Info.	Date
Start Date	End Date	Critical Path Y N	Predecessor Work Package(s)				Successor Work Package(s)		
		TASK							
No.	Name	Description		Time (days)	Responsibility			Contact Info.	
Prepared by		Date		Approved by		Date		Sheet 1 of 1	

Figure 10.3   Work package description report.

The work of planning the project is now complete. All that remains is to document the plan in the form of a project proposal and forward it to the appropriate manager(s) for approval. Approval at this stage is approval to do the project as defined in the project plan. In the next chapter we bring together all the discussions from earlier chapters on the Joint Project Planning session. While we have discussed various parts of project planning, we have not given you a complete picture of exactly how a project planning session is planned, organized, who should attend, and how one is conducted.

Case Exercise: Leveling the Resource Schedule

For this exercise, you will need to go to the file called GOLD.PDF on the companion CD-ROM. You will find a Table of Contents. Select "Construct a Project Activity Network" and follow the instructions for how to run the exercise.

Now that you've determined that the desired project finish date can be achieved based solely on the dependency schedule, the final question to be answered is this: Can we do it with the available resources? As you might imagine, with the number of activities occurring concurrently, some resources are going to be over-scheduled. There are several techniques for solving the over-allocation problem. The first is resource leveling. Others include stretching activity durations, smoothing the resource allocation with some overtime, and assigning alternative resources. You'll use all three of these techniques in this exercise.

Because of the number and complexity of the variables involved, there are no paper-based exercises with this lesson. Also, because of the number of resources involved, we show representative samples of different methods, rather than solutions for each of them.

If you are using Microsoft Project to follow along, the files are available on the CD-ROM for practice. We suggest that you look through our approach first and then try solving some of the over-allocation problems in the file.

Organize and Conduct the Joint Project Planning Session

This report, by its very length, defends itself against the risk of being read.

—WINSTON CHURCHILL
ENGLISH PRIME MINISTER

Learn to write well, or not to write at all.

—JOHN DRYDEN
ENGLISH POET

If you don't get the reader's attention in the first paragraph, the rest of your message is lost.

—PUBLIC RELATIONS MAXIM

Joint Project Planning Sessions

In each of the chapters in Part Three we closed the chapter with a brief discussion of the JPP session as it relates to the chapter topics. In this chapter we bring all of that information together, along with a treatment of the logistics of planning projects using the Joint Project Planning session.

All of the planning activities we've discussed so far to create the detailed project plan take place in a *Joint Project Planning session* (JPP). We advocate and use a group process for generating the detailed project plan. The JPP is a group session in which all of the people who are involved in the project meet to develop the detailed plan. The session can last from one to three days, and it can be work-intensive. Often, there is conflict between session attendees, but the final result of this meeting is an agreement about how the project can be accomplished within a specified time frame, budget, resource availabilities, and customer specification.

Our planning process shares many of the same features as Joint Requirements Planning (JRP) and Joint Applications Design (JAD) sessions. The JRP session is commonly used to design computer applications. Our JPP is robust—that is, it can be used for any type of project including the design and development of computer applications.

The objective of a JPP session is very simple: Develop a project plan that meets the Conditions of Satisfaction as negotiated between the requestor and the provider, and as described in the Project Overview Statement. Sounds simple, doesn't it?

Unfortunately, it doesn't happen with any regularity. There are many reasons for this. People are generally impatient to get on with the work of the project. After all, there are deadlines to meet and other projects demanding our attention. We don't have time for planning; we have too much work to do and too many customers to satisfy. Regrettably, at the project's eleventh hour, when it is too late to recover from a poor plan, we bow in defeat. Next time, we promise ourselves, we will pay more attention to the planning details. Somehow that next time never seems to come. *It's time for change!*

Planning the JPP Session

Team planning has always been viewed as advantageous over other forms of project planning, such as the project manager planning the project by walking around gathering data for the plan. In our experience, the synergy of the group provides far more accurate activity duration estimates, and we expect more complete information input to the planning process itself. Perhaps the best advantage of all is that it creates a much stronger commitment to the project for all those who lived through the pain of generating and agreeing to the complete project plan. If all else fails, it is more fun than doing planning in isolation.

Sometimes, we feel that planning is a necessary evil. It is something we all do because we *have to* and because we can then say that we have thought about where we want to go and how we are going to get there. Once written, plans are often bound in nice notebooks and become bookends gathering dust on someone's shelf.

Make up your mind right now to change that! Planning is essential to good project management. The plan that you generate is a dynamic document. It changes as the project commences. It will be a reference work for you and the team members when questions of scope and change arise. We make no bones about it—to do good planning is painful, but to do poor planning is even more painful. Take your choice.

The first document considered in the JPP session is the POS. One may already exist and therefore will be the starting point for the JPP. If one doesn't exist, it must be developed as the initial part or prerequisite to starting the JPP. The situation will dictate how best to proceed. The POS can be developed in a number of ways. If it is an idea for consideration, it will probably be developed by one individual—typically the person who will be the project manager. It can be departmentally based or cross-departmentally based. The broader the impact on the enterprise, the more likely it will be developed as the first phase of a JPP session. Finally, the POS may have been developed through a Conditions of Satisfaction exercise. In any case, the JPP session begins by discussing and clarifying exactly what is intended by the POS. The project team might also use this opportunity to write the PDS—their understanding of the project.

The JPP session must be planned down to the last detail if it is to be successful. Time is a scarce resource for all of us, and the last thing we want to do is to waste it. Recognize before you start that the JPP session will be a very intense session. Participants often get emotional and will even dig their heels in to make a point.

Before we discuss how the session is planned and conducted, let's talk about who should attend.

Attendees

The JPP participants are invited from among those who might be affected by or have input into the project. If the project involves deliverables or is a new process or procedure, anyone who has input to the process, receives output from the process, or handles the deliverables should be invited to participate in the JPP. The customer falls into one or more of these categories and must be present at the JPP. Any manager of resources that may be required by the project team also will attend the JPP session. In many organizations the project has a project champion (not necessarily the project manager or customer manager) who may wish to participate at least at the start.

Facilitator. A successful JPP session requires an experienced facilitator. This person is responsible for conducting the JPP. It is important that the facilitator not have a vested interest or bring biases to the session because that would diminish the effectiveness of the plan. It must be developed with an open mind, not with a biased mind. For this reason, we strongly suggest that the project manager should not facilitate the session. If using an outside consultant is not possible, we recommend a neutral party for facilitator, such as another project manager.

Project manager. Because the project manager is not leading the planning session, he or she can concentrate on the plan itself; that is the project manager's major role in the JPP. Having the proposed project manager (if known) facilitate the JPP session may seem to be an excellent choice, but it can be the wrong choice if the project is politically charged or has customers from more than one function, process, or resource pool. The project manager must be comfortable with the project plan. After all, the project manager is the one who has final responsibility when it comes to getting the project done on time, within budget, and according to specification.

Another project manager. Skilled JPP facilitators are hard to find. If the project manager is not a good choice for facilitator, then maybe another project manager—presumably unbiased—would be a good choice, especially if he or she has JPP experience.

JPP consultant. Project management consultants will often serve as another source of qualified JPP facilitators. Their broad experience in project management and project management consulting will be invaluable. This will be especially true in organizations that have recently completed project management training and are in the process of implementing their own project management methodology. Having an outside consultant facilitate the JPP session will be as much a learning experience as it is an opportunity to get off to a good start with a successful JPP session.

Technographer. The JPP facilitator is supported by a technographer, a professional who not only knows project management, but also is an expert in the software tools used to support the project. While the JPP facilitator is coordinating the planning activities, the JPP technographer is recording planning decisions on the computer as they occur in real time. At any point in time—and there will be several—the technographer can print out or display the plan for all to see and critique.

Core project team. Commitment is so important that to exclude the core team from the JPP session would be foolish. Estimating activity duration and resource requirements will be much easier with the professional expertise these people can bring to the planning session. The core project team is made up of those individuals who will stay with the project from first day to last day. This does not mean that they are with the project full time. In today's organization that is not to be expected unless the organization is totally projectized or uses self-directed teams.

Customer representative. This is always a bit tricky. Let's face it: Some customers really don't want to be bothered. It is up to the project manager or champion to convince customers of the importance of their participation in the JPP Session. We don't claim that this will be easy, but it is nevertheless important. There must be customer buy-in to the project plan. The customer won't get that if the project manager simply mails a copy of the plan. The customer must be involved in the planning session. To not have the customer's buy-in is to court disaster. Changes to the project plan will occur, and problems will arise. If the customer is involved in preparing the plan, he or she can contribute to resolution of change requests and problem situations.

Resource managers. These managers control resources that the project will require. To put a schedule together without input and participation from these managers would be a waste of time. They may have some suggestions that will make the plan all that more realistic, too. In some cases they may send a representative who might also be part of the project team. The important factor here is that someone from each resource area is empowered to commit resources to the project plan.

Project champion. The project champion drives the project and sells it to senior management. In many cases, the champion can be the customer—an ideal situation because commitment is already there. In other cases, the project champion can be the senior managers of the division, department, or process that will be the beneficiary of the project deliverables.

Functional managers. Because functional managers manage areas that can either provide input to or receive output from the project deliverables, they or a representative should participate in the planning session. They will ensure that the project deliverables can be smoothly integrated into existing functions or that the functions will have to be modified as part of the project plan.

Process owner. For the same reasons that functional managers should be present, so should process owners. If the project deliverables do not smoothly integrate into their processes, either the project plan or the affected process(es) will have to be altered.

A formal invitation, announcing the project, its general direction and purpose, and the planning schedule, should be issued to all these individuals. RSVPs are a must! Full attendance is so important that we have cancelled a JPP session because certain key participants were not able to attend. On one occasion, we acted as the project manager for a client and cancelled the JPP session because the customer did not think his attendance was important enough. Our feedback to the customer was that as soon as it was a high enough priority for him to attend, we would schedule the JPP session. Pushback like this is tough, but we felt that the JPP is so critically important to the ultimate success of the project that we were willing to take this strong position with the customer.

Facilities

Because the planning team may spend as many as three consecutive days in planning, it is important that the physical facility is comfortable and away from the daily interruptions (off-site is best if you wish to minimize distractions). While off-site seems preferable, we prefer on-site planning sessions. This has both advantages and disadvantages, but, with proper planning, they can be controlled. Easy access to information has been a major advantage to on-site planning sessions in our experience; interruptions due to the daily flow of work have been the major disadvantage. With easy access to the office made possible by cell phones and e-mail, the potential for distraction and interruptions has increased. These need to be minimized in whatever way makes sense. You need to allocate enough space so that groups of four or five planning members each have separate work areas with tables, chairs, and flip charts. All work should be done in one room. In our experience, we have found that breakout rooms tend to be dysfunctional. To the extent possible everybody needs to be present for everything that takes place in the planning session. The room should have plenty of whiteboard space or blank walls. In many cases, we have taped flip-chart paper or butcher paper to the walls. You can never have enough writing space in the planning room.

Equipment

An ample supply of Post-It notes, tape, scissors, and colored marking pens is what you will need. Add high-tech equipment: an LCD projector and a PC are all you need for everyone in the room to see the details as they come together.

The Complete Planning Agenda

The agenda for the JPP session is straightforward. It can be completed in one, two, or three sessions. For example, an early meeting with the requestor can be scheduled, at which time the Conditions of Satisfaction are drafted. These will be input to the second session in which the POS is drafted. In those cases where the POS must be approved before detailed planning can commence, there will be an interruption until approval can be granted. Once approval is obtained, the third session can be scheduled. At this session (usually two or three days long) the detailed project plan can be drafted for approval.

Here's a sample agenda for the JPP session:

Session # 1

1. Negotiate the Conditions of Satisfaction.

Session #2

1. Write the Project Overview Statement.

Session #3 (JPP session)

1. Entire planning team creates the first-level WBS.
2. Subject matter experts develop further decomposition with the entire planning team observing and commenting.
3. Estimate activity durations and resource requirements.
4. Construct project network diagram.
5. Determine critical path.
6. Revise and approve project completion date.
7. Finalize resource schedule.
8. Gain consensus on the project plan.

Deliverables

The deliverables from the JPP session are given in the project management life cycle and have already been discussed in detail in the appropriate chapters. They are repeated here.

Work Breakdown Structure. Recall that the Work Breakdown Structure (WBS) is a graphical or indented outline list of the work (expressed as activities) to be done to complete the project. It is used as a planning tool as well as a reporting structure.

Activity duration estimates. The schedule, which is also a major deliverable, is developed from estimates of the duration of each work activity in the project. Activity duration estimates may be single-point estimates or three-point estimates, as discussed in Chapter 8, "Estimate Activity Duration, Resource Requirements, and Cost."

Resource requirements. For each activity in the project an estimate of the resources to perform the work is required. In most cases the resources will be the technical and people skills, although they can also include such things as physical facilities, equipment, and computer cycles.

Project network schedule. Using the WBS, the planning team will define the sequence in which the project activities should be performed. Initially this sequence is determined only by the technical relationships between activities, not by management prerogatives. That is, the deliverables from one or more activities are needed to begin work on the next activity. This sequence is most easily understood by displaying it graphically. The definition of the network activities and the details of the graphical representation are covered in Chapter 9, "Construct and Analyze the Project Network Diagram."

Activity schedule. With the sequence determined, the planning team will schedule the start and end date for each activity. The availability of resources will largely determine that schedule.

Resource assignments. The output of the activity schedule will be the assignment of specific resources (such as skill sets) to the project activities.

Project notebook. Documentation of any type is always a chore to produce. Not so in the five-phase project management life cycle that we have used in this book. Project documentation happens as a natural byproduct of the project work. All that is needed is to appoint a project team member to be responsible. His or her responsibilities include gathering information that is already available, putting it in a standard format, and electronically archiving it. This responsibility begins with the project planning session and ends when the project is formally closed.

Project Proposal

The culmination of all the planning is the project proposal. The project proposal is the deliverable from the JPP session and is forwarded to the senior management team for approval to do the project. It states the complete business case for the project. This includes expected business value as well as cost and time estimates. In addition to this information, the proposal details what is to be done, who is going to do it, when it is going to be done, and how it is going to be done. It is the roadmap for the project.

Expect feedback and several revisions before approval is granted. It is not the purpose of this section to spell out in detail what a project proposal should look like. The organization will have a prescribed format to follow. Rather, it is our intention to outline the contents you will be expected to submit.

Contents of the Project Proposal

Each organization will have a prescribed format for its project proposal, but most proposals will have sections similar to the ones listed here. You will see a remarkable resemblance to the topics we have covered in Chapters 6 through 10. Rightly so, for the project proposal is a restatement of all the planning work that has been done so far.

Background. This brief description details the situation that led to the project proposal. It often states the business conditions, opportunities, and/or problems giving rise to the project. It sets the stage for later sections and puts the project in the context of the business.

Objective. This is another short section that gives a very general statement of what you hope to accomplish through this project. Avoid jargon because you don't know who might have reason to read this section. Use the language of the business, not the technical language of your department. The objective should be clearly stated so that there is no doubt as to what is to be done and what constitutes attainment of the objective.

Overview of approach to be taken. For those who might not be interested in the details of how you are going to reach your objective, this section provides a high-level outline of your approach. Again, avoid jargon whenever possible. Give a brief statement of each step and a few sentences of supporting narrative. Brevity and clarity are important.

Detailed statement of work. Here is where you give the details of your approach. Include what will be done, when it will be done, who will do it, how much time will be required of them, and what criteria will be used to measure completeness. This is the roadmap of all the project work. We have found Gantt charts useful for presentations of schedule data. They are easily understood and generally intuitive even for people who are seeing them for the first time.

Time and cost summary. It is our practice to include a summary page of time and cost data. This usually works best if done as a Gantt chart. Often the data will have been stated over several pages and is brought together here for easy review and comment by the customer.

Appendices. We reserve the appendix for all supporting data and details that are not germane to the body of the proposal. Anticipate questions your customer might have and include answers here. Remember that this is detail beyond the basic description of the project work. Supporting information is generally found here.

There are no hard and fast rules as to format. You will surely be able to find examples of successful proposals in your department to be used as guides. Once you have your ideas sketched out, share the proposal with a trusted colleague. His or her feedback may be the most valuable advice you can get.

In this chapter we have provided a structure for you to follow as you organize and conduct the planning session that will produce a detailed description of the project. Most books on project management devote very little space to the mechanics of producing a project plan. In our experience poor planning is one of the major obstacles to successful project execution, and so we have given you our best advice on planning a project garnered from our many years of experience in planning projects with our clients.

This chapter also completes Part Three, "Planning." The next two chapters cover implementation beginning with a chapter on team organization (Chapter 12, "Recruit, Organize, and Manage the Project Team") and monitoring and controlling the project work (Chapter 13, "Monitor and Control Progress"). Finally, Chapter 14, "Close Out the Project," covers the closing activities that take place once the project work has been completed.

PART FOUR

Implementation

The implementation phase begins with management's approval of the project proposal.

Chapter 12, "Recruit, Organize, and Manage the Project Team," discusses the final details of assembling the project team and establishing the rules and procedures governing how the team will work together.

Despite the best efforts to plan and document the project work, things seldom go according to plan. Chapter 13, "Monitor and Control Progress," introduces a number of monitoring and control tools for analyzing and reporting project progress. These tools include procedures for managing change and resolving problems.

Finally, when the project work has been completed and accepted by the requestor, a series of closing activities begin. These are discussed in Chapter 14, "Close Out the Project."

Recruit, Organize, and Manage the Project Team

*The productivity of a workgroup seems to depend on how
the group members see their own goals in relation
to the goals of the organization.*

—PAUL HERSEY AND KENNETH H. BLANCHARD

*When the best leader's work is done the
people say, 'We did it ourselves.'*

**—LAO-TZU
CHINESE PHILOSOPHER**

*When a team outgrows individual performance
and learns team confidence, excellence becomes reality.*

**—JOE PATERNO
FOOTBALL COACH, PENN STATE**

The project plan has been approved, and it's time to get on with the work of the project. Before we turn the team loose, we must attend to a few housekeeping chores.

Project Manager vis-a-vis the Functional Manager

First, let's juxtapose the roles of the project manager with those of the functional manager. The distinction is an important foundation to the material presented in this chapter.

The objective of the project manager is clear. Complete the project on time, within budget, and according to the customer's conditions of satisfaction, in other words—according to specification. Staff development is not on the list! The only cases when staff development is an objective of the project manager occur when the project manager also has line responsibility for the project team, in self-managed teams, or in project forms of organizational structures. In these cases staff development is definitely part of the project manager's objectives. The project manager must develop the skills on his or her project team to handle whatever assignments come along.

On the other hand, the functional (or resource) manager's objectives include development of staff skills to meet project requirements and deployment of staff to projects. These objectives pertain regardless of the organizational structure.

Conflicting Objectives

The project manager's objectives and the functional (or resource) manager's objectives will often conflict. Part of the program for developing staff skills will occur through on-the-job training. Functional (or resource) managers will look for opportunities to deploy staff to project assignments that provide opportunities to learn new skills. The project manager, on the other hand, would rather have experienced staff assigned to project activities, especially activities that are critical to the completion of the project according to plan. The project manager will not be interested in being the training ground for professional staff.

A further complication arises in those situations where the functional (or resource) manager is also a project manager. In matrix organizations this occurs frequently. Here the functional (or resource) manager is torn between assigning the best professionals to the activity and assigning professionals so that they can learn new skills or enhance current skills.

The last conflict arises when the choice between assigning a skilled professional to a project not in his or her area of responsibility to a project in his or her area of responsibility. In matrix organizations this can occur with regularity. The primary issues arise when the manager must assign staff to projects. He or she not only has to staff projects internal to functional responsibilities but also assign staff to projects outside the functional area. The project manager must address such questions as these: What projects have priority? Should I assign my best staff to my projects? After all, I do have to take care of my needs although that stance may be hard to explain to the other project managers. Or do I assign the best staff to outside projects? Am I shooting myself in the foot? After all, I do have responsibilities to meet and do want to succeed in doing them. Always assigning the best professionals to projects within their area of responsibility will cause senior managers to wonder whether the functional (or resource) manager has the proper corporate focus.

We don't want you to think that the project manager is totally insensitive to staff development and motivation. He or she needs the commitment of each project team member and in that sense will have to provide opportunities for development, but only with the goal of the project in mind. To the extent that the two are compatible, development will be an objective of the project manager.

Projects as Motivation and Development Tools

Not everyone can be motivated. In fact, in most cases all the manager can do is create an environment in which the subordinate might be motivated and then hope that he or she is. It's really like farming. All the farmer can do is pick the crop to plant, the acreage to plant it on, the fertilizer to use, and then hope that nature supplies the right amounts of rain, wind, and sunshine. The same scenario applies to the project manager. He or she must create a working environment that is conducive to and encourages development of the team member and leave it up to the team member to respond positively.

Fortunately, we do have some information on what professional staff perceive as motivators and demotivators on the job.[1] Motivators are those behaviors or situations that have a positive impact on the worker—they motivate the worker to better performance. Demotivators, on the other hand, are those things that, by their absence, have a negative impact on performance. To put it another way, there are certain expectations that the worker has, and to not have them is to demotivate him or her. For example, workers expect a reasonable vacation policy; to not have one acts as a demotivator. On the other hand, having a good vacation policy does not motivate the worker. The following list was created as a result of a 1959 survey of professionals by Herzberg. While the survey was conducted over 40 years ago, it has become a classic study and still applies today.

MOTIVATORS

Herzberg identified the following motivators:

- Recognition
- Advancement and growth
- Responsibility
- Work itself

DEMOTIVATORS

Herzberg identified the following demotivators:

- Company policy
- Administrative practices
- Working conditions
- Technical supervision
- Interpersonal relations
- Job security
- Salary

Note that the motivators are related to the job, specifically to its intrinsic characteristics; the demotivators are related to the environment in

[1]Both the Herzberg and Cougar studies are reported in Toledo Mata and Elizabeth A. Unger, "Another Look at Motivating Data Processing Professionals," Department of Computer Science, Kansas State University, Manhattan, KS, p.4., 1988.

which the job is performed. This list offers both good news and bad news for the manager. The good news is that the motivators relate to the job and to the aspects of it over which the manager has some amount of control. The bad news is that the demotivators, being environmental, are beyond the control of the manager. Managers can bring them to the attention of their senior management but are otherwise powerless to change them.

Daniel Cougar of Colorado State conducted a similar survey in 1988. Here the respondents were analysts and programmers. The responses were grouped by those areas that the respondents considered motivators and those that they considered demotivators. The combined list represents the areas ordered from highest motivator to lowest motivator:

- The work itself
- Opportunity for achievement
- Opportunity for advancement
- Pay and benefits
- Recognition
- Increased responsibility
- Technical supervision
- Interpersonal relations
- Job security
- Working conditions
- Company policy

The motivators that are high on the list tend to be intrinsic to the job, such as providing opportunities for advancement and for recognition, while the demotivators, which are lower on the list, tend to be environmental factors, such as working conditions (parking areas) and company policy (sick leave and vacation time).

Several of the motivators are directly controlled or influenced by actions and behaviors of the project manager regarding the work itself that the team member will be asked to do. They are briefly discussed next.

Challenge. Professionals always have responded to challenge. In general, if you tell a professional that something cannot be done, his or her creative juices begin to flow. The result: a solution. Professionals dread nothing more than practicing skills, long since mastered, over and over again. Boredom can lead to daydreaming and lack of attention to detail, which results in errors. Challenging the professional does not mean that every moment of every day should be spent solving previously unsolved problems. Usually, an hour or two on a new and challenging task per day is sufficient to keep a professional motivated throughout the day.

Recognition. Professionals want to know that they are progressing toward a professional goal. Publicly and personally recognizing their achievements and following it with another challenge tells the professional that his or her contribution is valued. Recognition therefore does not necessarily mean dollars, promotions, or titles.

Job design. Because the job itself is such an important part of the motivators, let's look at job design for just a moment. Five dimensions define a job:

Skill variety. Jobs that do not offer much task variety or the opportunity to learn and practice new skills become boring for most people. In designing jobs, it is important to consider building in some task variety. The variety, at the least, provides a diversion from what otherwise would be a tedious and boring workday. On the other hand, it also can provide a break during which the person can learn a new skill. With a little bit of forethought, the manager can find opportunities for cross-training by introducing some task variety for new skills development. The manager will want to consider the risk involved in such actions. The person may not rise to the challenge of the new task or might not have the native ability to master the skills needed to perform the new task.

Task identity. People need to know what they are working on. This is especially true for contracted team members. The project manager should help them understand their work in relation to the entire project. Knowing that their task is on the critical path will affect their attitude and the quality of their work.

Task Significance. Does it make any difference if I am successful? Will anybody notice? Just how important is my work to the overall success of the project? Am I just doing busy work to pass the day? Team members need to know whether their effort and success make any difference to the success of the project.

Autonomy. Professionals want to know what is expected from them—what are the deliverables? They don't want to hear every detail of how they will accomplish their work. Systems people are rugged individualists. They want to exercise their creativity. They want freedom, independence, and discretion in scheduling their work and determining the procedures they will follow to carry it out.

Feedback. Good, bad, or indifferent, professionals want to know how effective they are in their work. Paying attention to a professional is motivating in itself. Having something good to say is even better. When performance is below expectations, tell them. If you can convince them that they own the problem, then ask them for an action plan to correct their marginal performance.

Recruit the Project Team

Project plans and their execution are only as successful as the manager and team who implement them. Building effective teams is as much an art as a science.

When recruiting and building an effective team, you must consider not only the technical skills of each person, but also the critical roles and chemistry that must exist between and among the project manager and the team members. The selection of project manager and team members will not be perfect—there are always risks with any personnel decision.

A project team has three separate components:

- Project manager
- Core team
- Contracted team

It is important to be aware of the characteristics that should be part of an effective project manager and project team. The following sections describe the responsibilities of each of the three components to a project team. We give you a checklist that should assist you in your selection process, and we also suggest guidelines for organizing the project in an organization.

The Project Manager

Project managers are the leaders of the projects. They are responsible for completing the project on time, within budget, and according to specification. They have the authority to get the job done. The project manager represents the project to the organization and to external groups. In many cases, the project manager has responsibility for more than one project simultaneously.

The timing in selecting a project manager varies. Ideally, you want the project manager in the chair at the very beginning of the project. In some cases, the project manager might not be identified until the project has been approved for implementation. For example, in contemporary organizations, senior management assigns project managers to projects after the project proposal has been approved. In those instances, the project manager will not have participated in the scoping and definition phases. This leads to a number of significant problems, one of which is short schedules. Short schedules arise in projects that are defined generally between the account representative and the customer (whether internal or external). These agreements usually constrain all sides of the triangle as well as the scope. All too often the project manager will have been put in a no-win situation. One rule that we all learned a long time ago is, "The sooner the project manager and team are involved in planning the project, the more committed they will be to its implementation." (This is also true for other members in the organization whose expertise and resources are required to implement the project.) Another problem with assigning the project manager after the project has been approved for implementation is buy-in by the project manager. Even when placed in situations that are not to his or her liking, the project manager must outwardly display enthusiasm and support for the project.

Selection Criteria

Harold Kerzner[2] states that because the roles and responsibilities of the project manager are so important, his or her selection should be general management's responsibility. If you are working in a large organization, a group or committee is usually assigned to help screen project manager candidates.

[2]Harold Kerzner, Project Management: A Systems Approach to Planning, Scheduling, and Controlling (New York, NY: Van Nostrand Reinhold Co., 1984).

A project manager must be experienced, capable, and competent in getting the project done on time, within budget, and according to specifications. Easier said than done. The potential project manager should have the following general skills:

Background and experience. Background and experience in good project management practices are difficult to find in many organizations. The problem is that the demand for experienced project managers outstrips the supply. The solution for many organizations is to create a learning laboratory for *wanna-be* project managers, those who are acquiring project management skills and competencies. To help develop a cadre of project managers of varying backgrounds and experiences, a hierarchy of project management assignments is commonly put in place. That hierarchy might start at team member and then progress to activity manager, project manager, and finally to program manager. (These assignments have a one-to-one correspondence to projects ranging from Type D to Type A as discussed in Chapter 4, "What Is a Project?") Project managers progress through this hierarchy as a result of training and experience in the skill areas needed to take on projects of increasing scope and complexity

In addition to on-the-job experience training, several alternatives to "build your own" project managers are available. The most common training method is to learn the project management skills through reviewing project documentation, attending and later supporting JPP sessions, observing project status meetings, maintaining project documentation, and playing the role of technographer in JPP sessions. By participating in whatever way is practical the individual can gain the skills through on-the-job experiences.

Leadership and strategic expertise. The project manager is generally not the line manager of the team members. The project manager's job is to manage the work of the project. That puts him or her in relationships with the team members that are very different from the relationship that would evolve if the team members reported directly to the project manager. The project manager must get the team members' cooperation and support without having direct authority over them. It simply means that the project manager's skills as a leader are more important to his or her role. The project manager's success as a leader is also related to his or her ability to link the project to the strategy of the business. Often that will be at the heart of his or her relationship and any leverage he or she might have with the project team.

Technical expertise. There are two schools of thought regarding the level of technical expertise that a project manager should have. One school suggests that managing one project is like managing any other project. These are the same pundits who would say that if you can manage one department you can manage any department. We'll ignore the comment on managing departments, but we do take issue with the statement that implies that project management is independent of the project being managed. Despite all that has been written and said about project management, the discipline is primitive. There is a lot we do not know about the successful management of projects. If that were not the case, how would you explain the high project failure rates as reported by the Standish Group and discussed in Chapter 5, "What Is Project Management?" While we would agree that the project manager does not need an intimate knowledge of and to be skilled in working with the technology involved, he or she does need to have sufficient knowledge to know what questions to ask, how to interpret the answers, and whether he or she is being given the technical information needed to make a management decision.

Interpersonal competence. Sooner or later the job of the project manager reduces to his or her ability to interact successfully with another individual. In the course of the project, the project manager will interact with the team, other project managers, business managers, functional managers, senior managers, the customer, outside contractors, and suppliers. These interactions will challenge all of the project manager's interpersonal skills as they relate to such areas as negotiations, conflict resolution, and problem resolution.

Managerial ability. Certain managerial skills are a superset of project management skills. By superset we mean that they apply to project management but are more appropriate on a larger scale to the business. These tend to be strategic and tactical in nature and include skills such as strategic planning, budget planning, staff planning, quality management, business process reengineering, and personnel development.

The Core Team Members

Core team members are with the project from cradle to grave. They typically have a major role to play in the project and bring a skill set that has broad applicability across the range of work undertaken in the project.

They might also have responsibility for key activities or sets of activities in the project.

Similar to the project manager's assignment, this assignment is usually not full-time. In matrix organizations, professional staff can be assigned to more than one project at a time. This is especially true when a staff member possesses a skill not commonly found in the staff. A core team member will have some percentage of his or her time allocated to the project, say a .25 full-time equivalent person.

Because the core team will be needed for the JPP session, its members should be identified as early as possible. The core team is usually identified at the beginning of the scoping phase. This means that the members can participate in the early definition and planning of the project.

Selection Criteria

Because of the downsizing, rightsizing, and capsizing going on in corporate America, much of the responsibility for choosing core team members has been designated to the project manager. While the situation differs from organization to organization, the project manager may have little or no latitude in picking core team members even though he or she may have been given that responsibility. The problem stems from several causes:

- Most organizations have a very aggressive portfolio of projects with constantly changing priorities and requirements.
- The work load on the individual is so large that the thought of joining another team is not in his or her mind.
- Staff turnover, especially among highly technical and scarce professionals, is out of control in many organizations.

All of these situations make it difficult for the project manager to select the core "dream team." For example, suppose a project manager has a choice between the "A Team" and the "B Team." The "A Team" is the most skilled in a particular technology. Its members are the company's experts. The "B Team," on the other hand, is made up of those individuals who would like to be on the "A Team" but just don't have the experience and skills to justify "A Team" membership. The project manager would like to have all "A Team" members on the core team but realizes that this is just not going to happen. Even suggesting such a core team would be rejected out of hand by the managers of such highly skilled professionals. The politically savvy project manager would determine the project work that must have an "A Team" member and the project work that could get done with a "B Team" member and negotiate accordingly with the managers of these potential team members.

The project manager will have to pick his or her battles carefully because he or she may want to consider the "A Team" for critical path activities, high-risk activities, and high-business-value projects and accept the "B Team" for activities and projects of lesser criticality. Be ready to horse trade between projects, too! Give the resource managers an opportunity to use noncritical path activities as on-the-job training for their staff. Remember that they have as many staff development and deployment problems as you have project planning and scheduling problems. Trading a favor of staff development for an "A Team" member may be a good strategy.

In our project management consulting work, we identified a list of characteristics that many project managers have offered as successful characteristics in their core teams. For the most part, these characteristics are observed in individuals based on their experiences and the testimony of those who have worked with them. Typically these are not characteristics whose presence or absence in an individual are determined through interviews.

In many cases, the project manager will just have to take a calculated risk that the team member possesses these characteristics even though the individual has not previously demonstrated that he or she has them. It will become obvious very quickly whether the individual possesses these characteristics. If not, and if it is critical to the team member's role in the project, the project manager or the team member's line manager will have to correct the team member's behavior.

The characteristics that we consider important for the core team members are as follows:

Commitment. Commitment to the project by the core team is critical to the success of the project. The project manager must know that each core team member places a high priority on fulfilling his or her roles and responsibilities in the project. The core team must be proactive in fulfilling those responsibilities and not need the constant reminders of schedule and deliverables from the project manager.

Shared responsibility. Shared responsibility means that success and failure are equally the reward and blame of each team member. To have shared responsibility means that you will never hear one team member taking individual credit for a success on the project nor blaming another team member for a failure on the project. All share equally in success and failure. Furthermore, when a problem situation arises all will pitch in to help in any way. If one team member is having a problem, another will voluntarily be there to help.

Flexibility. Team members must be willing to adapt to the situation. "That is not my responsibility" doesn't go very far in project work. Schedules may have to change at the last minute to accommodate an unexpected situation. It is the success of the project that has priority, not the schedule of any one individual on the project team.

Task orientedness. In the final analysis it is the team members' ability to get their assigned work done according to the project plan that counts. In other words, they must be results-oriented.

Ability to work within schedule and constraints. Part of being results-oriented means being able to complete assignments within the time frame planned and not offer excuses for not doing so. It is easy to blame your delay on the delay of others—that is the easy way out. The team member will encounter a number of obstacles, such as delays caused by others, but he or she will have to find a way around those obstacles. The team depends on its members to complete their work according to plan.

Willingness to give trust and mutual support. Trust and mutual support are the hallmarks of an effective team. That means that every member must convey these qualities. Team members must be trusting and trustworthy. Are they empathetic and do they readily offer help when it is clear that help is needed? Their interaction with other team members will clearly indicate whether they possess these characteristics. Individuals that do not will have a difficult time working effectively on a project team.

Team-orientedness. To be team-oriented means to put the welfare of the team ahead of your own. Behaviors as simple as the individual's frequency of use of "I" versus "we" in team meetings and conversations with other team members are strong indicators of team orientation.

Open-mindedness. The open-minded team member will welcome and encourage other points of view and other solutions to problem situations. His or her objective is clearly to do what is best for the team and not look for individual kudos.

Ability to work across structure and authorities. In the contemporary organization, projects tend to cross organizational lines. Cross-departmental teams are common. Projects such as these require the team member to work with people from a variety of business disciplines. Many of these people will have a different value system and a different approach than the team member might be used to working with. Their adaptability, flexibility, and openness will be good assets.

Ability to use project management tools. The team member must be able to leverage technology in carrying out his or her project responsibilities. Projects are planned using a variety of software tools, and the team member must have some familiarity with these tools. Many project managers will require the team member to input activity status and other project progress data directly into the project management software tool.

The Contracted Team Member

The business-to-business environment is changing, and those changes are permanent. Organizations are routinely outsourcing processes that are not part of their core business or core expertise. There are two reasons for choosing to use contract team members instead of the company's own employees: shortage of staff or shortage of skills. Those shortages have made it possible for a whole new type of business to grow—tech-temps is the name we associate with this new business opportunity. The day of the small contractor and niche market player is here to stay. To the project manager, this brings the need to effectively manage a team whose membership will probably include outside contractors. Some may be with the project for only a short time. Others may be no different from core teams except they are not employees of your company.

Typically contracted team members are available for only short periods of time on the project. They possess a skill that is needed for just a brief time. They are assigned to the project when it is time for them to contribute their skills. As soon as they have completed their assigned task, they leave the project.

Implications of Contract Team Members

Contracted team members present the project manager with a number of problems. In most systems development efforts it is unlikely that professionals would be assigned full-time to the project team. Rather, people will join the project team only for the period of time during which their particular expertise is needed. The project manager must be aware of the implications to the project when contracted professionals are used.

- There may be little or no variance in the time contracted team members are available, so the activities on which they work must remain on schedule.

- They must be briefed on their role in the project and how their activity relates to other activities in the project.

- Commitment of contracted members is always a problem because their priorities probably lie elsewhere.

- Quality of work may be an issue because of poor levels of commitment. They just want to get the job done and get on with their next assignment. Often anything will do.

- Contracted team members will often require more supervision than core team members.

Selection Criteria

If the project manager (PM) has made the decision to buy rather than build a project team, the PM must determine who will get the business. Contracted team members are usually employed or represented by agencies that cater to technical professionals who prefer free-lancing to full-time employment. These professionals are available for short-term assignments in their area of specialization. To employ these professionals the project manager must make several decisions: what process to follow, who should be invited to submit information, and how to evaluate the information received. The evaluation often takes the form of a score sheet. The score sheet contains questions grouped by major features and functions, with weights attached to each answer. A single numeric score is often calculated to rank vendor responses. Nonquantitative data such as customer relations and customer service are also collected from reference accounts provided by the vendor.

The steps the project manager follows to engage the services of a contracted team member might look something like the following:

- Identify the types of skills needed, the number of personnel, and the time frame within which they will be needed.

- Identify a list of companies that will be invited to submit a proposal.

- Write the request for proposal.

- Establish the criteria for evaluating responses and selecting the vendor(s).

- Distribute the request for proposal.

- Evaluate the responses.

- Reduce the list of vendors to a few who will be invited on site to make a formal presentation.

- Conduct the onsite presentations.

- Choose the final vendor(s), and write and sign the contract.

Types of Proposals

A project manager might consider three types of proposals as he or she looks for a vendor or agency to provide contracted team members: Request for Information, Request for Proposal, Request for Quote.

Request for Information. A Request for Information (RFI) is used when an organization is looking for information relevant to a particular process or product. It usually does not have a written specification. The purpose of an RFI is to discover vendors and products that the organization will investigate further with one of the other two types of proposals.

Request for Proposal. A Request for Proposal (RFP) is used to find the vendor or vendors that can provide the best solution and price. The RFP always includes a specification that identifies the features, functions, physical specifications, performance requirements, and environment in which the requested deliverable must operate. Generally descriptions of steps to be followed to select the vendor and the method of evaluation are included. In some cases, more than one vendor will be chosen. Each vendor will provide a piece of the final solution. Using several vendors presents special challenges to the project manager.

Request for Quote. The Request for Quote (RFQ) is used to find the best price-to-performance ratio for a given solution. In this case, the company knows exactly what it wants; it is only a matter of finding the vendor that best meets the Conditions of Satisfaction. The definition of what the company wants will often include the exact hardware, software, and more. This approach offers the project manager an easier-to-manage situation than the multivendor alternative.

Types of Contracts

There are four types of contracts:

Retainer. These arrangements pay the contractor a fixed fee per period (usually monthly). Often no end date is specified. At some time the organization will decide that the arrangement can terminate because the contractor's services are no longer needed. The retainer will state how many days per period are expected of the contractor and the deliverables the contractor will provide. The deliverables are often only vaguely described because such arrangements are usually investigative or design related.

Time and materials. In these cases a little more specificity exists, but a detailed specification is not available or cannot be provided. The company is willing to accept the risk of high costs in the face of unknowns.

Time and materials—not to exceed. Here the vendor assumes more of the risk. A detailed specification may not exist, but enough is known so that the contractor will meet the customer's requirements at a cost not to exceed a specified figure and within a specified time frame.

Fixed bid. In these cases a detailed specification exists, and the vendor is willing to meet the deliverables and a deadline date for a specified figure. Obviously, the vendor assumes most of the risk here. Fixed bid contracts usually include a payment schedule, too. In our consulting practice we use the 40-40-20 rule: 40 percent is due on contract signing, 40 percent is due at an agreed-on midpoint in the project, and the remaining 20 percent is due once the final deliverables have been accepted and the company signs off that the contract is complete.

Contract Administration

Once the contract is signed and the vendor begins to deliver the contracted work, contract administration for that vendor has begun. Contract administration is the responsibility of the project manager. Our general advice is to have the contract spell out in detail exactly how business will be done. This is not a detailed list of what will be done for every possible occurrence during the contract period, but rather clear guidelines that everyone understands. The guidelines might include obligations, responsibilities, performance goals and deadline dates, penalties for missed dates, rewards for early delivery, status reporting dates, problem discovery, escalation and resolution, change management procedures, milestone dates, project status meeting dates, acceptance test criteria, cancellation conditions, cancellation policies, and closing criteria.

Contract Cancellation

The contract should clearly spell out the conditions under which the contract may be cancelled. For example, can either party cancel for any reason by simply notifying the other according to a defined procedure? Or does cancellation require both party's mutual agreement? Cancellation will often be the result of performance not meeting expectations.

Contract Closing

Once the acceptance criteria have been met, a series of events occurs. These are generally debriefing sessions and hand-offs of deliverables and documentation. A final payment to the vendor is commonly withheld pending receipt of these items.

Organize the Project Team

Now that you have identified the individuals who will become the project team, it is time to make them function as a team. Remember right now that they are a herd of cats; they are not a team—at least not yet. First a few words on authority and responsibility. Then we will discuss several procedural matters that the team will have to discuss and agree on.

Authority

Authority and responsibility go hand in hand. To have one and not the other makes no sense. How often have we been in situations where we were responsible for making a certain thing happen but had no authority over the resources needed to make it happen or no authority to make and carry out a decision? To be effective the project manager must have authority over the project. It is his or her job to get the project done on time, within budget, and according to specification. That authority is often delegated, but it is the project manager who is ultimately responsible.

The major difficulty that project managers have is that the project team is not their line responsibility. Team members are assigned based on their expertise but report to other managers. This means that the project manager will have to exercise the best leadership skills and diplomacy to get the job done. The key is in the project planning activities that schedule resources to windows of time. It is here that the resource manager makes the commitment of people resources. Honoring that commitment within the time allotted reduces the incidence of problems. If the project manager remembers to keep the resource managers involved and aware of all project changes, negotiations will proceed better when circumstances warrant.

Responsibility

There is no question where the responsibility lies. This cannot be delegated. The project manager assigns activity management responsibility to team members. They are then responsible for completing their assigned activity within its scheduled window of time and for producing the activity deliverables on time according to specification. It is the project manager, though, who is ultimately responsible for completing the project as expected. In conveying this sense of responsibility to each team member the project manager must exercise sound leadership and management skills. He or she will do this by maintaining a consistent level of interest in and communication with each of their activity managers, by involving them and engaging them in planning, change management deliberations, and problem resolution. He or she will keep everybody on the team informed of project status.

Establish Team Operating Rules

Project teams all too often fail to define and agree on the team operating rules. These operating rules define how the team works together, makes decisions, resolves conflicts, reports progress, and deals with a host of other administrative chores.

There are several areas to consider when you create the operating rules that govern how the team conducts itself.

Decision Making

The first operating rule is the establishment of how the team will make decisions. There are three major types of decision-making models:

Directive. In this model, the person with the authority—the project manager for the project and the activity manager for the activity—makes the decision for all team members. While this approach is certainly expedient, it has obvious drawbacks. The only information available is the decision maker's information, which may or may not be correct or complete. An added danger is that those who disagree or were left out of the decision may not carry it out.

Participative. In this model, everyone on the team contributes to the decision-making process. A synergy is created as the best decision is sought. Because everyone has an opportunity to participate, commitment will be much stronger than in the directive approach. Obviously, there are additional benefits to team building—empowerment of the team. Whenever possible we recommend this participative approach.

Consultative. This middle-ground approach combines the best of the other two approaches. While the person in authority makes the decision, the decision is made only after consulting with all members to get their input and ideas. This approach is participative at the input stage but directive at the point of decision. In some cases, when expediency is required, this approach is a good one to take.

Which model to use in a specific situation is generally a function of the gravity and time sensitivity of the pending decision. Some organizations have constructed categories of decisions, with each category defined by some financial parameters, such as the value of the decision, or by some scope parameters, such as the number of business units or customers affected by the decision. The person responsible for making the decision is defined for each decision category. The more serious the category, the higher the organizational level of the decision maker. Some decisions might be made by an individual team member, some by an activity manager, some by the project manager, some by the customer, and some by senior management. Yet others might require a group decision, using either a participative or a consultative approach.

Conflict Resolution

The second operating rule deals with how the team resolves conflicts. Conflicts arise when two or more team members have a difference of opinion, when the customer takes issue with an action to be taken by the project team, or in a variety of other situations involving two parties with different points of view. In all of these examples, the difference must be resolved. Clearly conflict resolution is a much more sensitive situation than the decision-making rule because it is confrontational and situational, whereas the decision-making rule is procedural and structured. Depending on the particular conflict situation, the team might adopt one of three conflict resolution styles:

Avoidant. Some people will do anything to avoid a direct confrontation. They agree even though they are opposed to the outcome. This style cannot be tolerated on the project team. Each person's input and opinion must be sought. It is the responsibility of the project manager to make sure that this happens. A simple device is to ask each team member in turn what he or she thinks about the situation and what he or she suggests be done about it. Often this approach will diffuse any direct confrontation between two individuals on the team.

Combative. Some avoid confrontation at all costs; others seem to seek it out. Some team members play devil's advocate at the least provocation. There are times when this is advantageous—testing the team's thinking before making the decision. At other times it tends to raise the level of stress and tension, when many view it as a waste of time and not productive. The project manager knows who these team members are and must act to mitigate the chances of these situations arising. One technique we have used with success is to put such individuals in charge of forming a recommendation for the team to consider. Such an approach offers less opportunity for combative discussion because the combative team member is sharing recommendations before others give reason for disagreement.

Collaborative. In this approach, the team looks for win-win opportunities. The approach seeks out a common ground as the basis for moving ahead to a solution. This approach encourages each team member to put his or her opinions on the table and not avoid the conflict that may result. At the same time, team members do not seek to create conflict unnecessarily. The approach is constructive, not destructive.

The choice of conflict resolution styles is beyond the scope of this book. There are several books on the topic that you can consult. Of particular importance will be the variety of collaborative models that might be adopted.

Consensus Building

Consensus building is a process that a team can follow to reach agreement on which alternative to proceed with for the item (action, decision, and so forth) under consideration. The agreement is not reached by a majority vote, or any vote for that matter. Rather the agreement is reached through discussion where each participant in the discussion reaches a point where he or she has no serious disagreement with the decision that is about to be taken. The decision will have been revised several times for the participants to reach the point where they have no serious disagreement.

This is an excellent tool to have in the project team tool kit. In all but a few cases, there will be a legitimate difference of opinion as to how a problem or issue should be addressed. There will be no clear-cut action on which all can agree. In such situations the team must fashion an action or decision with which no team members have serious disagreement even though they may not agree in total with the chosen action. To use the method successfully, make sure that everyone on the team gets to speak. Talk through the issue until an acceptable action is identified. Conflict is good, but try to be creative as you search for a compromise action. As soon as no one has serious objections to the defined action, you have reached consensus. Once a decision is reached, all team members must support it.

If the project manager chooses to operate on a consensus basis, he or she must clearly define the situations in which consensus will be acceptable. The team needs to know this.

Brainstorming

Brainstorming is an essential part of the team operating rules because, at several points in the life of the project, the creativity of the team will be tested. Brainstorming is a technique that can focus that creativity and help the team discover solutions. There will be situations where acceptable ideas and alternatives have not come forth from the normal team deliberations. In such cases the project manager might suggest a brainstorming session. A brainstorming session is one in which the team contributes ideas in a stream-of-consciousness mode, as described in the next paragraph. Brainstorming sessions have been quite successful in uncovering solutions where none seemed present. The team needs to know how the project manager will conduct such sessions and what will be done with the output.

When you have exhausted all other avenues for solving a problem, try brainstorming. You may find it to be a diamond in the rough! The method is simple and quick, too. First, assemble together those individuals who may have some knowledge of the problem area. They don't need to be experts. In fact, it may be better if they are not. You need people to think creatively and "outside the box." Experts tend to think inside the box. The session begins with everyone throwing any idea out on the table. No discussion (except clarification) is permitted. This continues until no new ideas are forthcoming. Silence and pauses are fine. Once all the ideas are on the table, you discuss the items on the list. Look to combine ideas or revise ideas based on each member's perspective. In time, some solutions begin to emerge. Don't rush the process, and by all means test each idea with an open mind. Remember that you are looking for a solution that no individual could identify but that, we hope, the group is able to identify. This is a creative process, one that must be approached with an open mind. Convention and *"We've always done it that way"* have no place in a true brainstorming session.

Team Meetings

The project manager needs to define team meetings in terms of frequency, length, meeting dates, submission/preparation/distribution of the agenda, who calls the meeting, and who is responsible for recording and distributing the minutes. The entire team needs to participate in and understand the rules and structure of the meetings that will take place over the life of the project. Different types of team meetings, with perhaps different rules governing their conduct and format, may occur.

Team meetings are held for a variety of reasons including problem definition and resolution, scheduling work, planning, discussing situations that affect team performance, and decision making. The team will need to decide on several procedural matters, including the following:

Meeting frequency. How often should the team meet? If it meets too frequently, precious work time will be lost. If it meets too infrequently, problems may have arisen and the window of opportunity will have been closed for lack of a meeting to discuss and solve the problem. Too infrequently, and the project manager risks losing management control over the project. Meeting frequency will vary as the length and size of the project varies. There is no formula for frequency. The project manager must simply make a judgment call.

Agenda preparation. When the project team is fortunate enough to have a project administrative assistant, that person can receive agenda items and prepare and distribute the agenda. In the absence of an administrative assistant, the assignment should be rotated to each team member. The project manager may set up a template agenda so that each team meeting covers essentially the same general topics.

Meeting coordinator. Just as agenda preparation can be circulated around to each team member so can the coordination responsibility. Coordination involves reserving a time, place, and equipment.

Recording and distributing meeting minutes. Meeting minutes are an important part of project documentation. In the short term, they are the evidence of discussions of problem situations and change requests, the actions taken, and the rationale for those actions. When confusion arises in the project and clarifications are needed, the meeting minutes can settle the issue. Recording and distributing the minutes are important responsibilities and should not be treated lightly. The project manager should establish a rotation among the team members for recording and distributing the meeting minutes.

Summary

In this chapter we discussed the team, its membership, skills needed of the members, and the rules that the team will follow as it goes about the work of the project. Even though you have done your best to put the team together and set and agree on the operating rules, much is yet to be done. The team needs to learn to work together by working together. Mistakes will be made, procedures will not always be followed as intended, the first few team meetings will be clumsy. Learning is taking place, and it must be allowed to take place. The team is passing through a stage called norming, where it is learning to work together as teams should. It is a phase of development that must occur. Unfortunately, we can't wait for the team to become a lean, mean machine. The work of the project must begin. In the next chapter we discuss monitoring and reporting project progress against the plan and the changes that we can expect as the project work is done.

Monitor and Control Progress

Chapter Learning Objectives

After reading this chapter you will be able to:

- ✔ Understand the reasons for implementing controls on the project
- ✔ Track the progress of a project
- ✔ Determine an appropriate reporting plan
- ✔ Measure and analyze variances from the project plan
- ✔ Understand and use cost/schedule control
- ✔ Determine the appropriate corrective actions to restore a project to its planned schedule
- ✔ Use Gantt charts to track progress and identify warning signs of schedule problems
- ✔ Understand the change control process
- ✔ Reallocate resources to maintain the project schedule
- ✔ Report project status with graphical tools
- ✔ Establish trend charts for early warning signals
- ✔ Properly identify corrective measures and problem escalation strategies

When you are drowning in numbers you need a system
to separate the wheat from the chaff.

—ANTHONY ADAMS
VICE PRESIDENT, CAMPBELL SOUP CO.

If two lines on a graph cross, it must be important.

—ERNEST F. COOKE
UNIVERSITY OF BALTIMORE

Control versus Risk

At this point, you have put considerable effort into building and getting approval for a project plan that describes in great detail how you will accomplish the goal of the project. The project work has begun, and you want to make sure that it is progressing as planned. To do this, you will institute a number of reports that are designed to tell exactly how well the project is doing with respect to the plan and how to correct variances from this plan. The first question to consider is the extent to which you want to maintain control through the reports you require.

The project plan is a system. As such it can get out of balance, and a get-well plan must be put in place to restore the system to equilibrium. The longer the project manager waits to put the fix in place, the longer it will take for the system to return to equilibrium. The controls are designed to discover out-of-balance situations early and put get-well plans in place quickly.

You can use a variety of reports as control tools. Most can be used in numeric and tabular form, but we suggest using graphics wherever possible. Graphics are particularly effective as part of your status report to management. Senior managers generally aren't interested in reading long reports only to find out that everything is on schedule. While they will be pleased that your project is on schedule, their time could have been spent on other pursuits that require their attention. If projects are not on schedule, they want to know so right away and see what corrective action you plan to take.

Purpose of Controls

Controls are actions taken as a result of reports. When implemented, controls are designed to bring actual project status back into conformance with the project plan. These reports are designed to support control activities by drawing attention to certain aspects or characteristics of the project, such as planned versus actual schedule, trends in the schedule, and actual versus planned resource use.

We typically track performance levels, costs, and time schedules. There are three reasons to use reports in your project (Weiss & Wysocki, 1991)[1]:

[1]Joseph W. Weiss and Robert K. Wysocki, *5-Phase Project Management: A Practical Planning and Implementation Guide* (Reading, MA: Addison Wesley Publishing Co., 1991).

To track progress. The project manager will want to use a periodic (at least biweekly, but weekly is best) reporting system that identifies the status of every activity scheduled for work since the last progress report. These reports summarize progress for the current period as well as the cumulative progress for the entire project.

To detect variance from plan. Variance reports are of particular importance to management. They are simple and intuitive, and they give managers an excellent tool by which to quickly assess the health of a project. In order to detect variance, the project manager needs to compare planned performance to actual performance. In larger projects (those with 50 or more activities) reports that indicate everything is on schedule and on budget are music to the ears of the project manager, but these reports can be too long and boring. Exception reports, variance reports, and graphical reports give management the information necessary for decision making in a concise format.

To take corrective action. To take corrective action it is necessary to know where the problem is and to have that information in time to do something about it. Once there is a significant variance from plan, the next step is to determine whether corrective action is needed and then act appropriately. In complex projects, this requires examining a number of "what ifs." When problems occur in the project, delays result and the project falls behind schedule. For the project to get back on schedule, resources might have to be reallocated. In larger projects, the computer can assist in examining a number of resource reallocation alternatives and help to pick the best.

High Control—Low Risk

There is a trade-off between the amount of control (through reports and their frequency) that you can achieve and the protection you buy against out-of-control situations that may arise undetected and hence unfavorably affect risk. Simply exerting more controls can reduce project risk.

Low Control—High Risk

At the other extreme, having no controls in place and just assuming that the project work will get done according to the plan are foolish. Knowing that the project is sick in time to formulate and implement a get-well plan is critical to project success. Answering the question "How long am I willing to wait before I find out that there is a problem?" may provide

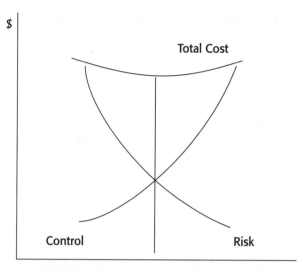

Figure 13.1 The total cost of control and risk.

the clue about how much control to put in place. We will analyze these situations with the Milestone Trend Charts presented later in this chapter.

Balancing the Control System

It is very easy to get carried away with controls and reports. The more controls that are put in place, the lower the project risk, and the less likely it will be for the project to get in trouble. As Figure 13.1 shows, however, there is a point of diminishing returns. Cost aside, there is another impact to consider. To comply with the project controls, project team members will have to spend time preparing and defending progress reports. This subtracts from the time spent doing project work.

The project manager needs to strike a balance between the extent of the control system and the risk of unfavorable outcomes. Just as in the insurance industry, compare the cost of the policy against the dollar value of the loss that will result from the consequences. Figure 13.1 shows the relationship between risk and control. Conceptually, there is a balance point that minimizes the total cost exposure for having chosen a particular level of control.

Control also implies rigidity and structure. Both tend to stifle creativity. The project manager should allow the team members to have some latitude to exercise their individuality. The cost of the control must be weighed against the value of empowering team members to be proactive (hence risk takers).

Control versus Quality

Quality will not happen by accident. It must be designed into the project management process. Chapter 5, "What Is Project Management?," discussed the continuous quality management and process quality management models. You might want to refer to Chapter 5 if you have forgotten what those management models are and what they do regarding quality.

Fortunately, control and quality are positively correlated with one another. If we do not take steps to control the product and the process, we will not enjoy the benefits that quality brings to the equation.

Progress Reporting System

Once project work is underway, you want to make sure that it proceeds according to plan. To do this you need to establish a reporting system that keeps you informed of the many variables that describe how the project is proceeding as compared to the plan.

A reporting system has the following characteristics:

- Provides timely, complete, and accurate status information
- Doesn't add so much overhead time as to be counterproductive
- Is readily acceptable to the project team and senior management
- Warns of pending problems in time to take action
- Is easily understood by those who have a need to know

In order to establish this reporting system you will want to look into the hundreds of reports that are standard fare in project management software packages. Once you decide what you want to track, these software tools will give you several suggestions and standard reports to meet your needs. Most project management software tools allow you to customize their standard reports to meet even the most specific needs.

Types of Project Status Reports

There are five types of project status reports:

Current period reports. These reports cover only the most recently completed period. They report progress on those activities that were open or scheduled for work during the period. Reports might highlight activities completed and variance between scheduled and actual completion dates. If any activities did not progress according to plan, the report should include a discussion of the reasons for the variance and the appropriate corrective measures that will be implemented to correct the schedule slippage.

Cumulative reports. These reports contain the history of the project from the beginning to the end of the current report period. They are more informative than the current period reports because they show trends in project progress. For example, a schedule variance might be tracked over several successive periods to show improvement. Reports can be at the activity or project level.

Exception reports. Exception reports report variances from plan. These reports are typically designed for senior management to be read and interpreted quickly. Reports that are produced for senior management merit special consideration. Senior managers do not have a lot of time to read reports that tell them that everything is on schedule and there are no problems serious enough to warrant their attention. In such cases, a one-page, high-level summary report that says everything is OK is usually sufficient. It might also be appropriate to include a more detailed report as an attachment for those who might wish to read more detail. The same might be true of exception reports. That is, the one-page exception report tells senior managers about variances from plan that will be of interest to them while an attached report provides more details for the interested reader.

Stoplight reports. Stoplight reports are a variation that can be used on any of the previous report types. We believe in parsimony in all reporting. Here is a technique you might want to try. When the project is on schedule and everything seems to be moving as planned, put a green sticker on the top right of the first page of the project status report. This will signal to senior managers that everything is progressing according to plan and they need not even read the attached report. When the project has encountered a problem—schedule slippage, for example—you might put a yellow sticker on the top right of the first page of the project status report. That is a signal to upper management that the project is not moving along as scheduled but that you have a get-well plan in place. A summary of the problem and the get-well plan may appear on the first page, but they can also refer to the details in the attached report. Those details describe the problem, the corrective steps that have been put in place, and some estimate of when the situation will be rectified. Red stickers placed on the top right of the first page signal that a project is out of control. Red reports are to be avoided at all costs. This means that the project has encountered a problem and you don't have a get-well plan or even a recommendation for upper management. Senior managers will obviously read these reports because they signal a major problem with the project. If this should occur, our advice is to find an empty box and pack your belongings in it; your days as project manager are numbered. On a more positive note, the red condition may be beyond your control. For example, there is a major power grid failure on the East Coast and a number of companies have lost their computing systems. Your hot site is overburdened with companies looking for computing power. Your company is one of them, and the loss of computing power has put your project seriously behind in final system testing. There is little you can do to avoid such acts of nature.

Variance reports. Variance reports do exactly what their name suggests—they report differences between what was planned and what actually happened. The report has three columns: the planned number, the actual number, and the difference, or variance, between the two. A variance report can be in one of two formats. The first is numeric and displays a number of rows with each row giving the actual, planned, and variance calculation for those variables in which such numbers are needed. Typical variables that are tracked in a variance report are schedule and cost. For example, the rows might correspond to the activities open for work during the report period and the columns might be the planned cost to date, the actual cost to date, and the difference between the two. The impact of departures from plan is signified by larger values of this difference (the variance). The second format is a graphical representation of the numeric data. It might be formatted so that the plan data is shown for each report period of the project and is denoted with a curve of one color; the actual data is shown for each report period of the project and is denoted by a curve of a different color. The variance need not be graphed at all because it is merely the difference between the two curves at some point in time. One advantage of the graphic version of the variance report is that it can show the variance trend over the report periods of the project while the numeric report generally shows data only for the current report period.

Typical variance reports are snapshots in time (the current period) of the status of an entity being tracked. Most variance reports do not include data points that report how the project reached that status. Project variance reports can be used to report project as well as activity variances. For the sake of the managers who will have to read these reports, we recommend that one report format be used regardless of the variable being tracked. Top management will quickly become comfortable with a reporting format that is consistent across all projects or activities within a project. It will make life a bit easier for the project manager, too.

There are five reasons why you would want to measure duration and cost variances:

Catch deviations from the curve early. The cumulative actual cost or actual duration can be plotted against the planned cumulative cost or cumulative duration. As these two curves begin to display a variance from one another, the project manager will want to put corrective measures in place to bring the two curves together. This reestablishes the agreement between the planned and actual performance. This topic is treated in detail later in the chapter in the section *Cost Schedule Control.*

Dampen oscillation. Planned versus actual performance should display a similar pattern over time. Wild fluctuations between the two are symptomatic of a project that is not under control. Such a project will get behind schedule or overspent in one period, corrected in the next, and go out of control in the next report period. Variance reports can give an early warning that such conditions are likely and give the project manager an opportunity to correct the anomaly before it gets serious. Smaller oscillations are easier to correct than larger oscillations.

Allow early corrective action. As just suggested, the project manager would prefer to be alerted to a schedule or cost problem early in the development of the problem rather than later. Early problem detection may offer more opportunities for corrective action than later detection.

Determine weekly schedule variance. In our experience, we found that progress on activities open for work should be reported on a weekly basis. This is a good compromise on report frequency and gives the project manager the best opportunity for corrective action plans before the situation escalates to a point where it will be difficult to recover any schedule slippages.

Determine weekly effort (person hours/day) variance. The difference between the planned effort and actual effort has a direct impact on both planned cumulative cost and schedule. If the effort is less than planned, it may suggest a potential schedule slippage if the person is not able to increase his or her effort on the activity in the following week. Alternatively, if the weekly effort exceeded the plan and the progress was not proportionately the same, a cost over-run situation may be developing.

Early detection of out-of-control situations is also important. The longer we have to wait to discover a problem, the longer it will take for our solution to bring the project back to a stable condition.

How and What Information to Update

As input to each of these report types activity managers and the project manager must report the progress made on all of those activities that were open for work (in other words, those that were to have work completed on them during the report period) during the period of time covered by the status report. Recall that your planning estimates of activity duration and cost were based on little or no information. Now that you have completed some work on the activity, you should be able to provide a better estimate of the duration and cost exposure. This reflects itself in a reestimate of the work remaining to complete the activity. That update information should also be provided.

The following is a list of what should actually be reported.

Determine a set period of time and day of week. The project team will have agreed on the day of the week and time of day by which all updated information is to be submitted. A project administrator or another team member is responsible for seeing that all update information is on file by the report deadline.

Report actual work accomplished during this period. What was planned to be accomplished and what was actually accomplished are two different things. Rather than disappoint the project manager, activity managers are likely to report that the planned work was actually accomplished. Their hope is to catch up by the next report period.

Project managers need to verify the accuracy of the reported data rather than simply accept it as accurate. Spot checking on a random basis should be sufficient. If the activity was defined according to the completion criteria discussed in Chapter 5, "What Is Project Management?" verification should not be a problem.

Record historical and reestimate remaining (in-progress work only). Two kinds of information are reported. All work completed prior to the report deadline is *historical information*. It will allow variance reports and other tracking data to be presented and analyzed. The other kind of information is *futures-oriented*. For the most part, this information is reestimates of duration and cost and estimates to completion (both cost and duration) of the activities still open for work.

Report start and finish dates. These are the actual start and finish dates of activities started or completed during the report period.

Record days of duration accomplished and remaining. How many days have been spent so far working on this activity is the first number reported. The second number is based on the reestimated duration as reflected in the time-to-completion number.

Report resource effort (hours/day) spent and remaining (in-progress work only). Whereas the above numbers report calendar time these numbers report labor time over the duration of the activity. There are two numbers. One reports labor completed over the duration accomplished. The other reports labor to be spent over the remaining duration.

Percent Complete

Percent complete is the most common method used to record progress because it is the way we tend to think about what has been done in reference to the total job that has to be done. Percent complete isn't the best method to report progress, though, because it is a subjective evaluation. When you ask someone "What percent complete are you on this activity?" what goes through his or her mind? The first thing he or she thinks about is most likely: "What percent should I be?", followed closely by "What's a number that we can all be happy with?"

In order to calculate the percent complete for an activity, you need something quantifiable. At least three different approaches have been used to calculate the percent complete of an activity:

- Duration
- Resource work
- Cost

Each of these could result in a different percent complete! So when we say percent complete, what measure are we referring to?

If you focus on duration as the measure of percent complete, where did the duration value come from? The only value you have is the original estimate. You know that original estimates often differ from actual performance. If you were to apply a percent complete to duration, however, the only one you have to work with is the original estimated one. Therefore this is not a good metric.

Our advice is to never ask for and never accept percent complete as input to project progress. Always allow it to be a calculation. Many software products will let you do it either as an inputted value or as a calculated value. The calculated value that we recommend above all others is one based on the number of tasks actually completed in the activity as a proportion of the number of tasks that currently define the activity. Recall that the task list for an activity is part of the work package description. Here we count only completed tasks. Tasks that are underway but not reported as complete may not be used in this calculation.

Frequency of Gathering and Reporting Project Progress

A logical frequency for reporting project progress is once a week, usually on Friday afternoon. There are some projects, such as refurbishing a large jet airliner, where progress is recorded after each shift, three times a day. We've seen others that were of such a low priority or long duration that they were updated once a month. For most projects, start gathering the information about noon on Friday. Let people extrapolate to the end of the work day.

Variances

Variances are deviations from plan. Think of a variance as the difference between what was planned and what actually occurred. There are two types of variances: positive variances and negative variances.

Positive Variances

Positive variances are deviations from plan that indicate that an ahead-of-schedule situation has occurred or that an actual cost was less than a planned cost. This is good news to the project manager, who would rather hear that the project is ahead of schedule or under budget. Positive variances bring their own set of problems, which can be as serious as negative variances. Positive variances can allow for rescheduling to bring the project to completion early, under budget, or both. Resources can be reallocated from ahead-of-schedule projects to behind-schedule projects.

Not all the news is good news, though. Positive variances also can result from schedule slippage! Consider budget. Being under-budget means that not all dollars were expended, which may be the direct result of not having completed work that was scheduled for completion during the report period. We return to this situation later in the *Cost Schedule Control* section of this chapter. On the other hand, if the ahead-of-schedule situation is the result of the project team's finding a better way or a shortcut to completing work, the project manager will be pleased. This may be a short-lived benefit, however. Getting ahead of schedule is great, but staying ahead of schedule presents another kind of problem—staying ahead of schedule. To stay ahead of schedule the project manager will have to negotiate changes to the resource schedule. Given the aggressive project portfolios in place in most companies, there is not much reason to believe that resource schedule changes can be made. In the final analysis, being ahead of schedule may be a myth.

Negative Variances

Negative variances are deviations from plan that indicate that a behind-schedule situation has occurred or that an actual cost was greater than a planned cost. Being behind schedule or over budget is not what the project manager or his reporting manager wants to hear. Negative variances, just like positive variances, are not necessarily bad news. For example, you might have overspent because you accomplished more work during the report period than was planned. But in overspending during this period, you could have accomplished the work at less cost than was originally planned. You can't tell by looking at the variance report. More details are forthcoming on this in the *Cost Schedule Control* section later in this chapter.

In most cases, negative time variances affect project completion only if they are associated with critical path activities or if the schedule slippage on noncritical path activities exceeds the activity's total float. Variances use up the float time for that activity; more serious ones will cause a change in the critical path.

Negative cost variances can result from uncontrollable factors such as cost increases from suppliers or unexpected equipment malfunctions. Some negative variances can result from inefficiencies or error. We discuss a problem escalation strategy to resolve such situations later in this chapter.

Graphical Reporting Tools

Senior managers may have only a few minutes of uninterrupted time to digest your report. Respect that time. They won't be able to fully read and understand your report if they have to read 15 pages before they get any useful information. Having to read several pages only to find out that the project is on schedule is frustrating and a waste of valuable time.

Gantt Charts

A *Gantt chart* is one of the most convenient, most used, and easy-to-grasp depictions of project activities that we have encountered in our practice. The chart is formatted as a two-dimensional representation of the project schedule with activities shown in the rows and time shown across the horizontal axis. It can be used during planning, for resource scheduling, and for status reporting. The only down side to using Gantt charts is that they do not contain dependency relationships. Some project management software tools have an option to display these dependencies, but the result is a graphical report that is so cluttered with lines representing the dependencies that the report is next to useless. In some cases, dependencies can be guessed at from the Gantt chart, but in most cases they are lost.

Figure 13.2 shows a representation of the Cost Containment Project as a Gantt chart using the format that we prefer. The format shown is from Microsoft Project 2000, but it is typical of the format used in most project management software packages.

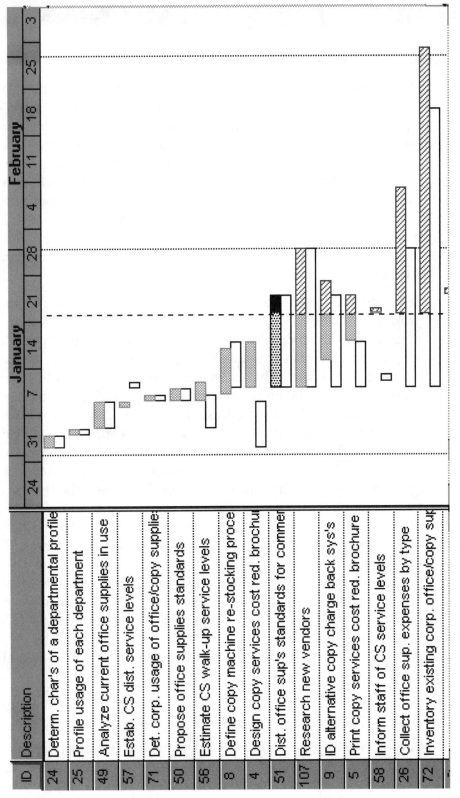

Figure 13.2 Gantt chart project status report.

Milestone Trend Charts

Milestones are significant events in the life of the project that you wish to track. These significant events are zero-duration activities and merely represent that a certain condition exists in the project. For example, a milestone event might be that the approval of several different component designs has been given. This event consumes no time in the project schedule. It simply reflects the fact that those approvals have all been granted. The completion of this milestone event may be the predecessor of several build-type activities in the project plan. Milestone events are planned into the project in the same way that activities are planned into the project. They typically have FS relationships with the activities that are their predecessors and their successors.

Let's look at a milestone trend chart (see Figure 13.3) for a hypothetical project. The trend chart plots the difference between the planned and estimated date of a project milestone at each project report period. In the original project plan the milestone is planned to occur at the ninth month of the project. That is the last project month on this milestone chart. The horizontal lines represent one, two, and three standard deviations above or below the forecasted milestone date. Any activity in the project has an expected completion date that is approximately normally distributed. The mean and variance of its completion date are a function of the longest path to the activity from the report date. In this example, the units of measure are one month. For this project the first project report (at month 1) shows that the new forecasted milestone date will be one week later than planned. At the second project report date (month two of the project) the milestone date is forecasted on target. The next three project reports indicate a slippage to two weeks late, then three weeks late, then four weeks late, and finally six weeks late (at month 6 of the project). In other words, the milestone is forecasted to occur six weeks late, and there are only three more project months in which to recover the slippage. Obviously, the project is in trouble. The project appears to be drifting out of control and, in fact, it is. Some remedial action is required of the project manager.

Certain patterns signal an out-of-control situation. These are given in Figures 13.3 through 13.6 and are described here:

Successive slippages. Figure 13.3 depicts a project that is drifting out of control. Each report period shows additional slippage since the last re-

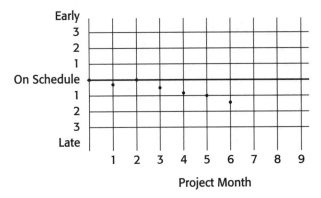

Figure 13.3 A run up or down of four or more successive data points.

port period. Four such successive occurrences, however minor they may seem, require special corrective action on the part of the project manager.

Radical change. Figure 13.4, while it does show the milestone to be ahead of schedule, reports a radical change between report periods. Activity duration may have been grossly over-estimated. There may be a data error. In any case, the situation requires further investigation.

Successive runs. Figure 13.5 signals a project that may have encountered a permanent schedule shift. In the example, the milestone date seems to be varying around one month ahead of schedule. Barring any radical shifts and the availability of resources over the next two months, the milestone will probably come in one month early. Re-

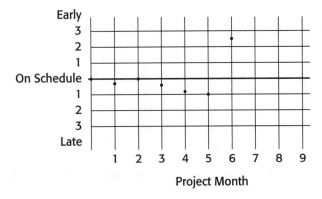

Figure 13.4 A change of more than three standard deviations.

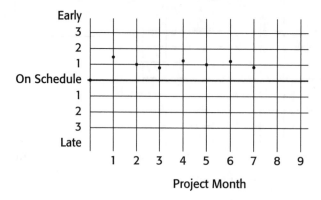

Figure 13.5 Seven or more successive data points above or below the planned milestone date.

member that you have negotiated for a resource schedule into these two months and now you will be trying to renegotiate an accelerated schedule.

Schedule shift. Figure 13.6 depicts a major shift in the milestone schedule. The cause must be isolated and the appropriate corrective measures taken. One possibility is the discovery that a downstream activity will not be required. Perhaps the project manager can buy a deliverable rather than build it and remove the associated build activities from the project plan.

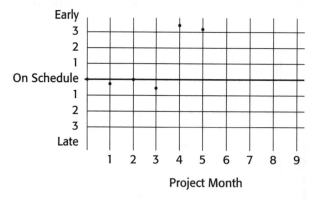

Figure 13.6 Two successive data points outside three standard deviations from the planned milestone date.

Cost Schedule Control

Cost schedule control is used to measure project performance and, by tradition, uses the dollar value of work as the metric. As an alternative, resource person hours/day can be used in cases where the project manager does not directly manage the project budget. Actual work performed is compared against planned and budgeted work expressed in these equivalents. These metrics are used to determine schedule and cost variances for both the current period and cumulative to date. Cost, or resource person hours/day are not good objective indicators with which to measure performance or progress. While this is true, there is no other good objective indicator. Given this we are left with dollars or person hours/day, which we are at least familiar working with in other contexts. Either one by itself does not tell the whole story. We need to relate them to one another.

One drawback that these metrics have is that they report history. Although they can be used to make extrapolated predictions for the future, they primarily provide a measure of the general health of the

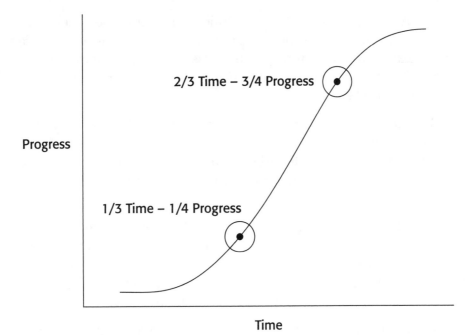

Figure 13.7 The standard S curve.

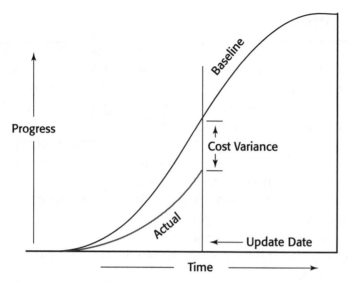

Figure 13.8 Baseline versus actual cost curve illustrating cost variance.

project, which the project manager can correct as needed to restore the project to good health.

Figure 13.7 shows an S curve, which represents the baseline progress curve for the original project plan. It can be used as a reference point. You can compare your actual progress to date against the curve and determine how well the project is doing. Again, progress can be expressed as either dollars or person hours/day.

By adding the actual progress curve to the baseline curve, you can now see the current status versus the planned status. Figure 13.8 shows the actual progress curve to be below the planned curve. If this represented dollars, we might be tempted to believe the project is running under budget. Is that really true?

Projects rarely run significantly under budget. A more common reason for the actual curve to be below the baseline is that the activities that should have been done have not been and thus the dollars or person hours/day that were planned to be expended have not been. The possible schedule variance is highlighted in Figure 13.9.

To determine whether there has really been a progress schedule variance, you need some additional information. Cost schedule control (CSC) comprises three basic measurements: budgeted cost of work scheduled, budgeted cost of work performed, and actual cost of work

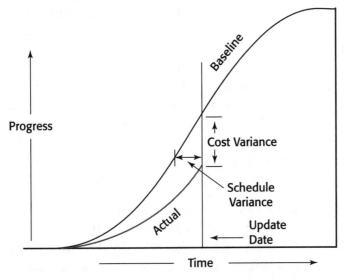

Figure 13.9 Baseline versus actual cost illustrating schedule variance.

performed. These measurements result in two variance values, schedule variance and cost variance. Figure 13.10 is a graphical representation of the three measurements.

The figure shows a single activity that has a five-day duration and a budget of $500. The budget is prorated over the five days at an average daily value of $100. The left panel of Figure 13.10 shows an initial (baseline) schedule with the activity starting on the first day of the week (Monday)

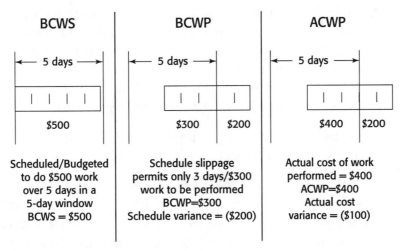

Figure 13.10 Cost/performance indicators.

and finishing at the end of the week (Friday). The budgeted $500 value of the work is planned to be accomplished all within that week. This is the budgeted cost of work scheduled (BCWS). The center panel shows the actual work that was done. Note that the schedule slipped and work did not begin until the third day of the week. Using an average daily budget of $100 we see that we were able to complete only $300 of the scheduled work. This is the budgeted cost of work performed (BCWP). The rightmost panel shows the actual schedule as in the center panel, but now we see the actual dollars that were spent to accomplish the three days work. This $400 is the actual cost of work performed (ACWP).

The BCWS, BCWP, and ACWP are used to compute and track two variances. The first is *schedule variance (SV)*. SV is the difference between the BCWP and BCWS, which is –$200 (BCWP – BCWS) for this example. That is, the SV is the schedule difference between what was done and what was planned to be done, expressed in dollar or person hours/day equivalents. The second is cost variance (CV). CV is the difference between the BCWP and the ACWP, which is $100 in this example. That is, we overspent by $100 (ACWP – BCWP) the cost of the work completed.

Management might react positively to the news shown in Figure 13.8, but they might also be misled by such a conclusion. The full story is told by comparing both budget variance and schedule variance, shown in Figure 13.11.

To correctly interpret the data shown in Figure 13.9, you need to add the BCWP data that was given in Figure 13.10 to produce Figure 13.11. Comparing the BCWP curve with the BCWS curve you see that you have underspent because all of the work that was scheduled has not been completed. Comparing the BCWP curve to the ACWP curve also indicates that you overspent for the work that was done. Clearly, management would have been misled by Figure 13.8 had they ignored the data in Figure 13.10. Either one by itself may be telling a half-truth.

In addition to measuring and reporting history, CSC can be used to predict the future status of a project.

Take a look at Figure 13.12. By cutting the BCWS curve at the height from the horizontal axis, which has been achieved by the BCWP, and then pasting this curve on to the end of the BCWP curve, you can extrapolate the completion of the project. Note that this is based on using the original estimates for the remaining work to be completed. If you

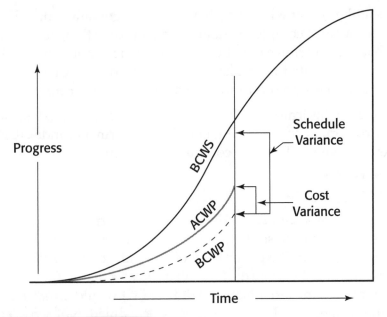

Figure 13.11 The full story.

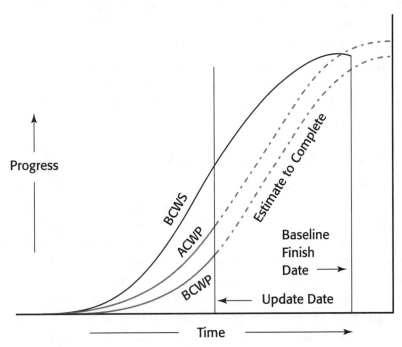

Figure 13.12 BCWS, BCWP, and ACWP curves.

continue at the rate at which you have been progressing, you will finish beyond the planned completion date. Doing the same thing for the ACWP shows that you will finish over budget. This is the simplest method of attempting to "estimate to completion," but it clearly illustrates that a significant change needs to occur in the way this project is running.

The three basic indicators yield one additional level of analysis for us. Schedule performance index (SPI) and Cost performance index (CPI) are a further refinement. They are computed as follows:

SPI = BCWP/BCWS

CPI = BCWP/ACWP

Schedule performance index. The schedule performance index (SPI) is a measure of how close the project is to performing work as it was actually scheduled. If we are ahead of schedule, BCWP will be greater than BCWS, and therefore the SPI will be greater than 1. Obviously this is desirable. On the other hand, an SPI below 1 would indicate that the work performed was less than the work scheduled. Not a good thing.

Cost performance index. The cost performance index (CPI) is a measure of how close the project is to spending on the work performed to what was planned to have been spent. If you are spending less on the work performed than was budgeted, the CPI will be greater than 1. If not, and you are spending more than was budgeted for the work performed, then the CPI will be less than 1.

Some managers prefer this type of analysis because it is intuitive and quite simple to equate each index to a baseline of 1. Any value less than 1 is undesirable; any value over 1 is good. These indices are displayed graphically as trends compared against the baseline value of 1.

Using the WBS to Report Project Status

Because the Work Breakdown Structure (WBS) shows the hierarchical structure of the work to be done, it can be used for status reporting, too. In its simplest form, each activity box can be shaded to reflect completion percentages. As lower-level activities are completed, the summary activities above them can be shaded to represent percent complete data. Senior managers will appreciate knowing that major parts of the project are complete. Unfortunately, the WBS does not contain scheduling or sequencing information. To the extent that this adds to the value of the report, narrative data or brief tabular data might be added to the report. Figure 13.13 shows an example status report using the WBS.

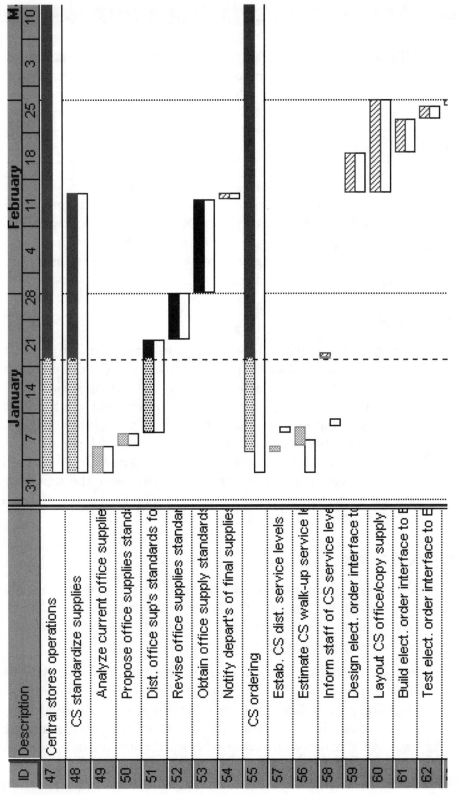

Figure 13.13 Status reporting with the WBS.

Although this report is rather intuitive it does not contain much detail. It would have to be accompanied by an explanatory note with schedule and cost detail.

Level of Detail

There are always questions about the level of detail and frequency of reporting in project status reports. Our feeling is that the more you report, the more likely it is that someone will object or find some reason to micro-manage your project. Let's examine this issue in more detail by considering the reporting requirements at the activity manager, project manager, and senior manager levels.

Activity Manager

The activity manager will want the most detailed and granular information available. After all, the activity manager is directly responsible for getting the work done. Because he or she manages the resources that are used to complete project work, he or she will want to know what happened, what was scheduled to happen, who did what (or didn't do what), why it happened as it did, what problems have arisen, what solutions are within reach, and what changes need to be made. Reports that reflect very detailed information are of use to the activity manager and the project manager but, because of their very detail, are of little value to anyone outside of the project team.

Project Manager

The project manager is concerned with the status information of all activities open for work during the report period. Just as is the case with activity-level reports, there are reports for the project manager and reports from the project manager to senior management.

Reports for the project manager present data at the activity level and show effects on the project schedule. If project management software is used, the posted data from the activity managers is used to update the project schedule and produce reports on overall project status. Any slippage at the activity level rippled through the successor activities, triggered a new activity schedule, and recomputed project completion dates. These reports display all scheduling information including float and resource schedule data. In effect, they become working documents for the project manager for schedule adjustments and problem resolution. Because these reports are at a very detailed level, they are not appropriate for distribution beyond the project team. In many cases, they may be for the project manager's eyes only.

Senior Management

We recommend using a graphical exception report structure to report project status to senior management. For many projects, reports at the activity level will be appropriate. For large projects either milestone-level or summary task-level reports are more effective. Senior managers have only a few minutes to review any single project report. Keeping a report to a single page is a good strategy. The best report format, in our experience, is the Gantt chart. These charts require little explanation. Activities should be listed in the order of scheduled start date, a line designating the report date should be given and all percent completed displayed.

If the project is sick, attach a one-page get-well plan to your report. This usually is in the form of a narrative discussion of the problem, alternative solutions, recommended action, and any other details relevant to the issue at hand.

Project Status Review Meetings

Project status review meetings do just what their name indicates—they review project status. They are not committee meetings where problems are solved. They are not discussion groups. These meetings have very specific timed agendas. They focus on a single project, but on occasion it can be useful to have multiple projects included on the agenda. Project status is reported weekly by the activity manager to the project manager. Biweekly, the project manager reports to senior management. It therefore makes sense that project status meetings occur biweekly. One of the purposes is to prepare the project manager to report to senior management.

Project size may be the determining factor, but in general we prefer a one-hour limit. This is the maximum, and an entire hour should not be needed at every project status meeting. Good judgment is needed here. Do not waste people's time.

The list of attendees will vary throughout the life of the project. The project team members often attend every meeting, but larger projects can include only those members that now contribute or will in the future contribute to the work. Managers of activities that were open for work or scheduled for work during the report period also attend. Those who are involved with successor activities may be invited as well. The customer, or the customer representative, will always be present. If any resource managers are affected by the status (presumed to have departed from the plan), they should be present, too. The project champion also attends every status meeting. Resource managers attend if the resources they command affect a current or future period schedule.

While the format of the status review meetings should be flexible, as project needs dictate, certain items are part of every status meeting. We recommend that you proceed in a top-down fashion:

1. The project champion reports any changes that may have a bearing on the future of the project.

2. The customer reports any changes that may have a bearing on the future of the project.

3. The project manager reports on the overall health of the project and the impact of earlier problems, changes, and corrective actions as they impact at the project level.

4. Activity managers report on the health of activities open or scheduled open for work since the last status meeting.

5. Activity managers of future activities report on any changes since the last meeting that might impact project status.

6. The project manager reviews the status of open problems from the last status meeting.

7. Attendees identify new problems and assign responsibility for their resolution (the only discussion allowed here is for clarification purposes).

8. The project champion, customer, or project manager, as appropriate, offers closing comments.

9. The project manager announces the time and place of the next meeting and adjourns the meeting.

Minutes are part of the formal project documentation and are taken at each meeting, circulated for comment, revised as appropriate, distributed, and filed in the project notebook (electronic, we hope). Because there is little discussion, the minutes contain any handouts from the meeting and list the items assigned for the next meeting. The minutes should also contain the list of attendees, a summary of comments made, and assigned responsibilities.

A project administrative support person should be present at the project status review meetings to take minutes and monitor handouts. The responsibility might also be passed around to the project team members. In some organizations the same person is responsible for distributing the meeting agenda and materials ahead of time for review. This is especially important if decisions will be made during the meeting. People are very uncomfortable if they are seeing important information for the first time, are expected to read and understand it, and then make a decision, all at the same time.

Change Control

It is difficult for anyone, regardless of his or her skills at prediction and forecasting, to completely and accurately define the needs for a product or service that will be implemented 6, 12, or 18 months in the future. Competition, customer reactions, technology changes, a host of supplier-related situations, and many other factors could render a killer application obsolete before it can be implemented. The most frequent situation starts something like this: "Oh, I forgot to tell you that we will also need…" or "We have to go to market no later than the third quarter instead of the fourth quarter." How often have you heard sentences that start something like those examples? Let's face it—change is a way of life in project management. We might as well face it and be prepared to act accordingly.

Because change is constant, a good project management methodology has a change management process in place. In effect, the change management process has you plan the project again. Think of it as a mini-JPP session.

Two documents are part of every good change management process: *project change request* and *project impact statement*.

Project change request. The first principle to learn is that every change is a significant change. Adopt that maxim and you will seldom go wrong. What that means is that every change requested by the customer must be documented. That document might be as simple as a memo but might also follow a format provided by the project team. In any case, it is the start of another round of establishing Conditions of Satisfaction. Only when the request is clearly understood can the project team evaluate the impact of the change and determine whether the change can be accommodated. Figure 13.15 is an example of a change request form that we have found useful.

Project impact statement. The response to a change request is a document called a *project impact statement*. It is a response that identifies the alternative courses of action that the project manager is willing to consider. The requestor is then charged with choosing the best alternative. The project impact statement describes the feasible alternatives that the project manager was able to identify, the positive and negative aspects of each, and perhaps a recommendation as to which alternative might be best. The final decision rests with the requestor.

Six possible outcomes can result from a change request:

It can be accommodated within the project resources and timelines. This is the simplest of situations for the project manager to handle. After considering the impact of the change on the project schedule, the project manager decides that the change can be accommodated without any harmful effect on the schedule and resources.

It can be accommodated but will require an extension of the deliverable schedule. The only impact that the change will have is to lengthen the deliverable schedule. No additional resources will be needed to accommodate the change request.

It can be accommodated within the current deliverable schedule but additional resources will be needed. To accommodate this change request the project manager will need additional resources but otherwise the current and revised schedule can be met.

It can be accommodated but additional resources and an extension of the deliverable schedule will be required. This change request will require additional resources and a lengthened deliverable schedule.

It can be accommodated with a multiple release strategy and prioritizing of the deliverables across the release dates. This situation comes up more often than you might expect. To accommodate the change request, the project plan will have to be significantly revised, but there is an alternative. For example, suppose that the original request was for a list of 10 features, and they are in the current plan. The change request asks for an additional 2 features. The project manager asks the customer to prioritize all 12 features. He or she will give the customer 8 of them earlier than the delivery date for the original 10 features and will deliver the remaining 4 features later than the delivery date for the original 10. In other words, the project manager will give the customer some of what is requested earlier than requested and the balance later than requested. We have seen several cases where this compromise has worked quite well.

It cannot be accommodated without a significant change to the project. These change requests are significant. They are so significant, in fact, as to render the current project plan obsolete. There are two alternatives here. The first is to deny the change request, complete the project as planned, and handle the request as another project. The other is to call a stop to the current project, replan the project to accommodate the change, and launch a new project.

An integral part of the change control process is the documentation. First, we strongly suggest that every change be treated as a major change until proven otherwise. To do otherwise is to court disaster. That means that every change request follows the same procedure. Figure 13.14 is an example of the steps in a typical change process. The change request is submitted by the customer using the form shown in Figure 13.15 and forwarded to the manager or managers charged with reviewing such requests. They may either accept the change as submitted or return it to the customer for rework and resubmission. Once the change request has been accepted, it is forwarded to the project manager, who will perform an impact study.

The impact study involves looking at the project plan, assessing how the change request impacts the plan, and issuing the impact study, which is forwarded to the management group for final disposition. They may return it to the project manager for further analysis and recommendations or reject it and notify the customer of their action. The project manager reworks the impact study and returns it to the management group for final disposition. If they approve the change, the project manager will implement it into the project plan.

The process is initiated by the customer, who submits a request for the change using a form much like the one shown in Figure 13.15.

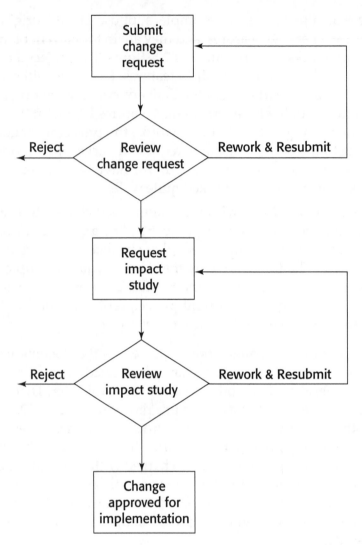

Figure 13.14 A typical change control process.

Problem Escalation

Something has happened that put the project plan at risk. Late ship-ments from suppliers, equipment malfunction, sickness, acts of nature, resignations, priority changes, errors, and a host of other factors give

Project Name	
Change Requested By	
Date Change Requested	
Description of Change	
Business Justification	
Action	
Approved by	Date

Figure 13.15 Change control form.

rise to problems that can affect deliverables, deliverable schedules, and resource schedules. The project manager owns the problem and must find a solution.

This situation is very different for the project manager than the case of a change request. When a change request has been made, the project manager has some leverage with the customer. The customer wants something and might be willing to negotiate to an acceptable resolution. That is not the case when a problem has arisen on the project team. The project manager does not have any leverage and is in a much more difficult position.

When the unplanned happens, the project manager needs to determine the extent of the problem and take the appropriate corrective measures. Minor variations from plan will occur and may not require corrective measures. There are degrees of corrective measures available to the project manager: In trying to resolve the problem the project manager will begin at the top of the following list and work down the list, examining each choice until one is found that solves the problem.

There are three levels of escalation strategy: project manager based, resource manager based, and customer based.

Project manager–based strategies. If the problem occurs within a non-critical path activity, it can be resolved by using the free float. One example is to reschedule the activity later in its ES to LF window or extend the duration to use some of the free float. Note that this strategy does not affect any other activities in the project. By using total float you impact the resource schedule for all activities that have this one as a predecessor. Another approach is to continue the schedule compression techniques employed in defining the original project plan. This can impact resource schedules just as in the prior case. The last option open to the project manager is to consider the resource pool under his or her control. Are there resources that can be reassigned from noncritical path activities to assist with the problem activity?

Resource manager–based strategies. Once the project manager has exhausted all the options under his or her control, it is time to turn to the resource managers for additional help. This may take the form of additional resources or rescheduling of already committed resources. Expect to make some trade-off here. For example, you might be accommodated now, but at the sacrifice of later activities in the project. At least you have bought some time to resolve the downstream problem that will be created by solving this upstream problem. If the project manager has other projects underway, some trades across projects may solve the problem.

Customer-based strategies. When all else fails, the project manager will have to approach the customer. The first strategy would be to consider any multiple release strategies. Delivering some functionality ahead of schedule and the balance later than planned may be a good starting point. The last resort is to ask for an extension of time. This is not as unpleasant as it may seem because the customer's schedule may have also slipped and the customer may be relieved to have a delay in your deliverable schedule, too.

The Escalation Strategy Hierarchy

Our problem escalation strategy is based on the premise that the project manager will try to solve the problem with the resources he or she controls. Failing to do that, the project manager will appeal to resource managers. As a last resort, the project manager will appeal to the customer.

One thing to note here that is very different from the change request situation discussed previously is the leverage to negotiate. As mentioned, the project manager has leverage when the customer has requested a change but has no leverage when he or she has a project problem to solve. The customer has nothing to gain and therefore is less likely to be cooperative. In most cases, the problem can be reduced to how to recover lost time. There are six outcomes to this problem situation.

No action required (schedule slack will correct the problem). In this case, the slippage involved a noncritical path activity, and it will self-correct.

Examine FS dependencies for schedule compression opportunities. Recall that you originally compressed the schedule to accommodate the requested project completion date by changing FS dependencies to SS dependencies. The project manager will use that same strategy again. The project schedule will have changed several times since work began, and there may be several new opportunities to accomplish further compression and solve the current problem.

Reassign resources from noncritical path activities to correct the slippage. Up to a point, the project manager controls the resources assigned to this project and others that he or she manages. The project manager may be able to reassign resources from noncritical path activities to the activities that have slipped. These noncritical path activities may be in the same project in which the slippage occurred, or they may be in another project managed by the same project manager.

Negotiate additional resources. Having exhausted all of the resources he or she controls, the project manager needs to turn to the resource managers as the next strategy. In order to recoup the lost time, the project manager needs additional resources. They may come in the form of added staff or dollars to acquire contract help.

Negotiate multiple release strategies. These last two strategies involve the customer. Just as in the case of a change request, the project manager can use multiple release strategies here to advantage. An example will illustrate the strategy. The project manager shares the problem with the customer and then asks for the customer to prioritize the features requested in the project plan. The project manager then offers to provide the highest-priority features ahead of their scheduled delivery date and the remaining priorities later than the scheduled delivery date. In other words, the project manager asks for an extended delivery schedule, but by giving the customer something better than the original bargain, namely something ahead of schedule.

Request schedule extension from the customer. This is the final alternative. Although similar to the multiple release strategy, it offers the customer nothing in trade. The slippage is such that the only resolution is to ask for a time extension.

The project manager tries to solve the problem by starting at the top of the list and working down until a solution is found. By using this approach the project manager will first try to solve the problem with resources he or she controls, then with resources the resource managers control, and finally with resources and constraints the customer controls.

Problem Management Meetings

Problem management meetings provide an oversight function to identify, monitor, and resolve problems that arise during the life of a project. Every project has problems. No matter how well planned or managed, there will always be problems. Many problems arise just as an accident of nature. For example, one of your key staff members has resigned just as he was to begin working on a critical path activity. His skills are in high demand, and he will be difficult to replace. Each day that his position remains vacant is another day's delay in the project. What will you do? Nevertheless, the project manager must be ready to take action in such cases. The problem management meeting is one vehicle for addressing all problems that need to be escalated above the individual for definition, solution identification, and resolution.

This is an important function in the management of projects, especially large projects. Problems are often identified in the project status meeting and referred to the appropriate persons for resolution. A group is assembled to work on the problem. Progress reports are presented and discussed at a problem management meeting.

Case Exercise: Recording Progress for Monitoring and Control

For this exercise, you will need to go to the file called GOLD.PDF on the companion CD-ROM. You will find a Table of Contents. Select "Recording Progress for Monitoring and Control" and follow the instructions for how to run the exercise.

Now that the project plan has reached the point where it appears reasonable, it's time to make a baseline of it and start running the project. This exercise takes you through the process of recording progress for the first week of the project using Microsoft Project.

Because of the number and complexity of the variables involved, we do not present any paper-based exercises with this lesson. We instead show examples of how it's done using views from Microsoft Project.

If you are using Microsoft Project to follow along, the appropriate file is available on the CD-ROM for practice. Instructions are included in the exercise. We suggest that you look through our approach first and then practice in the file.

Close Out the Project

Chapter Learning Objectives

After reading this chapter you will be able to:

✔ Understand the steps needed to effectively close a project
✔ Develop a closing strategy
✔ Identify the components of project documentation
✔ Conduct a post-implementation audit
✔ Explain the significance of each post-implementation audit question

We judge ourselves by what we feel capable of doing,
while others judge us by what we have already done.

—HENRY WADSWORTH LONGFELLOW
AMERICAN POET

We cannot afford to forget any experiences, even the most painful.

—DAG HAMMERSKJOLD
SECRETARY GENERAL OF THE UNITED NATIONS

Steps in Closing a Project

Closing the project is routine once we have the customer's approval of the deliverables. There are six steps to closing the project:

1. Get client acceptance of deliverables.
2. Ensure that all deliverables are installed.
3. Ensure that documentation is in place.
4. Get client sign-off on final report.
5. Conduct post-implementation audit.
6. Celebrate success.

Let's take a look at each of these steps in more detail.

Get Client Acceptance

The client decides when the project is done. It is the job of the project manager to demonstrate that the deliverables (whether product or service) meet client specifications. This can be very informal and ceremonial, or it can be very formal, involving extensive acceptance testing against the client's performance specifications.

Ceremonial Acceptance

Ceremonial acceptance is an informal acceptance by the customer. It does not have an accompanying sign-off of completion or acceptance. It simply happens. Two situations fall under the heading of ceremonial acceptance. The first involves deadline dates at which the client must accept the project as complete, whether or not it meets specification. For example, if the project was to plan and conduct a conference, the conference will happen whether or not the project work has been satisfactorily completed. The second involves a project deliverable requiring little or no checking to see if specifications have been met—for example, planning and taking a vacation.

Formal Acceptance

Formal acceptance occurs in those cases in which the client has written an acceptance procedure. In many cases, especially computer applications development projects, writing an acceptance procedure may be a joint effort by the customer and appropriate members of the project team; it typically is done very early in the life of the project. This acceptance procedure requires that the project team demonstrate compliance with every feature in the client's performance specification. A checklist is used and requires a feature-by-feature sign-off based on performance tests. These tests are conducted jointly and administered by the client and appropriate members of the project team. The checklist is written in such a fashion that compliance is either demonstrated by the test or it is not demonstrated by the test. It must not be written in such a way that interpretation is needed to determine whether compliance has been demonstrated.

Install Project Deliverables

The second step of closing a project is to go live with the deliverables. This commonly occurs in computer systems work. The installation can involve phases, cutovers, or some other rollout strategy. In other cases, it involves nothing more than flipping a switch. In either case, some event or activity turns things over to the customer. This triggers the beginning of a number of close-out activities that mostly relate to documentation and report preparation.

Document the Project

Documentation always seems to be the most difficult part of the project to complete. There is little glamour and no "attaboys" in doing documentation. That does not diminish its importance, however. There are at least five reasons why we need to do documentation:

Reference for future changes in deliverables. Even though the project work is complete, there will be further changes that warrant follow-up projects. By using the deliverables, the customer will identify improvement opportunities, features to be added, and functions to be modified. The documentation of the project just completed is the foundation for the follow-up projects.

Historical record for estimating duration and cost on future projects, activities, and tasks. Completed projects are a terrific source of information for future projects, but only if data and other documentation from them is archived so that it can be retrieved and used. Estimated and actual duration and cost for each activity on completed projects are particularly valuable for estimating these variables on future projects.

Training resource for new project managers. History is a great teacher, and nowhere is that more significant than on completed projects. Such items as how the WBS architecture was determined, how change requests were analyzed and decisions reached, problem identification, analysis and resolution situations, and a variety of other experiences are invaluable lessons for the newly appointed project manager.

Input for further training and development of the project team. As a reference, project documentation can help the project team deal with situations that arise in the current project. How a similar problem or change request was handled in the past is an excellent example.

Input for performance evaluation by the functional managers of the project team members. In many organizations, project documentation can be used as input to the performance evaluations of the project manager and team members. Care must be exercised in the use of such information, however. There will be cases where a project was doomed to fail even though the team members' performance may have been exemplary. The reverse is also likely. The project was destined to be a success even though the team members' performance may have been less than expected.

Documentation Contents

The documentation for a given project should include the following parts:

- Project Overview Statement
- Project proposal and backup data
- Original and revised project schedules
- Minutes of all project team meetings

- Copies of all status reports
- Design documents
- Copies of all change notices
- Copies of all written communications
- Outstanding issues reports
- Final report
- Sample deliverables (if appropriate)
- Client acceptance documents
- Post-implementation audit report

This is the "whole enchilada." For a given project, the project manager has to determine what documentation is appropriate. Always refer back to value-added considerations. If the document has value, and many will have good value for future projects, then include it in the documentation. Note also that the list contains very little that does not arise naturally in the execution of the project. All that is needed is to appoint someone to care and feed the project notebook. This involves collecting the documents at the time of their creation and ensuring that they are in a retrievable form (electronic is a must).

Post-Implementation Audit

The post-implementation audit is an evaluation of the project's goals and activity achievement as measured against the project plan, budget, time deadlines, quality of deliverables, specifications, and client satisfaction. The log of the project activities serves as baseline data for this audit. There are six important questions to be answered:

1. Was the project goal achieved?
   a. Does it do what the project team said it would do?
   b. Does it do what the client said it would do?

The project was justified based on a goal to be achieved. It either was or it wasn't, and an answer to that question must be provided in the audit. The question can be asked and answered from two different perspectives. The provider may have suggested a solution for which certain results were promised. Did that happen? On the other hand, the requestor may have promised that if the provider would only provide, say, a new or improved system, certain results would occur. Did that happen?

2. Was the project work done on time, within budget, and according to specification?

Recall from the scope triangle discussed in Chapter 6, "Scope the Project," that the constraints on the project were time, cost, and the customer's specification, as well as resource availability and quality. Here we are concerned with whether the specification was met within the budgeted time and cost constraints.

3. Was the client satisfied with the project results?

It is possible that the answers to the first two questions are "yes" while the answer to this question is "no." How can that happen? Simple; the Conditions of Satisfaction changed, but no one was aware that they had. The project manager did not check with the customer to see if the needs had changed; the customer did not inform the project manager that such changes had occurred. We remind you again that it is absolutely essential that the Conditions of Satisfaction be reviewed at every major event in the life of the project, including changes in the team membership, especially a new project manager, and changes in the sponsor. Reorganization of the company, acquisitions, and mergers are other reasons to recheck the Conditions of Satisfaction.

4. Was business value realized? (Check success criteria.)

The success criteria were the basis on which the business case for the project was built and were the primary reason why the project was approved. Did we realize that promised value? When the success criteria measure improvement in profit or market share or other bottom-line parameters we may not be able to answer this question until some time after the project is closed.

5. What lessons were learned about your project management methodology?

Companies that have or are developing a project management methodology will want to use completed projects to assess how well the methodology is working. Different parts of the methodology may work well for certain types of projects or in certain situations, and these should be noted in the audit. These lessons will be valuable in tweaking the methodology or simply noting how to apply the methodology when a given situation arises. This part of the audit might also consider how well the team used the methodology, which is related to yet different from how well the methodology worked.

6. What worked? What didn't?

The answers to these questions are helpful hints and suggestions for future project managers and teams. The experiences of past project teams are real "diamonds in the rough"; you will want to pass them on to future teams.

Unfortunately the post-implementation audit is seldom done. This is unfortunate because it does have great value for all stakeholders. Some of the reasons for skipping the audit include these:

Managers don't want to know. They reason that the project is done and what difference does it make whether things happened the way we said they would. It is time to move on.

Managers don't want to pay the cost. The pressures of the budget (both time and money) are such that they would rather spend resources on the next project than on those already done.

It's not a high priority. Other projects are waiting to have work done on them, and completed projects don't rate very high on the priority list.

There's too much other billable work to do. Post-implementation audits are not billable work, and they have billable work on other projects to do.

The Final Report

The final project report acts as the memory or history of the project. It is the file that others can check to study the progress and impediments of the project. Many formats can be used for a final report, but the content should include comments relative to the following points:

Overall success of the project. Taking into account all of the measures of success that we considered, can we consider this project to have been a success?

Organization of the project. Hindsight is always perfect, but now that we are finished with the project did we organize it in the best way possible? If not, what might that organization have looked like?

Techniques used to get results. By way of a summary list, what specific things did you do that helped to get the results?

Project strengths and weaknesses. Again by way of a summary list, what features, practices, processes did we use that proved to be strengths and/or weaknesses? Do you have any advice to pass on to future project teams regarding these strengths/weaknesses?

Project team recommendations. Throughout the life of the project there will have been a number of insights and suggestions. This is the place to record them for posterity.

Celebrating Success

There must be some recognition for the project team at the end of the project. This can be as simple as a commemorative mug, a tee shirt, a pizza party, tickets to a ball game, or something more formal such as bonuses. We recall that when Release 3 of the spreadsheet package Lotus 1-2-3 was delivered, each member of the project team was presented with a videotape showing the team at work during the last week of the project. That was certainly a good touch and one that will long be remembered by every member of the team.

Even though the team may have started out as a "herd of cats" the project they have just completed has honed them into a real team. Bonding has taken place, new friendships have formed, and mentor relationships have been established. The individual team members have grown professionally through their association with one another, and now it is time to move on to the next project. This can be a very traumatic experience for them, and they deserve closure: That is what celebrating success is all about. Our loud and continual message to the senior management team is: Don't pass up an opportunity to show the team your appreciation. Loyalty, motivation, and commitment by your professional staff are the result of this simple act on your part.

You have now completed all five phases of the project management life cycle. The current project is done, the customer is satisfied, you have celebrated your success, and now you are ready for the next assignment. We can only hope that the practical tools and techniques we have shared will provide a lasting and valuable store of resources for you to use as you grow in this exciting profession. Whether you are a full-time project manager, an occasional project manager, an experienced project manager, or a "wanna-be" project manager you should have found value in these pages.

Good luck!

PART FIVE

References

There are additional considerations that apply to managing multiple projects. Appendix A, "Managing Muliple Projects," briefly discusses shared resources, organizational considerations, staff development, and project schedule. It also lists some of the strategic and tactical issues project managers face.

You were given an opportunity to practice each project management skill discussed in the book with the case exercises. Appendix B, "About the CD-ROM" details how to use the CD-ROM to access those case exercises.

The Bibliography contains valuable resources for the project manager. Consult the text list to gain additional information about the topics mentioned in this book.

Managing Multiple Projects

In most management problems there are too many possibilities to expect experience, judgment, or intuition to provide good guesses even with perfect information.

—RUSSELL L. ACKOFF

Out of intense complexities intense simplicities emerge.

—WINSTON CHURCHILL

Efficiency and economy imply employment of the right instrument and material as well as their right use in the right manner.

—LOUIS DEMBITZ BRANDEIS
U. S. SUPREME COURT JUSTICE

Shared Resources

Contention can exist between projects that are vying for the same set of resources. The only link between the projects is the resources they share, which could be people, equipment, space, or any combination of the three. These are limited resources that can be used only in one place at one point in time. Scheduling these resources becomes the issue. A good example is managing the systems and programming group in the IS department.

One way of envisioning the project management problem is as a matrix whose rows represent available resources and whose columns are the projects that require use of one or more of the resources. This matrix is depicted in Figure A.1. The project manager's job is to make decisions about resource use so that the project requirements for cost, time, and quality are met.

The extension to multiple projects adds a number of issues that are not present in single project management situations. For example, if the programming resource pool does not have enough hours available to meet all project requirements by the required deadlines, then one of four alternatives is available to management:

- Use slack time across projects to resolve the scheduling conflict

- Delay one or more projects

- Increase available hours in the programmer pool

- Reduce the requirements of one or more projects

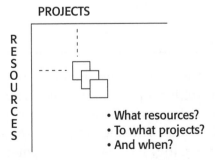

Figure A.1   A matrix visualization of the multiproject scenario.

Combinations of the three may be feasible. For example, some delay combined with additional hours in the resource pool can be less costly than any one of the strategies used by itself. In any case, all three strategies have far-reaching implications.

Enough has been written on project management to fill the Bible and the Congressional Record several times over. Despite this wealth of information, there is precious little devoted to the problems of managing multiple projects. Few would disagree that the real world is not one-dimensional (one project). Rather, we face a number of projects competing for scarce resources, narrowing windows of opportunity, and the changing demands of internal and external customers. Projects are continually added, changed, and removed in response to business activity and shifting market conditions. One thing is certain: The backlog of needed projects requires resources that exceed management's ability to provide. Of necessity, project priority changes as any one of a number of parameters change. Out of this seeming chaos project managers and resource managers are expected to create order.

This appendix discusses a number of considerations arising in multiple project management situations. It is not the purpose here to present solutions to all issues raised (although some are recommended). Rather, we attempt to raise the level of awareness and appreciation among those who must contend with these difficult situations.

It must be clear at the outset that this book does not cover *program management*. Program management is a special case of multiproject management. It has a single goal or purpose (put a man on the moon), whereas multiproject management treats the case of independent multiple goals (develop a client/server-based distribution system, install a new CIM package, and update the marketing information system).

Organizational Considerations

The matrix structure, or some hybrid of it, is the preferred organizational form for planning and controlling multiple projects. The traditional functional structure does not provide the necessary project management oversight required by today's businesses and is somewhat contrary to the trend toward right-sizing, worker empowerment, and business process management. Organizations try to shorten time to market, and the functional structure tends to work counter to that. While the pure project structure greatly simplifies resource scheduling, it is easily seen as an inefficient resource utilization. Resources committed to one project can be underutilized, and no formal mechanism exists to share excess capacity with other projects. The resulting cost inefficiencies are obvious. We could give examples of large projects in which the project structure has worked well; in general, though, these are the exception rather than the rule.

The matrix structure has both advantages and disadvantages, already discussed in this book. The matrix form is generally preferred in those organizations in which projects are an important component of departmental activity and where change and adaptability are expected.

There are two hybrids of the matrix structure. The first occurs in those organizations in which the project managers and resource managers report to the same manager. This variation is interesting because some of the political and decision-making situations that arise in the pure matrix structure do not exist here. The fact that one operational-level manager has a span of control that encompasses the projects and the resources that are scheduled to work on the projects means that scheduling revisions and project priority decisions are vested in the same individual. Obviously much of the politics can be avoided in this case.

The other hybrid arises when user managers function as project managers. As you move to client/server architectures and applications development at the user level, the project manager is more likely to come from the ranks of the user community. Although this brings a lot of political baggage and fairly intense negotiation situations, it does have a number of advantages. The most significant advantage is a much lower risk of project failure than the other hybrid. User managers will want the project to succeed. After all, the manager's reputation is on the line as is the success of his or her functional area. A related advantage is user buy-in. Commitment as project manager and buy-in as user go hand in hand.

The major disadvantages for this hybrid structure occur in those organizations in which the user manager accepts the role of project manager in name only. The user manager's deferring to the team members and not really taking a leadership role usually signal this. This often happens in cases in which senior management has not made a visible sign of endorsement and commitment to the project.

Of more recent vintage is the *self-directed work team* (SDWT). Peter Drucker, in a 1988 article in the *Harvard Business Review* ("The Coming of the New Organization," January/February 1988, pp. 45-53), writes of the emergence of a new organizational structure. It is based on information, rather than the command and control structures that have dominated the business landscape since the turn of the century. Drucker argues for a leaner organization—one in which several layers of management are no longer needed because of easy access to information for everyone on an as-needed basis. This article is required reading for any senior manager trying to redesign his or her organization to support the systems that are oriented to business processes rather than business functions. As the organization looks to improve customer service and empower the work force, the notion of the SDWT coupled with Drucker's task force begins to make good sense.

A typical organizational structure that supports these ideas was discussed earlier in the book. The functional areas are support to the *self-directed project teams* (SDPT). They provide highly technical consulting and training, as requested. All SDPTs are self-contained in terms of the technology and business knowledge required to complete their work. It is important to note that SDPT members must be multidisciplined. In the ideal all team members can perform any task required of the team. This is a marked departure from the current notion of specialization characteristics of all other organizational structures. The migration toward SDPTs does not appear to be an option. As organizations consider a customer-services orientation and a worker empowerment philosophy, they will come to realize that the SDPT, or some hybrid of it, is the only organizational design that makes sense given the current business landscape.

Staffing Considerations

The notion of a *learning organization* as described by Peter Senge in his book, *The Fifth Discipline* (New York: Doubleday/Currency, 1990), is quite compatible with good project management in the organization that uses a matrix or SDPT structure. Staff development has always been an issue, and with the migration away from centralized mainframe to client/server architectures, training and staff development are on the list of critical success factors. Of paramount importance is how to address the growing skills gap. The skills gap problem is further exacerbated by the focus on business processes rather than business functions. Information systems professionals soon realize that their skill set is lacking both in technology and business process knowledge.

In a matrix organization the managers of staff resources are responsible for developing the skill set in their staff that is required by the organization through the projects that it authorizes. Let's not overlook the fact that the project is a good vehicle for staff development. Researchers have concluded that the job itself is the most influential motivator of information technology professionals. Challenge, opportunity for advancement, and recognition head the list of job design parameters that contribute to motivation. Those who manage staff resources might examine the inventory of staff and their skills, then assign the individual whose skill set almost matches requirements. The needed skills will be developed in conjunction with the project task—just-in-time training. In choosing these types of on-the-job training assignments, care must be exercised so that the project is not exposed to greater risk because of the assignment. Obviously, critical path activities are not open to such assignments.

The project manager may not be all that willing to accept that model. His or her priority is to get the project done on time, within budget, and according to specification. The project manager is not particularly interested in the need for staff development unless it contributes directly to his or her ability to successfully complete their project.

Project-Related Considerations

There are two cases to consider. The first and most common situation is one where the resource pool is shared across multiple projects. In this case the projects are linked through one or more of the resources they share. For example, they both can require the services of a telecommunications expert. When the scheduled use of a common resource on one project conflicts with the scheduled use of that same resource on one or more other projects, the dependency becomes quite obvious and the resource manager must resolve the impasse.

The second case involves a dependency between the schedule of two or more projects. The scheduled start date of an activity in one project can depend on the actual finish date of an activity in another project. There can be multiple dependencies. These dependencies are particularly significant when the completion date of the predecessor activity in one project affects the start date of a successor activity in another project and that successor activity is on the critical path. In such cases, an early finish date on the predecessor activity is music to the ears of the successor activity manager. Further issues deal with who owns the slack on the predecessor activity. For any successor activities that are on the critical path, the manager of the successor activity and the manager of the associated project will make a strong argument for claiming ownership of the slack.

Even in the simplest of cases (say, two projects), the problem of resource scheduling could be intractable. The problem is exacerbated in cases in which resources are required on critical path activities of two projects whose schedules overlap. Let's step back from these multiple project scheduling problems and examine them in an orderly way.

Figure A.2, Multiple Project Situation, graphically displays the multiple project resource situation. The area of the triangle represents the collective specifications of currently scheduled projects. The sides of the triangle represent the budget, time, and resource available in the department to complete the currently scheduled projects. If a new project is requested, or if changes to an existing one are made, the area enclosed by the three sides must be able to accommodate the request; otherwise, one of four things must happen:

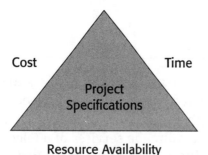

Figure A.2   Multiple project situation.

- The request can be accommodated without affecting the completion date of the changed project or the completion dates of any other scheduled projects. This is what they mean when they say you dodged a bullet!

- The request can be accommodated, but the scheduled completion of the changed project will be affected.

- The request can be accommodated, but the scheduled completion of the changed project and at least one other project will be affected. Get ready for some heated negotiations!

- The request cannot be accommodated with existing time, budget, and resources. A scope change of one or more projects may be required.

All but the first case requires negotiations between the project manager, the requesting unit, resource managers, and other project managers. This is not strange turf for any of these managers. It happens in all multiple project environments. More basic to the situation is how to determine exactly which of these four situations characterizes the issue at hand. The analysis is obviously complex for a variety of reasons:

- Problems are not well defined.

- There is no orderly way of examining alternatives.

- The solution requires sophisticated computer support.

- Alternatives will violate budget, time, resources, and/or specifications on one or more projects.

- Alternatives will have to be ranked.

The typical project management software tools provide some analytic support. Unfortunately, little is offered in the way of methodology. Managers are left to search the solution space in the absence of a search strategy.

Unfortunately, there is no corresponding version of the critical path for multiple projects. Furthermore, it is unlikely that any manual process could be found to solve the scheduling or schedule update problem. There is, however, an expert system solution. One software tool from Euridite Corporation offers a solution. The package is called Sagacity and is described in a recent book by Richard E. Westney, *Computerized*

Management of Multiple Small Projects (New York, NY: Marcel Dekker, 1992). Sagacity uses an expert systems approach called assignment modeling. Sagacity interacts with the decision maker to propose resource scheduling alternatives for multiple project scheduling problems. The system requires the decision maker to specify a series of prioritization rules based on a user-supplied criteria. The rules are generally duration-driven or effort-driven. Duration-driven rules calculate the total work hours of effort using inputs on the duration and inputs on the total work effort required and then calculate the resources required and activity duration. Sagacity uses user-determined prioritization rules to sequentially schedule projects based on their relative priority. The system can be used to establish initial project schedules as well as to update existing project schedules.

Slack Management

The first strategy for the project manager or the manager of project managers is to examine the available slack. In the case of a single project the available slack was embedded within the project, but in the case of multiple projects the slack is distributed across several projects. The project manager will have to look for opportunities to reschedule start and end dates for activities to make the slack available to other projects. Alternatively, the project manager might use slack time to train others in the skills needed to resolve the conflict. As in the case of single projects, the project manager will want to exhaust all possibilities before going to upper management with a request for additional resources, extended deadlines, or reduced project requirements.

Project Delay

Imposing project delays can affect customer relations, cause severe financial penalties for missed deadlines, affect other projects that are dependent on timely completion of the subject projects, and increase the risk of not meeting customer requirements. In deciding whether this strategy makes sense, management will have to weigh penalties for a delay in one project or some combination of projects. Before reaching a decision of this scope, the project managers will have to exhaust other possibilities for using slack time for noncritical path activities to resolve conflicts.

Strategic and Tactical Issues

There are strategic issues that project managers cannot resolve:

- What data and information are needed by senior management for strategic decision making?
- How do I communicate clearly to stakeholders?
- How do I decide which projects to delay, given insufficient resources to meet cost, time, and specification constraints?
- How do I determine the training and hiring mix for developing and inventorying staff skills?
- What are the strategic planning issues over the project management life cycle?

These are issues that must be dealt with at a higher level. In some cases, the manager of the project managers can suggest alternative strategies. In the final analysis the client will take part in the decision. This will occur for certain if the projects are for internal clients. When the projects are for external clients, their involvement may not be perfunctory. That is, the performance contract will often include penalty clauses for late completion or out-of-specification deliverables. The strategic decision will follow from a weighing of tangible (financial) and intangible (customer relations) factors.

There are tactical issues that will generally be settled at the middle-manager level (manager of project managers, resource managers, project managers):

- How do I identify interproject dependencies and their impact on project completion?
- How do I schedule my resources across projects?
- How do I add new projects to an existing schedule of projects?
- How do I determine the percentage of resources to allocate to projects and the percentage to contingencies?
- When do I use automated tools for planning and/or control?

We have just introduced the topic of multiple project management. Unfortunately, there is little in the theory and applications of project management to help the project manager with multiple project situations. Some project management software packages offer some help in resource scheduling and reporting, but only in terms of *what-if* functionality.

What's on the CD-ROM

The Companion CD-ROM accompanying the text contains two groups of exercises, one for each project example used in the book. The purpose of the exercises is to provide you with some examples of different situations that occur during the life span of most projects. The examples also provide some insight into the reports, graphs, and tables provided by Microsoft Project. Adobe Acrobat Reader 4.0 and Microsoft Project 2000 120-day Trial Edition are also included on the CD-ROM for your convenience.

The exercises are provided in Adobe PDF format and while any one of them may be opened independently, a table of contents is provided in the PDF file name *Office Supplies* for the first case presented in the book and *Gold* for the examples in the second case study.

When using the examples there are several conventions used to help you navigate. On each screen are hotspots. Placing the cursor over these hotspots causes the standard cursor to change into a hand or arrowhead. Clicking when the cursor is active will bring you to the next screen in sequence for the exercise.

There are several options provided on the displayed screen to navigate to other locations. The Return arrow in the lower left hand corner will send you back to the screen you just came from. Clicking on the EXIT icon, if present, will terminate the session and bring you back to the desktop.

There may be icons displaying an Astrolabe. The Astrolabe is an ancient navigational instrument used by mariners. There are two types of icons used in the exercises. The Gold Astrolabe will bring you back to the Table of Contents for the examples you are viewing. The Bronze Astrolabe will bring you to other locations within the current example.

On some screens yellow sticky notes may be displayed. These notes are usually found as responses to a YES or NO selection you have made. When one of these notes appear you can remove it from the screen by placing the cursor over the note and clicking. If you want to view the note again just make the same YES or NO selection.

The PDF file is set to provide a Full Screen view of the screens. To exit this mode press the Esc key on your keyboard. When in the Adobe reader all the functions normally available from Adobe are active. You can move from screen to screen using the paging facility, however this is not recommended as the order of the exercise screens is not sequential. Using the Adobe page function will not follow the logical sequence of the exercise.

Most of the screens were created using a standard screen capture software product. The PDF file was created on a 17″ monitor set at 800 by 600 pixel resolution. If the screen shots are difficult to view on your monitor, try changing the resolution of your desktop. Also the screens are displayed at Full Screen size. Adobe should adjust your desktop to accommodate this display setting. If the setting is unnatural for your monitor, try resetting using either your desktop resolution or the Adobe screen controls such as ZOOM or other window definition modes provided under the VIEW menu bar. Remember to press the Esc key to exit Full Screen mode and display the Adobe Reader screen format and control.

The software accompanying this book is being provided as is without warranty or support of any kind. Should you require basic installation assistance, or if your media is defective, please call our product support number at (212) 850-6194 weekdays between 9 am and 4 pm Eastern Standard Time. Or, we can be reached via e-mail at: **wprtusw@wiley.com**.

To place additional orders or to request information about other Wiley products, please call (800) 879-4539.

Bibliography

Ignorance never settles a question.

—BENJAMIN DISRAELI
ENGLISH PRIME MINISTER

Those who have read of everything are thought to understand everything, too; but it is not always so—reading furnishes the mind only with materials of knowledge; it is thinking that makes what is read ours. We are of the ruminating kind, and it is not enough to cram ourselves with a great load of collections; unless we chew them over again, they will not give us strength and nourishment.

JOHN LOCKE

Project Management References

The following listed books are a collection of current publications from our project management libraries. Some are dated but are written by leaders in our field or have a particularly valuable contribution to the literature and are classics. They will be of particular interest to professionals who have project management responsibilities, are members of project teams, or simply have a craving to learn about the basics of sound project management. The focus of many of the books is systems and software development, because that is our primary interest, although several also treat the basic concepts and principles of project management. We have also included books on closely related topics, which we have found to be of value in researching and writing this book. You might find value in them, too.

Adams, John R., C. Richard Bilbro, and Timothy C. Stockert. 1989. *An Organization Development Approach to Project Management.* Upper Darby, PA: Project Management Institute.

Adams, John R. and Bryan W. Campbell. 1990. *Roles and Responsibilities of the Project Manager.* Upper Darby, PA: Project Management Institute.

Baker, Sunny and Kim Baker. 1998. *The Complete Idiot's Guide to Project Management.* New York, NY: Alpha Books. (ISBN 0-02-861745-2)

Bennatan, E. M. 1992. *On Time, Within Budget: Software Project Management Practices and Techniques.* Wellesley, MA: QED Publishing Group. (ISBN 0-89435-408-6)

Block, R. 1983. *The Politics of Projects.* New York, NY: Yourdon Press.

Block, Thomas R. and J. Davidson Frame. 1998. *The Project Office.* Upper Darby, PA: Project Management Institute. (ISBN 1-56052-443-X)

Burman, J. 1972. *Precedence Networks for Project Planning and Control.* New York, NY: McGraw-Hill. (ISBN 0-07-010719-X)

Burr, Adrian and Mal Owen. 1996. *Statistical Methods for Software Quality.* London, England: International Thomson Computer Press. (ISBN 1-85032-171-X)

Cable, Dwayne P. and John R. Adams. 1989. *Organizing for Project Management.* Upper Darby, PA: Project Management Institute.

Cable, Dwayne P. and John R. Adams. 1997. *Principles of Project Management.* Upper Darby, PA: Project Management Institute. (ISBN 1-880410-30-3)

Capper, Richard. 1998. *A Project-by-Project Approach to Quality*. Hampshire, England: Gower Publishing Limited. (ISBN 0566079259)

CH2Mhill. 1996. *Project Delivery System: A System and Process for Benchmark Performance*. Denver, CO: CH2Mhill. (ISBN 0-9652616-0-3)

Chang, Richard Y. 1994. *Continuous Process Improvement*. Irvine, CA: Richard Chang Associates. (ISBN 1-883553-06-7)

Chang, Richard Y. 1995. *Process Reengineering in Action*. Irvine, CA: Richard Chang Associates. (ISBN 1-883553-16-4)

Chang, Richard Y. and Paul De Young. 1995. *Measuring Organizational Improvement Impact*. Irvine, CA: Richard Chang Associates. (ISBN 1-883553-17-2)

Chang Richard Y. and P. Keith Kelly. 1994. *Improving Through Benchmarking*. Irvine, CA: Richard Chang Associates. (ISBN 1-883553-08-3)

Chang, Richard Y. and Matthew E. Niedzwiecki. 1993. *Continuous Improvement Tools Vol I*. Irvine, CA: Richard Chang Associates. (ISBN 1-883553-00-8)

Chang, Richard Y. and Matthew E. Niedzwiecki. 1993. *Continuous Improvement Tools Vol II*. Irvine, CA: Richard Chang Associates. (ISBN 1-883553-01-6)

Chapman, Chris and Stephen Ward. 1997. *Project Risk Management: Processes, Techniques and Insights*. New York, NY: John Wiley & Sons. (ISBN 0-471-95804-2)

Charette, Robert N. 1989. *Software Engineering Risk Analysis and Management*. New York, NY: Intertext Publications/Multiscience Press, Inc. (ISBN 0-07-010719-X)

Cleland, David I., et al. 1998. *Project Management Casebook*. Upper Darby, PA: Project Management Institute. (ISBN 1-880410-45-1)

Cleland, David I., et al. 1998. *Project Management Casebook: Instructor's Manual*. Upper Darby, PA: Project Management Institute. (ISBN 1-880410-45-1)

Cleland, D. I. and W. R. King, eds. 1983. *Project Management Handbook*. New York, NY: Van Nostrand Reinhold.

Clifton, D. S. 1975. *Project Feasibility Analysis*. New York, NY: John Wiley & Sons.

DeGrace, Peter and Leslie Hulet Stahl. 1990. *Wicked Problems, Righteous Solutions*. Englewood Cliffs, NJ: Yourdon Press Computing Series. (ISBN 0-13-590126-X)

Dekom, Anton K. 1994. *Practical Project Management*. New York, NY: Random House Business Division. (ISBN 0-394-55077-3)

DeMarco, T. 1982. *Controlling Software Projects*. New York, NY: Yourdon Press.

DeMarco, T. and T. Lister. 1987. *Peopleware, Productive Projects and Teams*. New York, NY: Dorsett house Publishing. (ISBN 0-932633-05-6)

Fleming, Quentin W. 1992. *Cost/Schedule Control Systems Criteria*. Chicago, IL: Probus Publishing Company. (ISBN 1-55738-289-1)

Fleming, Quentin W., John Bronn, and Gary C. Humphreys. 1987. *Project & Production Scheduling*. Chicago, IL: Probus Publishing. (ISBN 0-917253-63-9)

Fleming, Quentin W. and Quentin J. Fleming. 1993. *Subcontract Planning and Organization*. Chicago, IL: Probus Publishing Company. (ISBN 1-55738-463-0)

Frame, J. Davidson. 1987. *Managing Projects in Organizations*. San Francisco, CA: Jossey-Bass Publishers.

Frame, J. Davidson. 1994. *The New Project Management*. San Francisco, CA: Jossey-Bass Publishers. (ISBN 1-55542-662-X)

Gilbreath, Robert D. 1986. *Winning at Project Management: What Works, What Fails, and Why*. New York, NY: John Wiley & Sons. (ISBN 0-471-83910-8)

Goldberg, Adele and Kenneth S. Rubin. 1995. *Succeeding with Objects: Decsion Frameworks for Project Management*. Reading, MA: Addison-Wesley Publishing. (ISBN 0-201-62878-3)

Goldratt, Eliyahu M. 1997. *Critical Chain*. Great Barrington, MA: The North River Press. (ISBN 0-88427-153-6)

Goldratt, Eliyahu M. (1992). "The Goal: A Process of Ongoing Improvement." Great Barrington, MA: The North River Press. (ISBN 0-88427-061-0)

Grady, Robert B. 1992. *Practical Software Metrics for Project Management and Process Improvement*. Englewood Cliffs, NJ: Prentice Hall. (ISBN 0-13-720384-5)

Grady, Robert B. and Deborah L. Caswell. 1987. *Software Metrics: Establishing a Company-Wide Program*. Englewood Cliffs, NJ: Prentice-Hall, Inc. (ISBN 0-13-821844-7)

Graham, Robert J. and Randall L. Englund. 1997. *Creating an Environment for Successful Projects*. San Francisco, CA: Jossey-Bass Publishers. (ISBN 0-7879-0359-0

Greer, Michael. 1996. *The Project Manager's Partner: A Step-by-Step Guide to Project Management*. Amherst, MA: HRD Press, Inc. (ISBN 0-087425-397-7)

Grey, Stephen. 1995. *Practical Risk Assessment for Project Management*, Chichester, England: John Wiley & Sons, Ltd. (ISBN 0-471-93979-X)

Hackos, JoAnn T. 1994. *Managing Your Documentation Projects*. New York, NY: John Wiley & Sons, Inc. (ISBN 0-471-59099-1)

Harrison, F. L. 1984. *Advanced Project Management*. New York, NY: John Wiley & Sons.

Haynes, Marion E. 1989. *Project Management: From Idea to Implementation*. Los Altos, CA: Crisp Publications. (ISBN 0-931961-75-0)

Hetzel, Bill. 1993. *Making Software Measurement Work*. New York, NY: John Wiley & Sons, Inc. (ISBN 0-471-56568-7)

Hiltz, Mark J. 1994. *Project Management Handbook of Checklists Volume 1: Conceptual/Definition and Project Initiation*. Ontario, Canada: Mark-Check Publishing. (ISBN0-9697202-2-X)

Hiltz, Mark J. 1994. *Project Management Handbook of Checklists Volume 2: Organizations/Communications/Management*. Ontario, Canada: Mark-Check Publishing. (ISBN0-9697202-3-8)

Hiltz, Mark J. (1994). *Project Management Handbook of Checklists Volume 3: Project Planning and Control*. Ontario, Canada: MarkCheck Publishing (ISBN0-9697202-4-6)

Hiltz, Mark J. 1994. *Project Management Handbook of Checklists Volume 4: Implementation/Termination*. Ontario, Canada: MarkCheck Publishing. (ISBN0-9697202-5-4)

Hoare, H. R. 1973. *Project Management Using Network Analysis*. New York, NY: McGraw-Hill.

House, Ruth Sizemore. 1988. *The Human Side of Project Management*. Reading, MA: Addison-Wesley.

Humphrey, Watts S. 1997. *Managing Technical People*. Reading, MA: Addison-Wesley. (ISBN 0-201-54597-7)

Huston, Charles L. 1996. *Management of Project Procurement*. New York, NY: The McGraw-Hill Companies, Inc. (ISBN 0-07-030552-8)

Ireland, Lewis R. 1991. *Quality Management for Projects and Programs*. Upper Darby, PA: Project Management Institute. (ISBN 1-880410-11-7)

Johnson, James R. 1991. *The Software Factory: Managing Software Development and Maintenance*. Wellesley, MA: QED Information Sciences, Inc. (ISBN 0-89435-348-9)

Johnston, Andrew K. 1995. *A Hacker's Guide to Project Management*. Oxford, England: Butterworth-Heinemann Ltd. (ISBN 0-7506-2230-X)

Kerzner, Harold. 1982. *Project Management for Executives*. New York, NY: Van nostrand Reinhold.

Kerzner, Harold. 1984. *Project Management: A Systems Approach to Planning, Scheduling and Controlling*. New York, NY: Van Nostrand Reinhold.

Kerzner, Harold. 1998. *In Search of Excellence in Project Management*. New York, NY: Van Nostrand Reinhold. (ISBN 0-442-02706-0)

King, David. 1992. *Project Management Made Simple*. Englewood Cliffs, NJ: Yourdon Press Computing Series. (ISBN 0-13-717729-1)

Kliem, Ralph L. and Irwin S. Ludin. 1997. *Reducing Project Risk*. Hampshire, England: Gower Publishing Limited. (ISBN 0-566-07799-X)

Kolluru, Steven, et al. 1996. *Risk Assessment and Management Handbook For Environmental, Health, and Safety Professionals*. New York, NY: McGraw-Hill, Inc. (ISBN 0-07-035987-3)

Kyle, Mackenzie. 1998. *Making It Happen: A Non-Technical Guide to Project Management*. Toronto, Canada: John Wiley & Sons, Canada Ltds. (ISBN 0-471-64234-7)

Lewis, James P. 1993. *The Project Manager's Desk Reference*. Chicago, IL: Probus Publishing. (ISBN 1-55738-461-4)

Lewis, James P. 1995. *Project Planning, Scheduling & Control*. Chicago, IL: Irwin. (ISBN 1-55738-869-5)

Lientz, Bennet P. and Kathryn P. Rea. 1995. *Project Management for the 21st Century*. New York, NY: Academic Press. (ISBN 0-12-449965-5)

Maguire, Steve. 1994. *Debugging the Development Process*. Redmond, WA: Microsoft Press. (ISBN 1-55615-650-2)

McConnell, Steve. 1996. *Rapid Development*. Redmond, WA: Microsoft Press. (ISBN 1-55615-900-5)

McConnell, Steve. 1998. *Software Project Survival Guide*. Redmond, WA: Microsoft Press. (ISBN 1-57231-621-7)

Megill, Robert E. 1984. *An Introduction to Risk Analysis*. Tulsa, OK: PennWell Books. (ISBN0-87814-257-6)

Meredith, Jack R. and Samuel J. Mantel, Jr. 1989. *Project Management: A Managerial Approach*. New York, NY: John Wiley & Sons.

Meyer, Christopher. 1993. *Fast Cycle Time: How to Align Purpose, Strategy, and Structure for Speed*. New York, NY: Free Press. (ISBN0-02-921181-6)

Michaels, Jack V. 1996. *Technical Risk Management*. Upper Saddle River, NJ: Prentice Hall. (ISBN 0-13-155756-4)

Miller, Dennis. 1994. *Visual Project Planning & Scheduling*. Boca Raton, FL: The 15th Street Press. (ISBN 0-9640630-1-8)

Moder, J. J. 1983. *Project Management with CPM, Pert, and Precedence Diagramming*. New York, NY: Van Nostrand Reinhold.

Muller, Robert J. 1998. *Productive Objects: An Applied Software Project Management Framework*. San Francisco, CA: Morgan Kaufmann Publishers, Inc. (ISBN 1-55860-437-5)

Norris, Mark, Peter Rigby, and Malcolm Payne. 1993. *The Healthy Software Project: A Guide to Successful Development and Management*. Chichester, England: John Wiley & Sons, Ltd. (ISBN 0-471-94042-9)

Page-Jones, Meilir. 1985. *Practical Project Management: Restoring Quality to DP Projects and Systems*. New York, NY: Dorsett House Publishing. (ISBN 0-932633-00-5)

Palisades Corp. 1994. *Risk Analysis & Modeling @Risk*. Newfield, NY: Palisades Corporation.

Pinto, Jeffrey K. 1998. *Project Management Handbook*. San Francisco, CA: Jossey-Bass Publishers. (ISBN 0-7879-4013-5)

Pressman, Roger S. 1988. *Making Software Engineering Happen: A Guide for Instituting the Technology*. Englewood Cliffs, NJ: Prentice Hall. (ISBN 0-13-547738-7)

Pritchett, Price and Brian Muirhead. 1998. *The Mars Pathfinder: Approach to Faster-Better-Cheaper*. Dallas, TX: Price Pritchett & Associates (ISBN 0-944002-74-9)

Project Management Institute. 1996. *A Guide to the Project Management Body of Knowledge*. Upper Darby, PA: Project Management Institute.

Project Management Institute. 1996. *Project Management Salary Survey*. Upper Darby, PA: Project Management Institute.

Project Management Institute. 1997. *The PMI Book of Project Management Forms*. Upper Darby, PA: Project Management Institute.

Project Management Institute. 1999. *Project Management Software Survey*. Newton Square, PA: Project Management Institute. (ISBN 1-880410-52-4)

Putnam, Lawrence H., and Ware Myers. 1992. *Measures for Excellence: Reliable Software On Time, Within Budget*. Englewood Cliffs, NJ: Yourdon Press Computing Series. (ISBN 0-13-56794-3)

Raferty, John. 1994. *Risk Analysis in Project Management*. London, England: E&FN SPON. (ISBN 0-419-18420-1)

Randolph, W. Allen and Barry Z. Posner. 1988. *Effective Project Planning & Management: Getting the Job Done*. Englewood Cliffs, NJ: Prentice Hall. (ISBN 0-13-244815-7)

Raynus, Joseph. 1999. *Software Process Improvement with CMM*. Boston, MA: Artech House. (ISBN 0-89006-644-2)

Roetzheim, William H. 1988. *Structured Computer Project Management*. Englewood Cliffs, NJ: Prentice Hall. (ISBN 0-13-853532-9)

Royce, Walker. 1998. *Software Project Management: A Unified Framework*. Reading, MA: Addison-Wesley. (ISBN 0-201-30958-0)

Saylor, James H. 1996. *TQM Simplified: A Practical Guide*. New York, NY: McGraw-Hill. (ISBN 0-07-057678-5)

Smith, Preston G., and Donald Reinertsen. 1991. *Developing Products in Half the Time*. New York, NY: Van Nostrand Reinhold. (ISBN 0-442-00243-2)

Stuckenbruck, Linn C., ed. 1981. *The Implementation of Project Management: The Professional's Handbook*. Reading, MA: Addison-Wesley Publishing Company. (ISBN 0-201-07260-2)

Thomsett, Michael C. 1990. *The Little Black Book of Project Management*. New York, NY: Amacom. (ISBN 0-8144-7732-1)

Thomsett, R. 1993. *Third Wave Project Management*. Englewood Cliffs, NJ: Yourdon Press Computing Series. (ISBN 0-13-915299-7)

Toney, Frank and Ray Powers. 1997. *Best Practices of Project Management Groups in Large Functinal Organizations*. Upper Darby, PA: Project Management Institute. (ISBN 1-880410-05-2)

Turner, W. S. III. 1980. *Project Auditing Methodology*. Amsterdam: North Holland.

Turtle, Quentin C. 1994. *Implementing Concurrent Project Management*. Englewood Cliffs, NJ: Prentice Hall. (ISBN 0-13-302001-0)

Vijay, Verma K. 1995. *Organizing Projects for Success*. Upper Darby, PA: Project Management Institute. (ISBN 1-880410-40-0)

Vijay, Verma, K. 1996. *Human Resource Skills for the Project Manager*. Newton Square, PA: Project Management Institute. (ISBN 1-880410-41-9)

Vijay, Verma K. 1997. *Managing the Project Team*. Upper Darby, PA: Project Management Institute. (ISBN 1-880410-42-7)

Weiss, Joseph W. and Robert K. Wysocki. 1992. *5-Phase Project Management: A Practical Planning and Implementation Guide*. Reading, MA: Addison-Wesley. (ISBN 0-201-56316-9)

Westney, Richard E. 1992. *Computerized Management of Multiple Small Projects*. New York, NY: Marcel Dekker. (ISBN 0-8247-8645-9)

Wheelwright, Steven C. and Kim B. Clark. 1992. *Revolutionizing Product Development: Quantum Leaps in Speed, Efficiency, and Quality*. New York, NY: The Free Press. (ISBN 0-02-905515-6)

Wheelwright, Steven C. and Kim B. Clark. 1995. *Leading Product Development: The Senior Manager's Guide to Creating and Shaping the Enterprise*. New York, NY: The Free Press. (ISBN 0-02-934465-4)

Whitten, Neal. 1990. *Managing Software Development Projects*. New York, NY: John Wiley & Sons. (ISBN 0-471-51255-9)

Wideman, R. Max. 1992. *Project & Program Risk Management: A Guide to Managing Project Risks & Opportunities*. Newton Square, PA: Project Management Institute. (ISBN 1-880410-06-0)

Wysocki, Robert K., Robert Beck, Jr, and David B. Crane. 1995. *Effective Project Management: How to Plan, Manage, and Deliver Projects on Time and within Budget*. New York, NY: John Wiley & Sons. (ISBN0-471-11521-5)

Zells, Lois. 1990. *Managing Software Projects: Selecting and Using PC-Based Project Management Systems*. Wellesley, MA: QED Information Sciences. (ISBN 0-89435-275-X)

Index

A

Acceptance, in project closeouts, 303–304
Accuracy, of progress reports, 272–273
Actions, in objective statements, 118
Activities, 105–106
   assigning staff to, 168–169
   crashing of, 160–162
   defined, 9–10, 65, 135
   measuring progress of, 144–145
   as parts of projects, 65–66, 139–143,
      151–154
   in project network diagrams, 179–181,
      181–196, 197–203, 203–206
   stretching of, 215–216
   in work hierarchies, 135–137, 151–154
   in work packages, 216–217
Activity duration, 106
   in case exercise, 173
   as completeness criterion, 144, 146
   defined, 10, 159
   estimates from Joint Project Planning
      session, 231
   estimating, 159–167

   Joint Project Planning sessions for
      estimating, 173–175
   percent complete and, 274
   in progress reports, 273
   in project network diagrams,
      179–181
   resource availability and, 170–172, 173
   resource loading versus, 160–162
   variation in, 162–163
   work effort versus, 159–160
Activity independence, as completeness
      criterion, 144, 146–147
Activity managers
   level of reporting detail for, 288
   at project status review meetings, 290
   work package reports for, 218–220
Activity nodes, in network diagraming,
      182–184
Activity-on-the-arrow (AOA) method, of
      network diagraming, 181–182
Activity-on-the-node (AON) method, of
      network diagraming, 182
Activity schedules, from Joint Project
      Planning sessions, 232

Actual cost of work performed (ACWP), 282–286

Adaptability, within project-driven structures, 21

Administration
of contracts, 254–255
project support offices and, 31

Aesop, 156

Agendas
for Joint Project Planning sessions, 230–231
operating rules for preparing team, 261

Agreement, in developing Conditions of Satisfaction, 110–111, 111–112

Ahead-of-schedule situations, 275

Analysis
in classifying project management competencies, 45, 47
financial, 122, 123–124
in Project Overview Statement, 122–124
of risk, 96–98, 122–123

Analysis units, in network diagraming, 182

Analytic thinking, assessing project manager's, 40

Appendixes, in project proposals, 234

Application, in classifying project management competencies, 45, 46

Approval, of Project Overview Statement, 125–128

Architectural design tool, Work Breakdown Structure as, 137

Assignability, in goal statements, 117–118

Assignment of resources
in estimating activity duration, 170–172, 173

from Joint Project Planning sessions, 232

Joint Project Planning sessions for estimating, 173–175

Assumptions, risks, obstacles part
of Project Definition Statement, 129
of Project Overview Statement, 114–115, 120–122, 125

"A Teams"
within matrix structures, 27
selection of, 248–249

Attachments, to Project Overview Statement, 122–124

Attendance
at Joint Project Planning sessions, 227–229
at project status review meetings, 289–291

Audits, after project closeouts, 306–308

Authority
in contemporary organizational environments, 29
of contracted teams, 255–256
in core team selection, 251
in task forces, 19

Autonomy, as motivator, 244

Avoidant conflict-resolution style, 258

B

Back-end activities, in estimating activity duration, 174

Background
of project manager, 246
in project proposals, 233

Backward pass, in scheduling, 191, 194

Balanced matrix structures, 27–28

Balanced systems
 for control, 267–268
 defined, 8–9
Baseline versus actual cost curve, 282, 283
Behind-schedule situations, 275–276
Best-practices constraints, in network diagramming, 187
Between-function problems, within functional structures, 23
Binary assessment, of skills, 169
Bloom's Taxonomy of Educational Objectives–Cognitive Domain, for classifying project management competencies, 45–49
Boredom, as demotivator, 243
Bottom-line impact statement, in Project Overview Statement, 119
Bottom-up approach, to generating Work Breakdown Structure, 141–142
Boundary-less organizations, 18
Boundedness, as completeness criterion, 144, 145. *See also* Project boundaries
Brainstorming, in generating Work Breakdown Structure, 141
 operating rules for, 259–260
Break-even analysis, in Project Overview Statement, 124
"B Teams," selection of, 248–249
Budgeted cost of work performed (BCWP), 282–286
Budgeted cost of work scheduled (BCWS), 282–286
Budgets, for projects, 67, 70, 275
Buffers, in critical chain project management, 202
Business awareness, of project managers, 39

Business competencies, of project managers, 38, 39
Business environment, in classifying projects, 34–35
Business function approach, in building Work Breakdown Structure, 151
Business partnership, assessing project manager's, 39
Business processes, in process quality management, 93–95
Business skills, required of project managers, 49
Business targeting, by project managers, 33–34
Business value, in project classification, 74–76
Buzan Centre, 142

C

Cancellation, of contracts, 255
Candidate list of risk drivers, 97
Career-path programs, 51–52. *See also* Project manager career path model
 within project-driven structures, 21
 in project management, 6–7
 project manager classification and, 36–37
 task forces and, 20
Career planning, 50–52
Careers
 jobs versus, 15
 task forces and, 20
Causal relationships, in Project Overview Statement, 122
CD-ROM, case exercises on, 12, 130–132, 155, 173, 203, 221, 299

Celebration of success, after project closeouts, 309–310

Center for Project Management, 34–35

Ceremonial acceptance, in project closeouts, 303

Challenge, as motivator, 242–243

Change, 5–6. *See also* Planning
after closeout, 304–305
contracted teams and, 251
controlling unplanned, 294–298
in project planning, 80–81
scope triangle and, 72–74

Change control, 291–294

Change control form, 295

Change management, 89–90, 294–298

Change requests, outcomes of, 292–294

Checks and balances, within functional structures, 24

Clarification, in developing Conditions of Satisfaction, 110–111

Clients. *See also* Customers
approval of Project Overview Statement by, 126, 128
at Joint Project Planning sessions, 228–229
in post-implementation audits, 307
in project classification, 35
in project closeouts, 90, 303–304
project managers and, 33
at project status review meetings, 290

Closing, of contracts, 255

Closing out. *See also* Success
in new product development, 101
in project management, 76, 82–83, 85, 86, 89–90, 91
of projects, 11, 82–83, 303–310
in systems development, 100

Collaborative conflict-resolution style, 258–259

Combative conflict-resolution style, 258

Commitment
in contemporary organizational environments, 29
of contracted teams, 252
in core team selection, 249–250

Commitment to quality, assessing project manager's, 39

Common sense, project management as organized, 84

Communication
within functional structures, 23
within matrix structures, 25
project support offices and, 31

Communication skills, assessing, 43

Competencies
required of project managers, 38–47
skills versus, 37–38

Competency profiles, assessing management skills via, 38–47

Completeness criteria, for Work Breakdown Structure, 135, 141, 143–147

Completion dates
of projects, 67
shifting of, 212, 213–214

Complex activities, in projects, 66

Complexity
assessment of, 34–35
of matrix structures, 27
in project classification, 75–76
project support offices and, 31–32

Complexity Assessment Grid, 34–35
project manager classification and, 36

Comprehension
in classifying project management competencies, 45, 46

in project planning, 81
Conceptual thinking, assessing
        project manager's, 40
Conditions of Satisfaction, 128
    development of, 109–113
    in project definition, 109
    Project Overview Statement and,
        119, 125
Conflicting goals
    within matrix structures, 26
    of project and functional managers,
        239–240
Conflict resolution, operating rules
        for, 258–259
Connected activities, in projects, 66
Connected networks, 184
Consensus
    in estimating activity duration, 174
    operating rules for building, 259
Constraints
    in core team selection, 250
    in critical chain project
        management, 202
    in network diagramming, 186–190
Consultants, at Joint Project Planning
        sessions, 227, 228
Consultative decision-making model,
        257
Contemporary organizational
        environments, project
        management in, 28–30
Continuous quality management,
        91–92, 93
Contracted teams
    problems with, 252
    recruitment of, 244, 251–253
Contracts
    administration of, 254–255
    cancellation of, 255
    closing of, 255
    types of, 254

Control
    in case exercise, 299
    network diagrams in, 181
    in new product development, 101
    in project management, 76, 82, 84,
        86, 89–90, 91, 265–268
    quality versus, 268
    risk versus, 265–268
    in systems development, 100
Controlling ability, assessing project
        manager's, 43
Core project teams
    approval of Project Overview
        Statement by, 127
    at Joint Project Planning sessions,
        228
    recruitment of, 244, 247–251
Corporate Education Center, 41
Corporate initiative, in developing
        Project Overview Statement,
        116
Corporations, relationship of project
        managers to, 15. See also
        Organizations
Corrective action, via reports and
        controls, 266, 269–270, 271–272
Cost. See also Money
    percent complete and, 274
    of a project, 68, 70
    in project classification, 75–76
    in scope triangle, 71–72
    time versus, 70
Cost/benefit analysis, in Project
        Overview Statement, 124
Cost containment, 17
Cost control, 265–266
    within matrix structures, 27
    within project-driven structures, 21
    for projects, 70
Cost estimates, 172
    as completeness criteria, 144, 146

Cost performance index (CPI), 286

Cost/performance indicators, 281–286

Cost schedule control (CSC), 281–286

Cost summaries, in project proposals, 233

Cost variance (CV), 284–286

Cougar motivation survey, 241–242

Coworkers, in competency assessment, 38

Crashing an activity, 160–162

Crashpoints, of activities, 161

Creativity
control and, 267–268
as motivator, 244

Credibility, assessing project manager's, 41

Creep, in scope, 72–74

Critical chain project management (CCPM), 201–203

Critical path, in scheduling, 192

Critical path activities
in schedule compression, 197–200
in scheduling, 192, 194–196

Critical success factors (CSFs), in process quality management, 93–95

Cross-functional teams, 28. *See also* Project teams

Cultural factors, in Project Overview Statement, 122

Cumulative reports, 269

Current period reports, 269

Customer-based strategies, for change control, 296

Customer-driven organizations, 16
quality management in, 93
role of project managers in, 16–17

Customer orders, processing of, 17

Customers. *See also* Clients

approval of Project Overview Statement by, 128

changes in projects by, 293–294

at Joint Project Planning sessions, 228–229

organizations and, 16–17

in project closeouts, 303–304

at project status review meetings, 290

unplanned changes by, 295

Customer satisfaction, in Project Overview Statement, 119

Cycle times, evolution of, 5–6

D

Date constraints, in network diagramming, 186, 190

Deadlines
for progress reports, 272
for projects, 67, 70

Decision-making models, types of, 257

Decomposition, of work, 136, 138–139, 148–149, 214–215

Definition, in project management, 76, 79–80, 90–91, 109

Deliverables
as completeness criteria, 144, 145
from Joint Project Planning sessions, 231–232
in project closeouts, 303–304
in project documentation, 304–305

Delphi technique, in estimating activity duration, 163, 164–166, 167

Demotivators, 241–244

Departmental approach, in building Work Breakdown Structure, 150

Dependencies
  in network diagraming, 184–186
  in schedule compression, 198–200
Deployment facilitation, project
    support offices and, 31
Design-build-test-implement
    approach, in building Work
    Breakdown Structure,
    149–150
Design tool, Work Breakdown
    Structure as, 137
Detail, in project status reports,
    288–289
Development opportunities
  within functional structures, 23
  within matrix structures, 25, 26
  project support offices and, 31
Development tools, projects as,
    240–244
Directive decision-making model,
    257
Discretionary constraints, in network
    diagramming, 187
Documentation
  in change control, 292–294
  contents of closeout, 305–306
  from Joint Project Planning
    sessions, 232
  in project closeouts, 304–306
  reasons for, 304–305
Document of Understanding, 87
Doneness statement, in Project
    Overview Statement, 119
Double bosses, within matrix
    structures, 26
Downsizing
  and core team selection, 248
  employee empowerment after, 18
  matrix structures and, 24–25
Dual reporting, within matrix
    structures, 25

Duration. *See* Activity duration; Time
Dynamism
  of Conditions of Satisfaction,
    112–113
  of project planning, 80–81

E

Earliest finish (EF) time
  in scheduling, 192–194
  slack time and, 195, 213
Earliest start (ES) time, in scheduling,
    192–194
Early schedule, 191–192
Efficiency, in project planning, 81
Efficiency of work time, in estimating
    activity duration, 162–163
Effort creep, 73
Elapsed time, work time versus,
    159–160
Electronic commerce, in
    contemporary organizational
    environments, 30
Employees, empowerment of, 18, 19,
    20. *See also* Resources
Enterprise Information Insights, Inc.,
    41, 47
Environmental factors, in Project
    Overview Statement, 121
Equipment
  for Joint Project Planning sessions,
    230
  as project resource, 168
Estimates, 70. *See also* Cost estimates
  of activity duration, 159–167
  as completeness criteria, 144, 146
  precision of, 167
Evaluation, in classifying project
    management competencies, 45,
    47

Exception reports, 269

Execution, of project plans, 81–82. *See also* Launching

Exercises, on CD-ROM, 12, 130–132, 155, 173, 203, 221, 299

Experience, of project manager, 246

Expert advice, in estimating activity duration, 163, 164

Expertise
of contracted teams, 252
of project manager, 246–247

F

Facilitators, at Joint Project Planning sessions, 227–228

Facilities
for Joint Project Planning sessions, 230
as project resource, 168

Failure
of project managers, 37
risk and probability of, 96–98
of task forces, 20

Feasibility studies, in Project Overview Statement, 123

Feature creep, 73–74

Feedback, as motivator, 244

Feedback loops, in continuous quality management, 92, 93

Final reports, after project closeouts, 308–309

Financial analysis, in Project Overview Statement, 122, 123–124

Financial chart of accounts (CoA), in building Work Breakdown Structure, 149

Finish dates. *See* Completion dates

Finish to finish (FF) dependency, in network diagramming, 185–186

Finish to start (FS) dependency, in network diagramming, 184–185

Fish-net organizational structure, 18

5-Phase Project Management: A Practical Planning and Implementation Guide (Weiss & Wysocki), 83, 144, 265

Fixed bid contracts, 254

Flexibility
assessing project manager's, 41
in core team selection, 250
within matrix structures, 25

Float, in scheduling, 195

Flow diagrams, for project networks, 180–181

Focused labor, 159–160

Formal acceptance, in project closeouts, 304

Formal change requests, 74

40–40–20 rule, 254

Forward pass, in scheduling, 191, 193

Free slack
in resource leveling, 213
in scheduling, 195–196

Frequency, of project status reports, 274

Front-end activities, in estimating activity duration, 174

Functional decomposition, in building Work Breakdown Structure, 149

Functional managers, 23–24, 25
closeout documentation for, 305
at Joint Project Planning sessions, 229
project managers versus, 239–240

Functional matrix structures, 27
Functional silos, 16–17
Functional specification, 69
Functional structures, 23–24
Function/process managers,
    approval of Project Overview
    Statement by, 128

G

Gantt charts, 148–149, 276–277
    for project networks, 180–181
    in project proposals, 233
Gap analysis, in attaining goals,
    51–52
Gaps, 51
Geographic approach, in building
    Work Breakdown Structure, 150
Goals
    in career planning, 50–51
    of programs, 68
    of projects, 66–67, 85–87, 114–115,
    116–118
Goal statements
    in Project Overview Statement,
    116–118
    in work hierarchies, 135–136
"Gold Medallion Organ" project, 55,
    57–58
GOLD.PDF file, 130, 155, 173, 203,
    221, 299
Graphics, in reports, 265, 276–288

H

Herzberg motivation survey, 241–242
Hierarchies
    activities and tasks in work,
    135–137, 151–154

for controlling problem escalation,
    297–298
Historical data, 82–83
    in closeout documentation, 305
    cost schedule control and, 281–286
    in estimating activity duration, 163,
    164
    in final report, 308–309
    in progress reports, 273
Hope creep, 73
Hybrid organizational structures, 24

I

IBM (International Business
    Machines), Delphi technique
    at, 165
Impact anticipation
    assessing project manager's, 42
    in change control, 291–294
Implementation
    network diagrams in, 181
    of projects, 235
Independence
    as completeness criterion, 144,
    146–147
    as motivator, 244
Individuals
    in contemporary organizational
    environments, 29
    control and, 267–268
    within functional structures, 23
    within matrix structures, 26
    within project-driven structures, 21
Influence, assessing project
    manager's, 42
Information gathering, assessing
    project manager's, 40
Inherited projects, 113–114

Initial Project Definition, 87

Initial project network schedules, creating, 191–196

Initiative. *See also* Unsolicited individual initiatives

assessing project manager's, 40

in developing Project Overview Statement, 116

Innovation, within project-driven structures, 21

Installation of deliverables, in project closeout, 304

Interdependency, of subprojects, 67

Interenterprise organization, 30

Interpersonal awareness, assessing project manager's, 42

Interpersonal competencies, of project managers, 38, 42, 247

Interpersonal factors, in Project Overview Statement, 121–122

Interpersonal skills, required of project managers, 49

Interproject constraints, in network diagramming, 186, 189–190

Interruptions, effects on activity duration of, 159–160

Inventory control, in contemporary organizational environments, 30

Invitations, to Joint Project Planning sessions, 229

Invoicing, in contemporary organizational environments, 30

as motivators, 243–244

of project managers, 32–34

Joint Applications Design (JAD) sessions, 225

Joint Project Planning (JPP) sessions, 11, 105–106, 225–232

agendas for, 230–231

for analyzing project networks, 203–206

attendees at, 227–229

deliverables from, 231–232

described, 225

developing Project Overview Statement during, 124–125

equipment for, 230

for estimating activity duration and resource requirements, 173–175

facilities for, 230

generating Work Breakdown Structure during, 138–139, 143

organizing, 10

planning of, 226–227

project proposals from, 232–234

Joint Requirements Planning (JRP) sessions, 225

K

Knowledge, in classifying project management competencies, 45–46

J

Job design, as motivator, 243–244

Jobs. *See also* Work

careers versus, 15

L

Labor costs, estimating, 172

Lag variables, in network diagramming, 191

Large projects, Work Breakdown Structures for, 142–143
Late schedule, 191–192
Latest finish (LF) time
  in scheduling, 193–194
  slack time and, 195, 213
Latest start (LS) time, in scheduling, 193–194
Launching
  in new product development, 101
  in project management, 76, 81–82, 84, 86, 89
  in systems development, 100
Leadership, of project manager, 246
Learning
  in career planning, 52
  as motivator, 243
  from post-implementation audits, 307–308
  by project teams, 261–262
Length (duration), in project classification, 74–76. *See also* Activity duration; Time
Leveling resources, 209–221
  strategies for, 212–216
Level *n* activities, in work hierarchies, 135–137
Level of detail, in project status reports, 288–289
Life cycles, 61
  for new product development, 99–102
  pain curve in, 102–103
  in project management, 83–91
  for software development, 99
Listening skills, developing good, 109
Logical constraints, in network diagraming, 187–188
Logic diagrams, 180

M

Management competencies, of project managers, 38, 43–44
Management constraints, in network diagramming, 186, 188–189
Management reserve
  defined, 201
  in scheduling, 200–203
Management skills, required of project managers, 48
Managerial ability, of project manager, 247
Mandated requirements, in developing Project Overview Statement, 116
Material costs, estimating, 172
Materials, as project resource, 168
Matrix structures, 24–28
  advantages and disadvantages of, 25–27
  in management skill assessment, 47–49
  in process quality management, 93–95
  project versus functional managers and, 239–240
  types of, 27–28
Max availability, 212
Max units, 212
Measurability
  as completeness criterion, 144–145
  in goal statements, 117–118
Measures of success
  in objective statements, 118
  in post-implementation audits, 306–308
Meeting coordinators, 261
Meeting frequency, for project teams, 261

Meeting minutes, 261, 290–291
Meetings
  operating rules for team, 260–261
  for problem management, 298
  for project status review, 289–291
Mentoring, project support offices and, 31
Micro-management, activity independence and, 147
Middle management, evolution of, 6
Milestones, 278
Milestone trend charts, 278–280
MindMan software, 142, 143
Mindmapping, in generating Work Breakdown Structure, 142, 143
Minutes. *See* Meeting minutes
Mistakes, in estimating activity duration, 163
Misunderstandings, in estimating activity duration, 163
Money, as project resource, 168. *See also* Cost
Monitoring
  in case exercise, 299
  in new product development, 101
  in project management, 10, 76, 82, 84, 86, 89–90, 265–299
  in systems development, 100
Monitoring ability, assessing project manager's, 43
Morale
  within matrix structures, 26
  in task forces, 19
Most likely estimates, in three-point technique, 166
Motivation of others, by project managers, 43, 240–244
Motivation tools, projects as, 240–244
Motivators, 241–244

Mutual support, in core team selection, 250

N

Near-critical path activities, in scheduling, 196
Negative variances, 274, 275–276
Negotiation, in developing Conditions of Satisfaction, 109–113
Network diagrams, 180–181
Network organizations, 18
New products, development life cycles for, 99–102
No-earlier-than constraints, in network diagramming, 190
No-later-than constraints, in network diagramming, 190
Nonverbal behavior, 37
Norming, of project teams, 261–262
Noun-type approaches, to building Work Breakdown Structure, 148–149

O

Objectives approach, in building Work Breakdown Structure, 150
Objective statements. *See also* Project objectives
  in project management, 87
  in Project Overview Statement, 118–119
  in project proposals, 233
Obstacles, in projects, 114–115, 120–122

"Office Supplies Containment" project, 55, 57
O'Neill & Preigh, 1, 8, 9, 55–60
   business situation of, 55–56
   preparing Project Definition Statement for, 130–132
   preparing Project Overview Statement for, 130–132
   project initiatives of, 56–58
   staff of, 58–60
On-this-date constraints, in network diagramming, 190
Open-mindedness, in core team selection, 251
Operating rules, for project teams, 256–261
Optimistic estimates, in three-point technique, 166
Organization, 106
   in project management, 90–91
Organizational approaches, to building Work Breakdown Structure, 148, 150–151
Organizational awareness, assessing project manager's, 42
Organizational structures, 18–22
   contemporary, 28–30
   in core team selection, 251
   evolution of, 5
   traditional, 22–28
Organizations. See also Corporations
   customer-driven, 16–17
   task forces in, 18–20
Organized common sense, project management as, 84
Outcomes, in objective statements, 118
Outline, decomposition as, 136, 151–154
Out-of-control situations
   early detection of, 271–272

in milestone trend charts, 278–280
Outsourcing, to contracted teams, 251
Overtime, in resource leveling, 212, 214

P

Padding, in scheduling, 200
Pain curve, 102–103, 112
Parallel (SS) dependencies, in schedule compression, 198–200
Parallel processing
   in generating Work Breakdown Structure, 139
   in project planning, 81
Participative decision-making model, 257
Partitionable activities, in schedule compression, 198–200
Partnership ability, assessing project manager's, 39
"Pay me now or pay me later," in project management, 102–103
People, as project resource, 71, 168–169, 209–211
Percent complete, in progress reports, 273–274
Percent/day, in estimating activity duration, 170–172
Performance levels, reports and controls on, 265–266
Permanent task forces, 18–19
Personal competencies, of project managers, 38, 40–41
Personal skills, required of project managers, 49
Personnel, at O'Neill & Preigh, 58–60

Personnel development
assessing project manager's, 43
via projects, 240–244
Pessimistic estimates, in three-point
technique, 166
Physical decomposition, in building
Work Breakdown Structure,
148–149
Planning, 105–106
in Joint Project Planning sessions,
203–206
of Joint Project Planning sessions,
226–227
network diagrams in, 181
in new product development, 101
pain curve in, 102–103
within project-driven structures, 21
in project management, 76, 80–81,
84, 86, 87–89, 90–91, 102–103
by project managers, 32, 40
scope triangle in, 72
in systems development, 100
Planning ability, assessing project
manager's, 43
Planning tool, Work Breakdown
Structure as, 137
PMBOK. *See Project Management Body
of Knowledge* (PMBOK)
Polaris Missile Program, network
diagrams and, 181–182
Politics
in core team selection, 249
within matrix structures, 26, 27
Positive variances, 274–275
Post-implementation audits, 306–308
reasons for skipping, 308
Post-It notes, in Joint Project Planning
sessions, 204
Power balance, within matrix
structures, 27

Precedence diagramming method
(PDM), of network
diagramming, 182–184
Problem escalation, controlling,
294–298
Problem management meetings, 298
Problem/opportunity part, of Project
Overview Statement, 114–115,
115–116, 125
Process-driven organizations, 17, 29
Process orientation, of contemporary
organizational environments,
29
Process owners, 28
at Joint Project Planning sessions,
229
Process quality, 69
Process quality management, 93–95
Process quality management model
(PQMM), 93–95
Process structures, 16–17
ownership within, 28
Product-based teams, 29
Productivity, of task forces, 19
Product quality, 69
Profile, in estimating activity
duration, 170–172
Program managers, skills required of,
36, 45
Programs, as collections of projects,
68. *See also* Career-path
programs
Progress
as motivator, 244
reports and controls on, 266
Progress reporting systems, 268–276
features of, 268
graphics in, 276–288
level of detail in, 288–289
purposes of, 271–272

reports in, 268–271
updating in, 272–274
Project administrative support
    person, at project status review
    meetings, 291
Project boundaries, 141, 150–151. *See
    also* Boundedness
Project champion
  at Joint Project Planning sessions,
    227, 229
  at project status review meetings,
    290
Project change requests, 291–292
Project Definition Statement (PDS),
    129–132, 226
  Project Overview Statement and,
    121
Project-driven organizations, 20–22
Project-driven structures, 21–22
  advantages and disadvantages of,
    21
Project goals part, of Project
    Overview Statement, 114–115,
    116–118, 125
Project impact statements, 291, 292
Project management, 1, 8, 32–34. *See
    also* Scheduling
  approval of Project Overview
    Statement in, 125–128
  closing projects in, 82–83
  control in, 82
  critical chain, 201–203
  defined, 9
  evolution of, 5–6
  execution in, 81–82
  five phases of, 83–84, 84–90
  within functional structures, 23–24
  hope creep and, 73
  implementation of projects in, 235
  levels of, 90–91

life cycles in, 83–91
within matrix structures, 24–28, 26
other methodologies versus, 99–102
pain curve in, 102–103
planning in, 80–81
principles of, 79–83
processes in, 76
as profession, 6–7
project definition in, 79–80
within project-driven structures,
    21–22
purpose of this book in, 7, 11–12
quality in, 91–95
risk in, 95–98
scope triangle and, 72–74
training paradigm for, 7
Project Management Body of Knowledge
    (PMBOK), 7, 83–84, 85
Project Management Institute, 7
Project management life cycle, 86
  origination of, 95
Project management skills, required
    of project managers, 48
Project management tools, in core
    team selection, 251
Project-manager-based strategies, for
    change control, 296
Project manager career path model, 1
Project Manager Competency
    Assessment, 38–45
Project managers, 15–52
  approval of Project Overview
    Statement by, 127–128
  authority and responsibility of,
    255–256
  becoming, 15, 52
  becoming world-class, 52
  career planning by, 50–52
  changes in projects and, 291–294
  classification of, 36–37

Project managers (*cont.*)
   in contemporary organizational
      environments, 28–30
   contracted team selection by,
      251–255
   core team selection by, 248–251
   demand for, 15–22
   determining competency profiles
      of, 38–47
   functional managers versus,
      239–240
   job functions of, 32–34
   at Joint Project Planning sessions,
      227–228
   level of reporting detail for,
      288–289
   motivation of others by, 240–244
   network constraints and, 187–188
   in post-implementation audits, 308
   problem escalation control by,
      294–298
   as process owners, 28
   Project Overview Statement and,
      121
   at project status review meetings,
      290
   recruitment of, 244, 245–247
   resource leveling by, 209–211
   skills and competencies required
      of, 34–49
   skills required of, 36, 45
   support offices for, 30–32
   team building by, 244–255, 255–256,
      256–261
   in traditional organizational
      environments, 22–28
   Work Breakdown Structure and,
      138
   work package reports for, 218–220
Project matrix structures, 27

Project network diagrams, 179–181
   analyzing of, 197–203
   building of, 181–196
   defined, 179
   Joint Project Planning sessions and,
      203–206
Project networks, 106
   constraints in, 186–190
   defined, 10
   dependencies in, 184–186
   diagrams of, 179–181, 181–184
   in Joint Project Planning sessions,
      203–206
   lag variables and, 191
   scheduling of, 191–196
   scheduling within, 197–203
Project network schedules, from Joint
      Project Planning sessions, 232
Project notebooks, 82–83 from Joint
      Project Planning sessions, 232
Project objectives. *See also* Objective
      statements
   within matrix structures, 26
   in project proposals, 233
Project objectives part
   of Project Definition Statement, 129
   of Project Overview Statement,
      114–115, 118–119, 125
Project Overview Statement (POS),
      87, 109, 111, 112, 226
   approval of, 125–128
   attachments to, 122–124
   Conditions of Satisfaction and, 113
   creation of, 113–124
   five parts of, 114–122
   Joint Project Planning sessions and,
      124–125
   Project Definition Statement and,
      129–132
   in project proposals, 233

Work Breakdown Structure and,
135, 136, 138, 140
Project plans, 81–82, 87–89
reports and controls on, 266
as systems, 265
Project proposals, 88. *See also*
Requests for proposals
from Joint Project Planning
sessions, 232–234
Projects
in career planning, 52
classification of, 8–9, 34–35, 74–76
closing out, 11
controlling changes in, 291–294
defined, 8–9, 65–68
as development tools, 240–244
history of, 82–83
implementation of, 235
inherited, 113–114
monitoring of, 10
as motivation tools, 240–244
multiple, 11
parameters constraining, 68–71
programs as collections of, 68
in project-driven organizations,
20–22
referents for, 113–114
scheduling of, 10
scope of, 9
Project shutdown, within matrix
structures, 26
Project status reporting tool, Work
Breakdown Structure as, 137
Project status reports, 89, 268–276
control via, 265–268
cost schedule control with, 281–286
frequency of, 274
graphics in, 276–288
level of detail in, 288–289
meetings reviewing, 289–291

purposes of, 271–272
tracking variances from plan with,
274–276
types of, 268–271
updating of, 272–274
Project status review meetings,
289–291
Project support offices (PSOs), 30–32
Project teams, 20. *See also* Contracted
teams; Core project teams;
Cross-functional teams; Task
forces
approval of Project Overview
Statement by, 126, 127
in contemporary organizational
environments, 28–30
within functional structures,
23–24
in launching projects, 89
management of, 33
operating rules for, 256–261
organizing, 10, 226–227, 244–255,
255–256, 261–262
product-based, 29
in traditional organizational
environments, 22–28

Q

Quality
assessing manager's commitment
to, 39
from contracted teams, 252
control versus, 268
of a project, 68, 69
in scope triangle, 71–72
from task forces, 19
Quality management, 69, 91–95
Quality Systems, 202

Quantifiable statements, in Project Overview Statement, 119–120

R

Radical changes, in milestone trend charts, 279
Random activities
in estimating activity duration, 162–163
in projects, 66
Realism, in goal statements, 117–118
Recall, knowledge and, 45–46
Recognition, as motivator, 243
Recording meeting minutes, 261, 290–291
Reengineering movement, 17
Remembering, knowledge and, 45–46
Reorders, in contemporary organizational environments, 30
Repetitiveness
within functional structures, 24
in projects, 65–66
Reports. *See* Dual reporting; Final reports; Project status reports; Work package description report
Request for Information (RFI), in selecting contracted teams, 253
Request for Proposal (RFP), in selecting contracted teams, 253
Request for Quote (RFQ), in selecting contracted teams, 253, 254
Requests
in developing Conditions of Satisfaction, 110–111
in developing Project Overview Statement, 115–116, 125
Requests for proposals, in selecting contracted teams, 253–254

Resource efficiency, within project-driven structures, 22
Resourcefulness, assessing project manager's,42
Resource limits, for projects, 67, 70, 71
Resource loading
activity duration versus, 160–162
risk and, 162
Resource-manager-based strategies, for change control, 296
Resource managers
approval of Project Overview Statement by, 128
at Joint Project Planning sessions, 229
at project status review meetings, 290
Resource requirements, from Joint Project Planning session, 231
Resources. *See also* Assignment of resources
leveling, 209–221
negotiating additional, 297–298
of a project, 68, 71, 167–169, 170–172, 173–175, 209
in project planning, 81–82
in scope triangle, 71–72
substitute, 216
Resource scheduling problem, 209–211
Resources maximum availability, 212
Response, in developing Conditions of Satisfaction, 110–111
Responsibilities
of project manager, 32–34
in task forces, 19
Responsibility
of contracted teams, 255–256
in core team selection, 250
Retainers, 254

Return on investment, in Project
Overview Statement, 124
Right-sizing. *See* Downsizing
Risk
control versus, 265–268
defined, 95
planning as reducing, 85, 114–115,
120–122
in project classification, 74–76
resource loading and, 162
Risk analysis, 96–98
in Project Overview Statement,
122–123
Risk analysis worksheet, 98
Risk drivers, 97–98
Risk management, 95–98
Routine projects, 35
Rules. *See* Operating rules

S

Schedule compression, 197–200
Schedule extensions, 298
Schedule performance index (SPI),
286
Schedule shifts, in milestone trend
charts, 279–280
Schedule variance (SV), 284–286
Scheduling, 10, 70, 106
activity independence and, 146–147
in core team selection, 250
hope creep and, 73
in Joint Project Planning sessions,
203–206
network diagrams in, 181, 191–196,
197–203
of people, 168–169
within project-driven structures, 21
of project plans, 81–82, 88–89
reports and controls on, 265–266

of resources, 209–211, 212–216
with subprojects, 67
Scope, 105
in new product development, 101
of a project, 68, 69
in project management, 79–80, 84,
85–87
in systems development, 100
Scope creep, 72–73
in project management, 80
Scope Statement, 87
Scope triangle, 71–74
Score sheets, for contracted teams,
252–253
S curves, 281–286
Security, in contemporary
organizational environments,
30
Self-confidence, assessing project
manager's, 41
Self-directed teams, 20
Self-managed teams, 20
in contemporary organizational
environment, 30
Self-sufficiency, in project-driven
organizations, 20
Senior project managers
approval of Project Overview
Statement by, 125–128
graphical reporting tools for,
276–288
level of reporting detail for, 289
Project Overview Statement and,
120, 121
skills required of, 36, 45
stoplight reports for, 269–270
Sequential activities, in projects, 65
Series (SF) dependencies, in schedule
compression, 198–200
Shared responsibility, in core team
selection, 250

Short schedules, project managers and, 245

Similarity of activities, in estimating activity duration, 163

Simple projects, 35

Skill categories, 169

Skill levels, 169
  in estimating activity duration, 162

Skills. *See* Business skills; Communication skills; Competencies; Expertise; Interpersonal skills; Listening skills; Management skills; Personal skills; Project management skills; Special skills

Skills matrices, 168–169

Skill variety, as motivator, 243

Slack time
  in resource leveling, 212–213
  in scheduling, 195–196

Small projects, Work Breakdown Structures for, 142

S.M.A.R.T. characteristics, in goal statements, 117–118

Smoothing, in resource leveling, 212, 214

Software
  for analyzing project networks, 203–206
  for calculating percent complete, 274
  development life cycles for, 99
  for mindmapping, 142, 143
  for progress reporting systems, 268

Software applications, evolution of, 5

Special skills
  competencies versus, 37–38
  within functional structures, 24
  within matrix structures, 25
  in project-driven organizations, 20

within project-driven structures, 21
  as project resources, 168–169
  project support offices and, 31, 32
  required of project managers, 34–49
  in task forces, 19–20

Specifications, for projects, 67–68

Specificity, in goal statements, 117–118

Stability
  within functional structures, 24
  within project-driven structures, 21

Staff turnover, 248

Standardization, within functional structures, 24

Standards, project support offices and, 30–31, 32

Standish Group, 96, 109

Start and finish dates, in progress reports, 273

Start to finish (SF) dependency, in network diagraming, 185

Start to start (SS) dependency, in network diagraming, 185

Statement of work, 69, 87
  in project proposals, 233

Stoplight reports, 269–270

Strategic expertise, of project manager, 246

Strategic planning
  for change control, 294–296, 297–298
  by project managers, 32

Stretching activities, 215–216

Subprojects, 66–67

Substitute resources, 216

Subteam approach, to generating Work Breakdown Structure, 140–141

Success. *See also* Closing out; Critical success factors (CSFs)
  auditing of, 306–308

celebrating, 309–310

in final reports, 308–309

of project managers, 37

Success criteria part, of Project Overview Statement, 114–115, 119–120, 125

Successive runs, in milestone trend charts, 279–280

Success measures, in objective statements, 118

Synthesis, in classifying project management competencies, 45, 47

T

Tactical planning, by project managers, 32

Task forces, 18–20. *See also* Project teams

permanent, 18–20

structure of, 19

Task identity, as motivator, 243

Task orientedness, in core team selection, 250

Tasks, 106

defined, 9–10, 135

measuring progress of, 144–145

of project managers, 32–34

in work hierarchies, 135–137, 151–154

in work packages, 216–217

Task significance, as motivator, 243

Team approach, to generating Work Breakdown Structure, 139

Team leaders, skills required of, 36, 45

Team-orientedness, in core team selection, 250

Team planning, 226–227

Teams. *See* Cross-functional teams; Project teams; Task forces

Teamwork, in resource leveling, 210–211

Technical constraints, in network diagraming, 186–188

Technical environment, in classifying projects, 34–35

Technical expertise, of project manager, 247

Technographers, at Joint Project Planning sessions, 228

Technological factors, in Project Overview Statement, 121

Tech-temps, 251

Texas Instruments (TI), 87

T-Form organizational structure, 18

Theory of Constraints, 202

Thought process tool, Work Breakdown Structure as, 137

Three-point technique, in estimating activity duration, 163, 166, 167

360 skill assessment tool, 38

Time. *See also* Completion dates; Cycle times; Date constraints

cost versus, 70

in goal statements, 117–118

percent complete and, 274

in progress reports, 272–273

of a project, 65, 70

in scope triangle, 71–72

Time and materials contracts, 254

Time estimates, 159–167

as completeness criteria, 144, 146

Time frames, in objective statements, 118

Time schedules

for progress reports, 272–273

reports and controls on, 265–266

Time summaries, in project proposals, 233

Time to market
  within product development life
      cycles, 99–102
  within project-driven structures,
      22
  in resource leveling, 213–214
Timing, in project manager selection,
      245
Top-down approach, to generating
      Work Breakdown Structure,
      139–141
Total cost, of control and risk, 267
Total slack
  in resource leveling, 213
  in scheduling, 195–196
Total work, in estimating activity
      duration, 170–172
Traditional organizational
      environments, project
      management in, 22–28
Training
  with closeout documentation, 305
  of project managers, 37
  project support offices and, 31
  skill development via, 20
Trend charts, 278–280
Trust, in core team selection, 250
Type A projects, 75–76
Type B projects, 75–76
Type C projects, 75–76
Type D projects, 75–76

U

Uncertainty, in project planning, 81
Unconnected activities, in projects, 66
Under-budget situations, 275,
      282–283
Understanding, in project planning,
      81

Unexpected events, in estimating
      activity duration, 162
Uninterrupted labor, 159–160
Unique activities, in projects, 65–66
Unique requirements constraints, in
      network diagramming, 188
Units of analysis, in network
      diagramming, 182
Unplanned interruptions, effects on
      work time of, 160
Unplanned project changes,
      controlling, 294–298
Unsolicited individual initiatives,
      Project Overview Statements
      for, 114

V

Variance reports, 270–271
  purposes of, 271–272
Variances from plans, 274–276
  detecting, 266, 269, 270–271,
      281–286
Vendors. *See* Contracted teams
Verb-type approaches, to building
      Work Breakdown Structure,
      148, 149–150

W

"Watercooler project," 110
Waterfall categories, in building Work
      Breakdown Structure, 149–150,
      151, 154
Weekly effort variance, 272
Weekly schedule variance, 271–272
Whiteboard space
  for analyzing project networks,
      204–205

in generating Work Breakdown Structure, 138–139

Wide-band Delphi technique, in estimating activity duration, 163, 167

Work, as motivator, 243–244. *See also* Jobs

Work accomplished, in progress reports, 272–273

Work Breakdown Structure, 11

Work Breakdown Structure (WBS), 135–155

    activities and tasks in, 135–137

    in case exercise, 155, 203

    completeness criteria for, 143–147

    creating, 138–143, 147–151

    defined, 135

    from Joint Project Planning session, 231

    Joint Project Planning session analysis of, 203–206

    project status reporting via, 286–288

    uses of, 137–138

    visualizing, 151–154

Work effort

    defined, 159

    duration versus, 159–160

    in estimating activity duration, 170–172

    percent complete and, 274

    in progress reports, 272–273

Work package assignment sheet, 218–219

Work package description report, 218, 219–220

Work package managers, 217

Work packages, 216–220

    defined, 136, 216–217

    format of, 218–220

    purpose of, 217

    in work hierarchies, 135–137, 151–154

Work time, elapsed time versus, 159–160

Z

Zero slack, in scheduling, 196